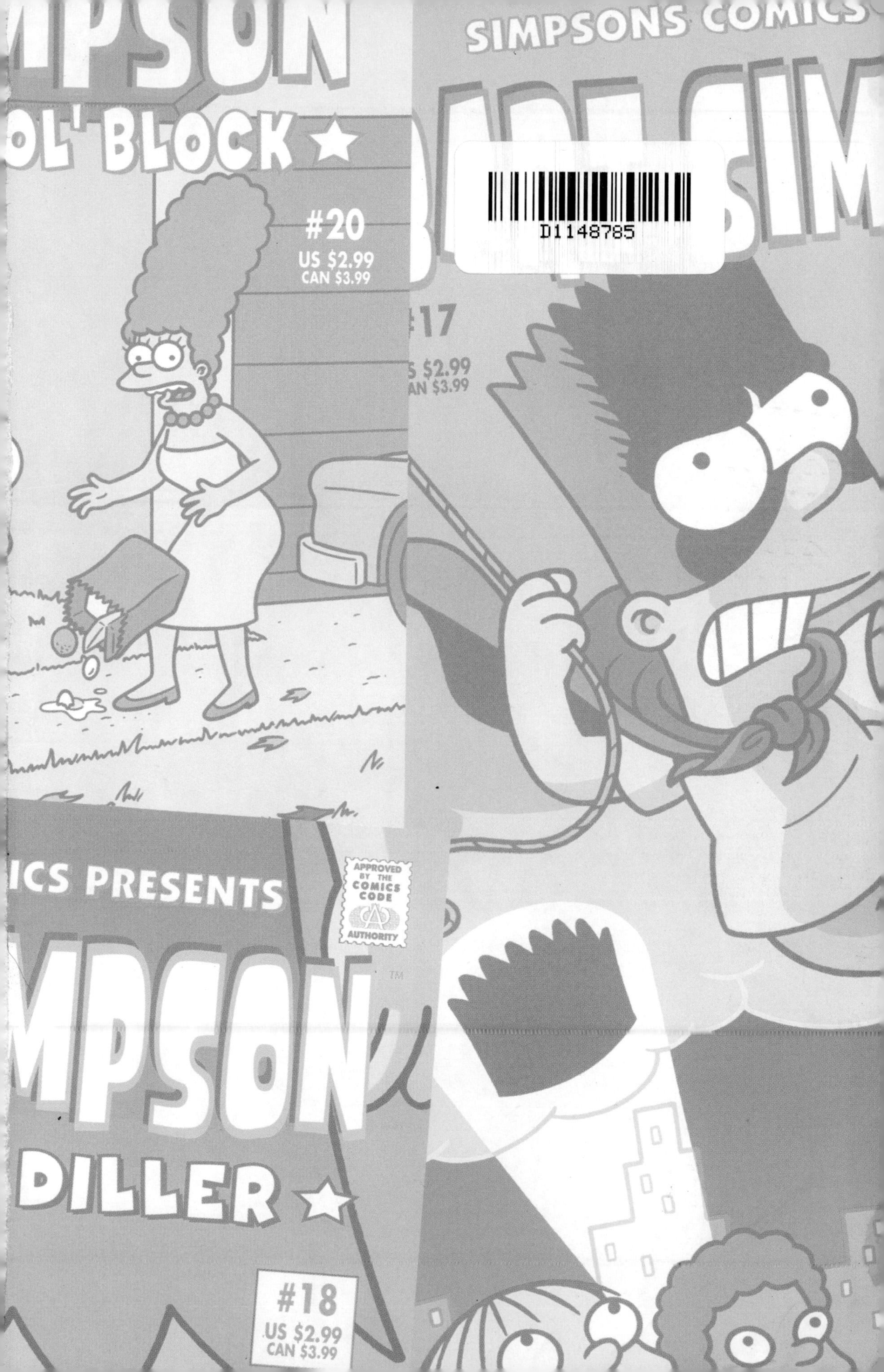
MPSON
OL' BLOCK
#20
US $2.99
CAN $3.99
SIMPSONS COMICS
#17
S $2.99
AN $3.99
ICS PRESENTS
APPROVED BY THE COMICS CODE AUTHORITY
MPSON
TM
DILLER
#18
US $2.99
CAN $3.99

BIG BOUNCY BOOK OF BART SIMPSON

TITAN BOOKS

BIG BOUNCY BOOK OF BART SIMPSON

Copyright © 2000, 2004 & 2006 by
Bongo Entertainment, Inc. All rights reserved.

Published in the UK by Titan Books, a division of Titan Publishing Group,
144 Southwark St., London SE1 0UP, under licence from Bongo Entertainment, Inc.

FIRST EDITION: MAY 2006

ISBN 1-84576-304-1

ISBN-13 9781845763046

06 07 08 09 00 QWM 10 9 8 7 6 5 4 3 2 1

Publisher: MATT GROENING
Creative Director: BILL MORRISON
Managing Editor: TERRY DELEGEANE
Director of Operations: ROBERT ZAUGH
Art Director: NATHAN KANE
Art Director Special Projects: SERBAN CRISTESCU
Production Manager: CHRISTOPHER UNGAR
Legal Guardian: SUSAN A. GRODE

Trade Paperback Concepts and Design: SERBAN CRISTESCU

Contributing Artists:
KAREN BATES, JOHN COSTANZA, SERBAN CRISTESCU, MIKE DECARLO,
MARK ERVIN, LUIS ESCOBAR, NATHAN HAMILL, JASON HO, JAMES HUANG,
NATHAN KANE, MIKE KAZALEH, BILL MORRISON, KEVIN M. NEWMAN, JOEY NILGES,
PHYLLIS NOVIN, PATRICK OWSLEY, RYAN RIVETTE, MIKE ROTE, SCOTT SHAW!, BOB SMITH,
TY TEMPLETON, CHRISTOPHER UNGAR, ART VILLANUEVA

Contributing Writers:
JAMES BATES, TONY DIGEROLAMO, BARRY DUTTER, BILL MORRISON,
SCOTT SHAW!, TY TEMPLETON, PATRIC M. VERRONE, CHRIS YAMBAR

PRINTED IN CANADA

TABLE OF CONTENTS

SIMPSONS COMICS PRESENTS
BART SIMPSON
#17
US $2.99
CAN $3.99
THE RETURN OF BARTMAN
APPROVED BY THE COMICS CODE AUTHORITY

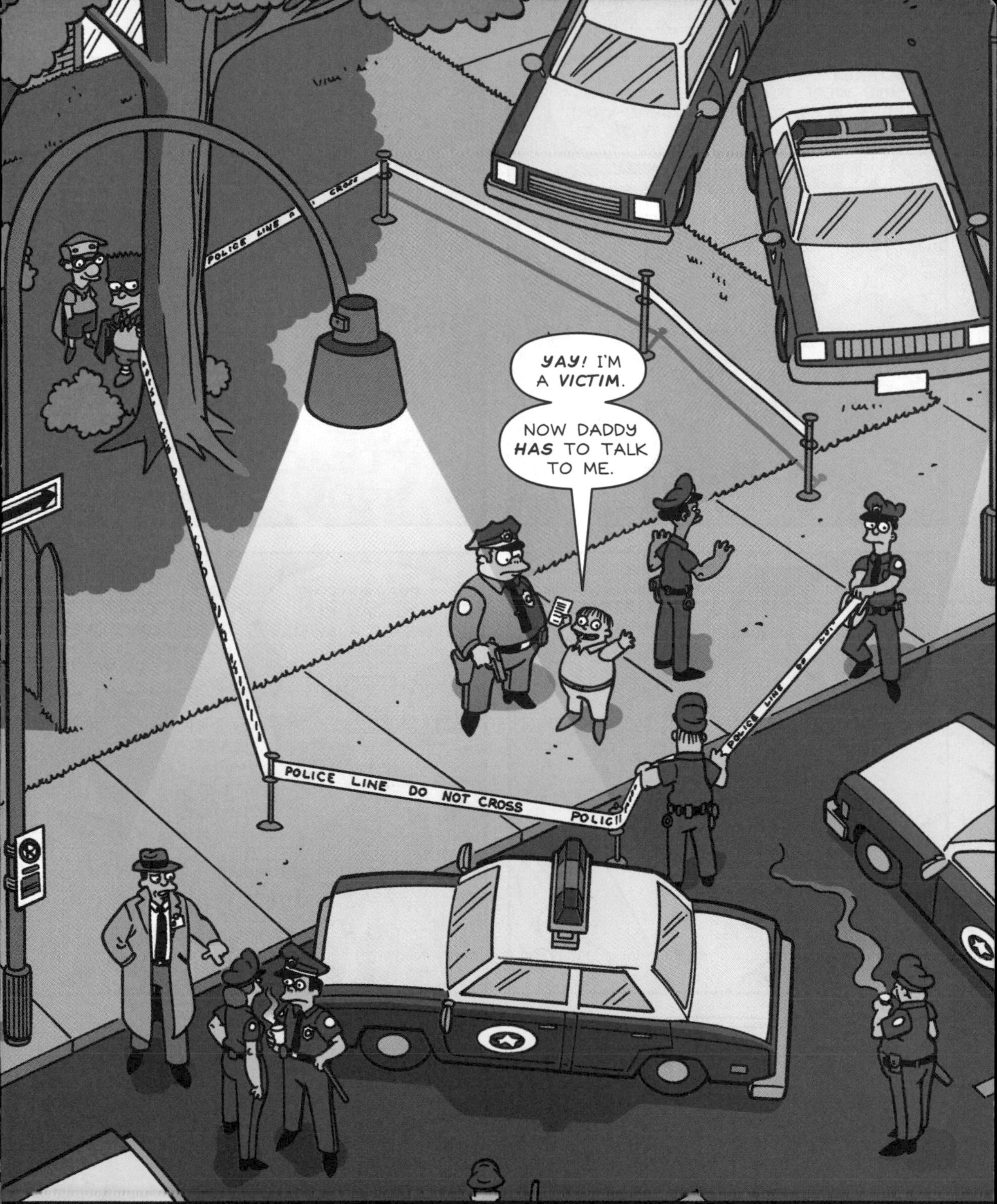
YAY! I'M A VICTIM.
NOW DADDY HAS TO TALK TO ME.
POLICE LINE DO NOT CROSS

MATT GROENING presents

LEGENDS OF THE BARTMAN FAMILY

TY TEMPLETON *SCRIPT & PENCILS*
BOB SMITH *INKS*
GUY INCOGNITO *COLORS*
KAREN BATES *LETTERS*
BILL MORRISON *EDITOR*

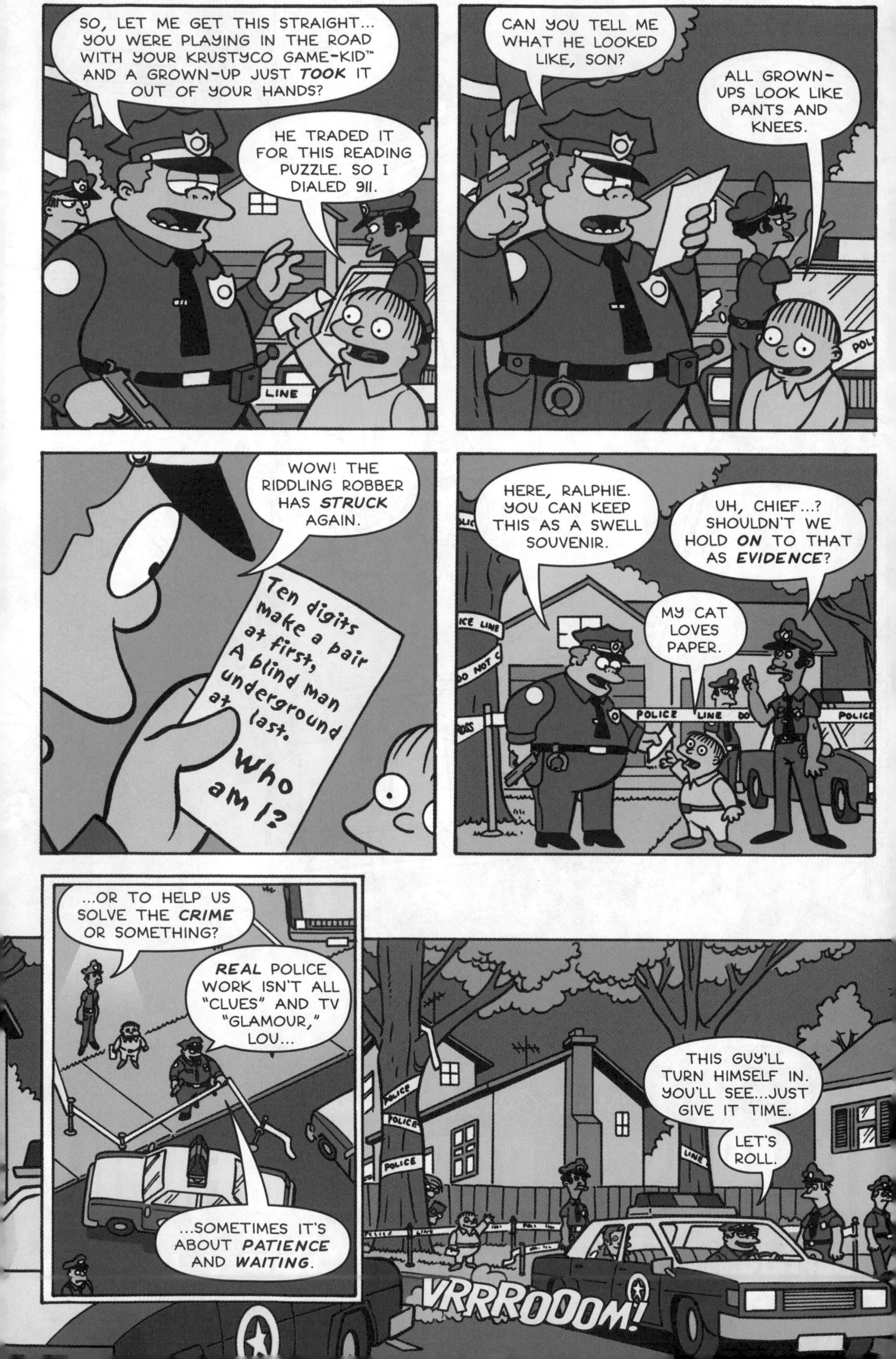

SO, LET ME GET THIS STRAIGHT... YOU WERE PLAYING IN THE ROAD WITH YOUR KRUSTYCO GAME-KID™ AND A GROWN-UP JUST *TOOK* IT OUT OF YOUR HANDS?
HE TRADED IT FOR THIS READING PUZZLE. SO I DIALED 911.
LINE
CAN YOU TELL ME WHAT HE LOOKED LIKE, SON?
ALL GROWN-UPS LOOK LIKE PANTS AND KNEES.
WOW! THE RIDDLING ROBBER HAS *STRUCK* AGAIN.
Ten digits make a pair at first, A blind man underground at last.
Who am I?
HERE, RALPHIE. YOU CAN KEEP THIS AS A SWELL SOUVENIR.
UH, CHIEF...? SHOULDN'T WE HOLD *ON* TO THAT AS *EVIDENCE*?
MY CAT LOVES PAPER.
POLICE LINE
...OR TO HELP US SOLVE THE *CRIME* OR SOMETHING?
REAL POLICE WORK ISN'T ALL "CLUES" AND TV "GLAMOUR," LOU...
...SOMETIMES IT'S ABOUT *PATIENCE* AND *WAITING*.
THIS GUY'LL TURN HIMSELF IN. YOU'LL SEE...JUST GIVE IT TIME.
LET'S ROLL.
VRRROOOM!

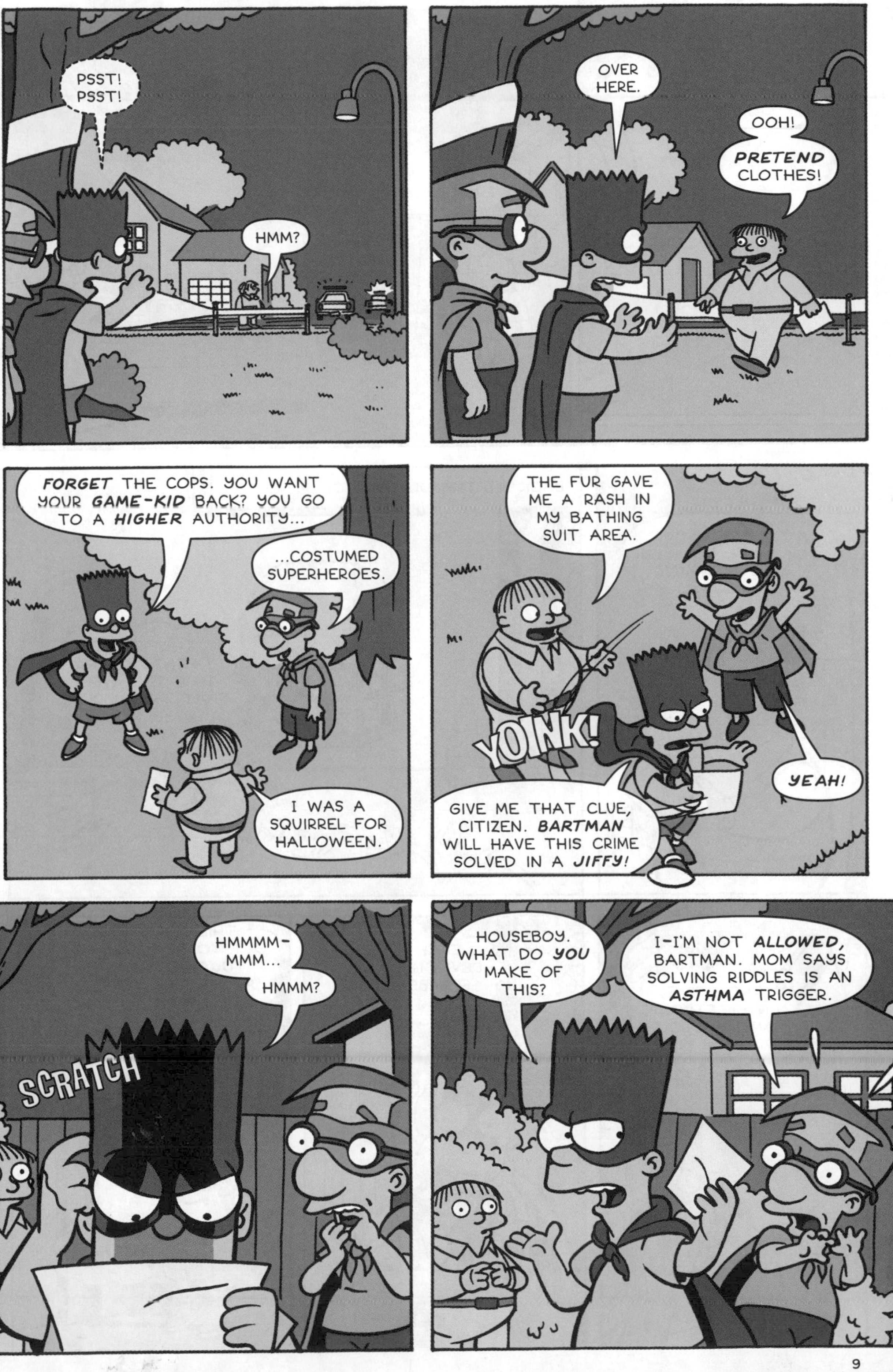
PSST!
PSST!
HMM?
OVER
HERE.
OOH!
PRETEND
CLOTHES!
FORGET THE COPS. YOU WANT YOUR GAME-KID BACK? YOU GO TO A HIGHER AUTHORITY...
...COSTUMED SUPERHEROES.
I WAS A SQUIRREL FOR HALLOWEEN.
THE FUR GAVE ME A RASH IN MY BATHING SUIT AREA.
YOINK!
GIVE ME THAT CLUE, CITIZEN. BARTMAN WILL HAVE THIS CRIME SOLVED IN A JIFFY!
YEAH!
HMMMM-
MMM...
HMMM?
SCRATCH
HOUSEBOY. WHAT DO YOU MAKE OF THIS?
I-I'M NOT ALLOWED, BARTMAN. MOM SAYS SOLVING RIDDLES IS AN ASTHMA TRIGGER.

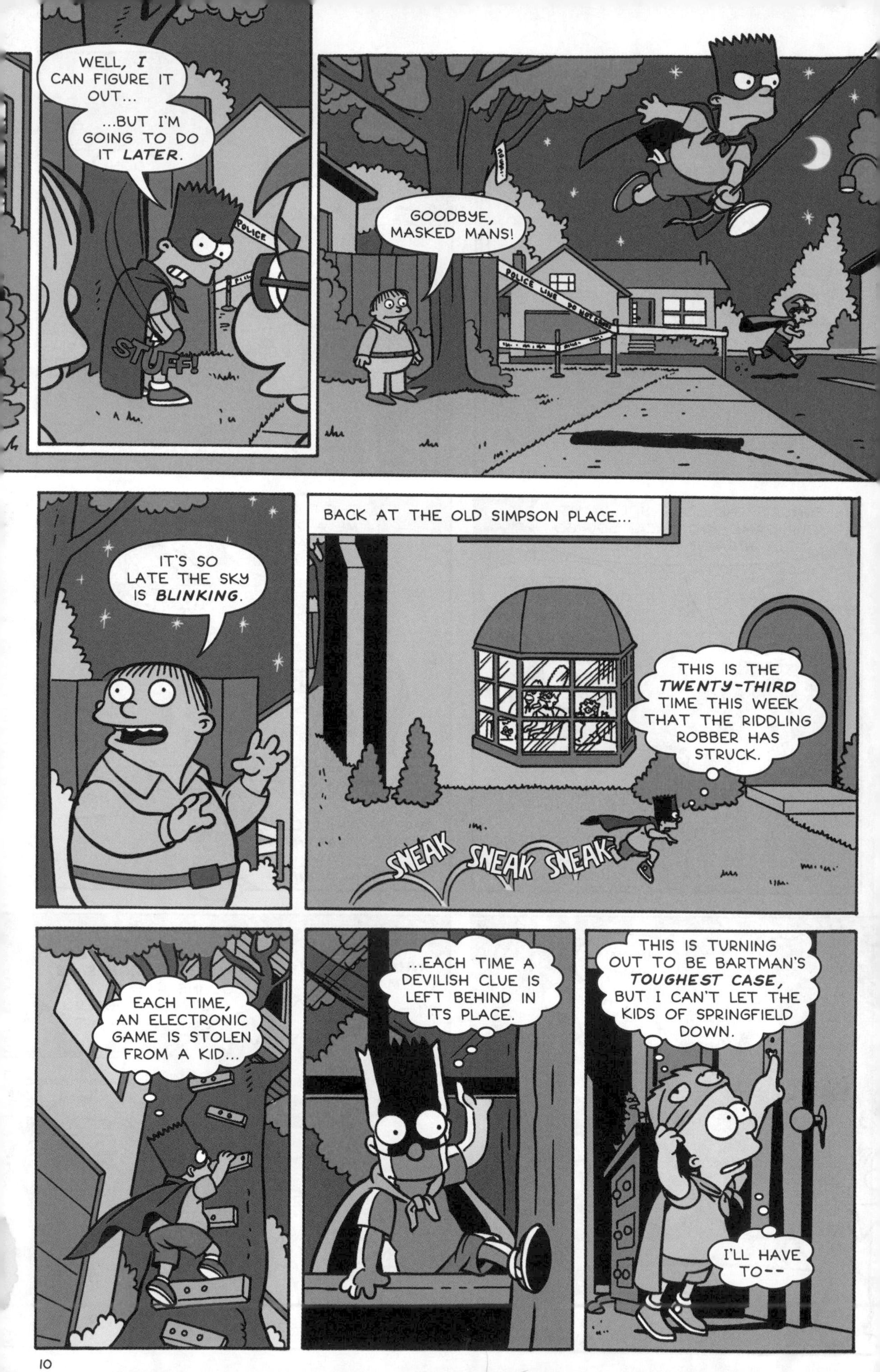
WELL, *I* CAN FIGURE IT OUT...
...BUT I'M GOING TO DO IT *LATER*.
STUFF!
GOODBYE, MASKED MANS!
IT'S SO LATE THE SKY IS *BLINKING*.
BACK AT THE OLD SIMPSON PLACE...
THIS IS THE *TWENTY-THIRD* TIME THIS WEEK THAT THE RIDDLING ROBBER HAS STRUCK.
SNEAK SNEAK SNEAK
EACH TIME, AN ELECTRONIC GAME IS STOLEN FROM A KID...
...EACH TIME A DEVILISH CLUE IS LEFT BEHIND IN ITS PLACE.
THIS IS TURNING OUT TO BE BARTMAN'S *TOUGHEST CASE,* BUT I CAN'T LET THE KIDS OF SPRINGFIELD DOWN.
I'LL HAVE TO--

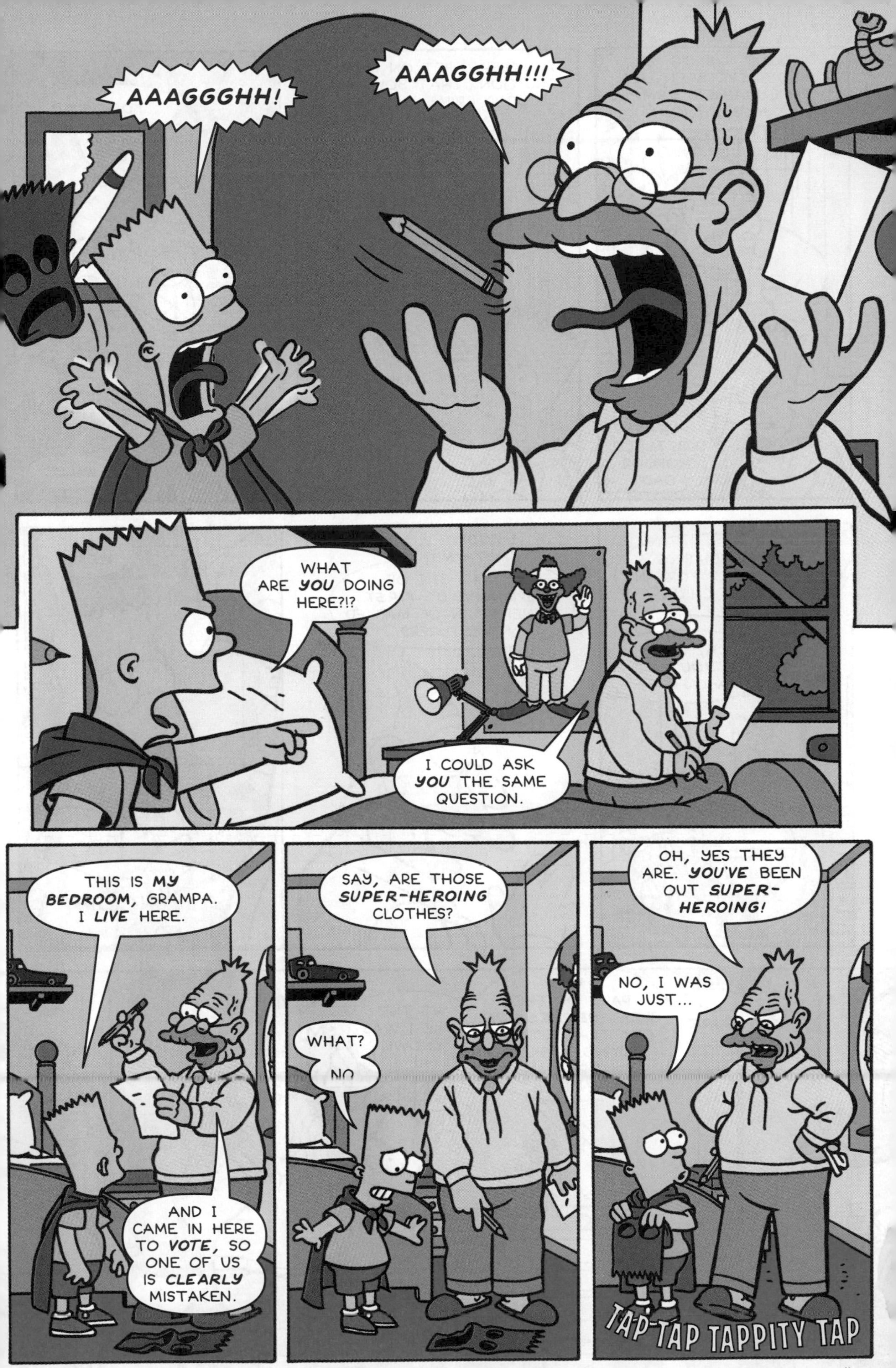
AAAGGGHH!
AAAGGHH!!!
WHAT ARE YOU DOING HERE?!?
I COULD ASK YOU THE SAME QUESTION.
THIS IS MY BEDROOM, GRAMPA. I LIVE HERE.
AND I CAME IN HERE TO VOTE, SO ONE OF US IS CLEARLY MISTAKEN.
SAY, ARE THOSE SUPER-HEROING CLOTHES?
WHAT?
NO
OH, YES THEY ARE. YOU'VE BEEN OUT SUPER-HEROING!
NO, I WAS JUST...
TAP-TAP TAPPITY TAP

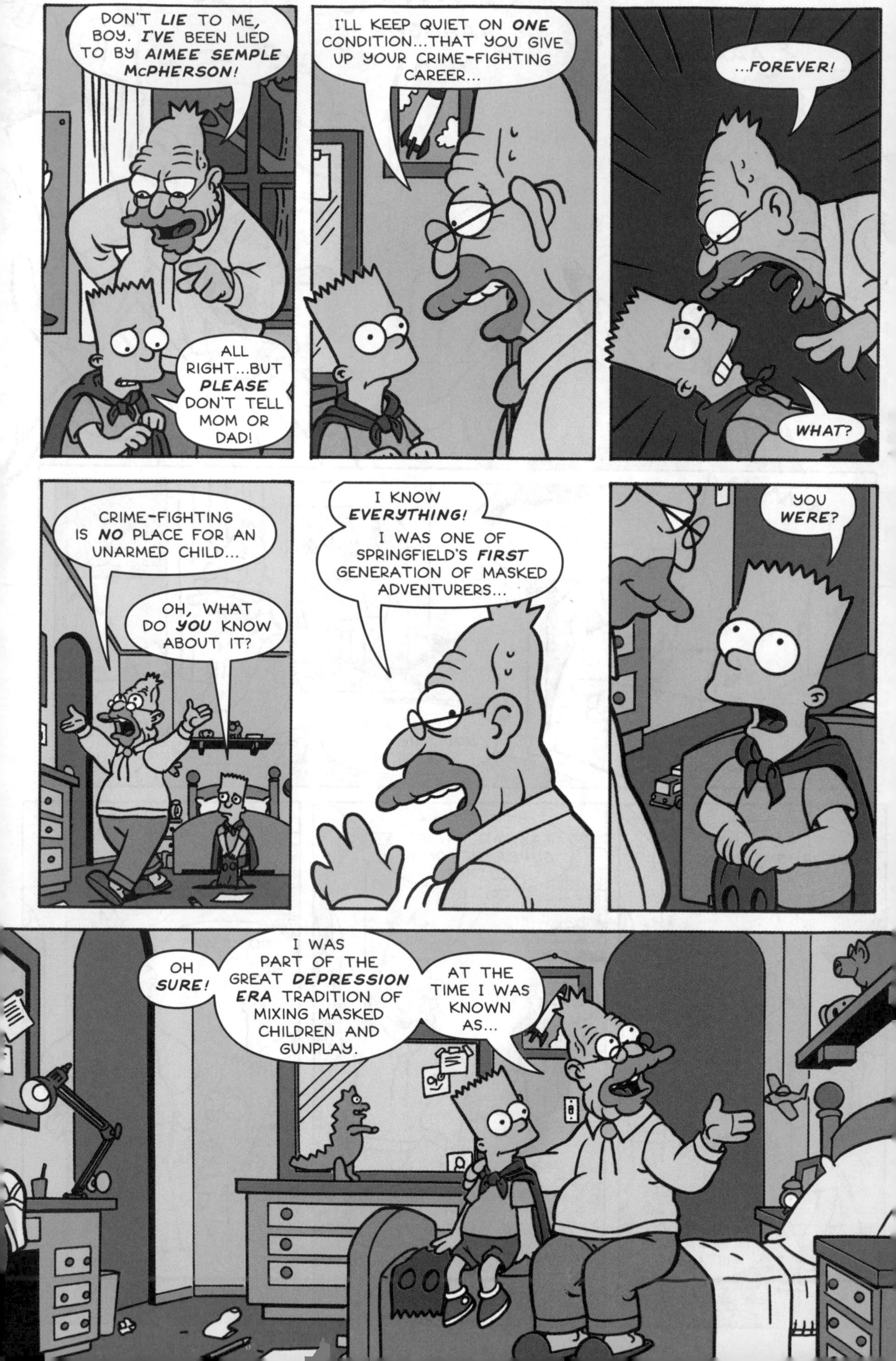
DON'T LIE TO ME, BOY. I'VE BEEN LIED TO BY AIMEE SEMPLE McPHERSON!
ALL RIGHT...BUT PLEASE DON'T TELL MOM OR DAD!
I'LL KEEP QUIET ON ONE CONDITION...THAT YOU GIVE UP YOUR CRIME-FIGHTING CAREER...
...FOREVER!
WHAT?
CRIME-FIGHTING IS NO PLACE FOR AN UNARMED CHILD...
OH, WHAT DO YOU KNOW ABOUT IT?
I KNOW EVERYTHING!
I WAS ONE OF SPRINGFIELD'S FIRST GENERATION OF MASKED ADVENTURERS...
YOU WERE?
OH SURE!
I WAS PART OF THE GREAT DEPRESSION ERA TRADITION OF MIXING MASKED CHILDREN AND GUNPLAY.
AT THE TIME I WAS KNOWN AS...

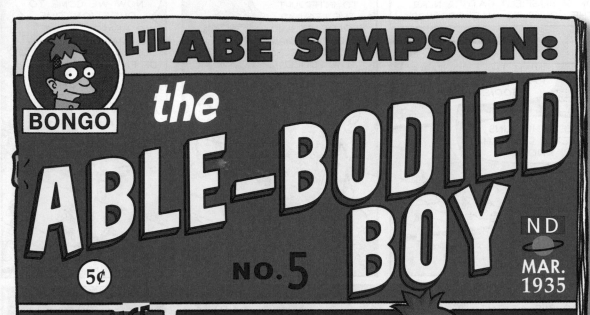

L'IL ABE SIMPSON:
the
ABLE-BODIED BOY

BONGO

5¢

NO. 5

ND
MAR.
1935

FREELANCE SIDEKICK TO AMERICA'S MASKED MEN!

WITH:

AVENGING PISTOL

THE MIGHTY ZEPPELIN

THE MYSTERY GUNMAN

ALL-NEW STORIES

13

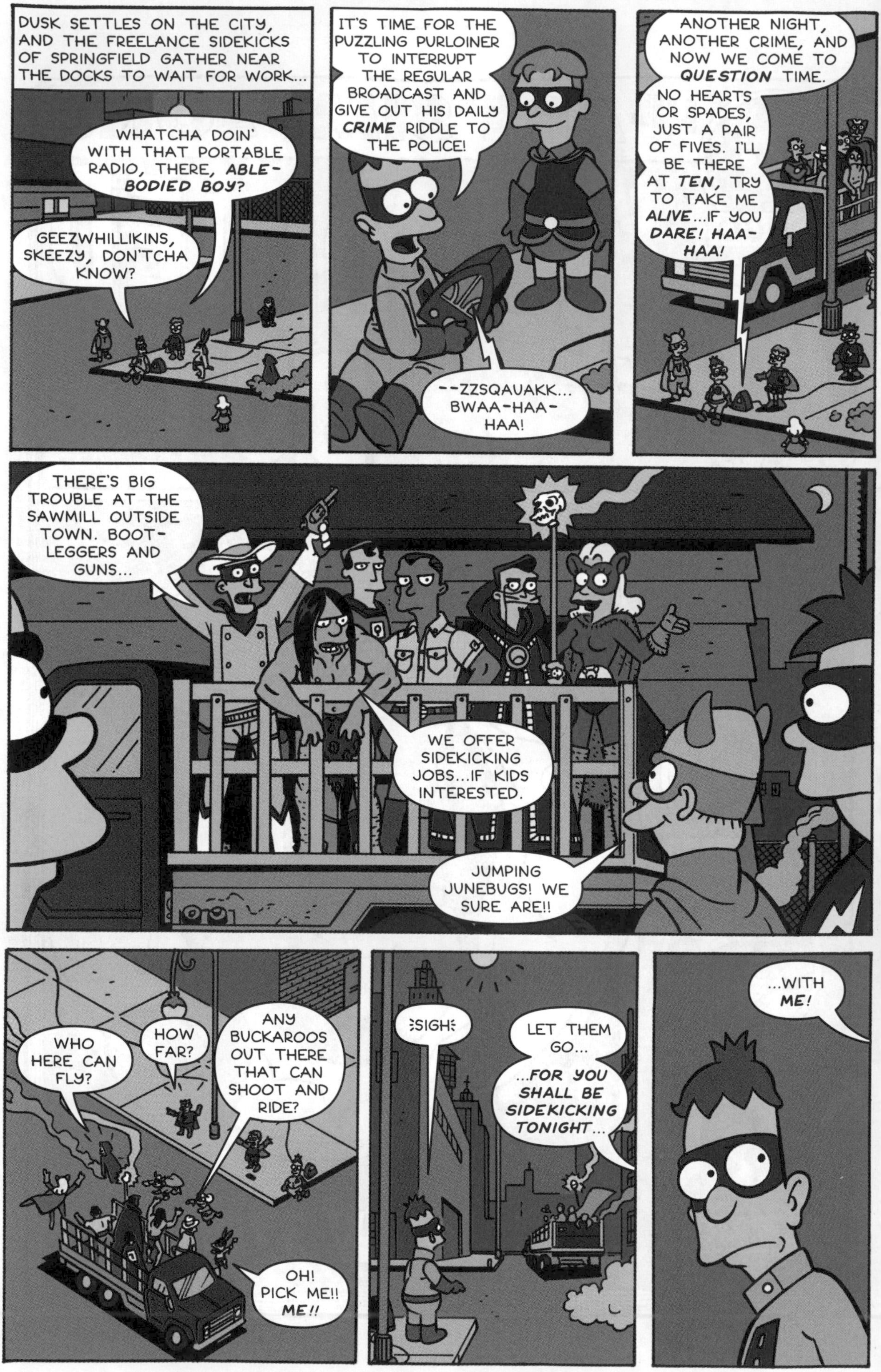
DUSK SETTLES ON THE CITY, AND THE FREELANCE SIDEKICKS OF SPRINGFIELD GATHER NEAR THE DOCKS TO WAIT FOR WORK...
WHATCHA DOIN' WITH THAT PORTABLE RADIO, THERE, ABLE-BODIED BOY?
GEEZWHILLIKINS, SKEEZY, DON'TCHA KNOW?
IT'S TIME FOR THE PUZZLING PURLOINER TO INTERRUPT THE REGULAR BROADCAST AND GIVE OUT HIS DAILY CRIME RIDDLE TO THE POLICE!
--ZZSQAUAKK... BWAA-HAA-HAA!
ANOTHER NIGHT, ANOTHER CRIME, AND NOW WE COME TO QUESTION TIME.
NO HEARTS OR SPADES, JUST A PAIR OF FIVES. I'LL BE THERE AT TEN, TRY TO TAKE ME ALIVE...IF YOU DARE! HAA-HAA!
THERE'S BIG TROUBLE AT THE SAWMILL OUTSIDE TOWN. BOOT-LEGGERS AND GUNS...
WE OFFER SIDEKICKING JOBS...IF KIDS INTERESTED.
JUMPING JUNEBUGS! WE SURE ARE!!
WHO HERE CAN FLY?
HOW FAR?
ANY BUCKAROOS OUT THERE THAT CAN SHOOT AND RIDE?
OH! PICK ME!! ME!!
SIGH
LET THEM GO...
...FOR YOU SHALL BE SIDEKICKING TONIGHT...
...WITH ME!

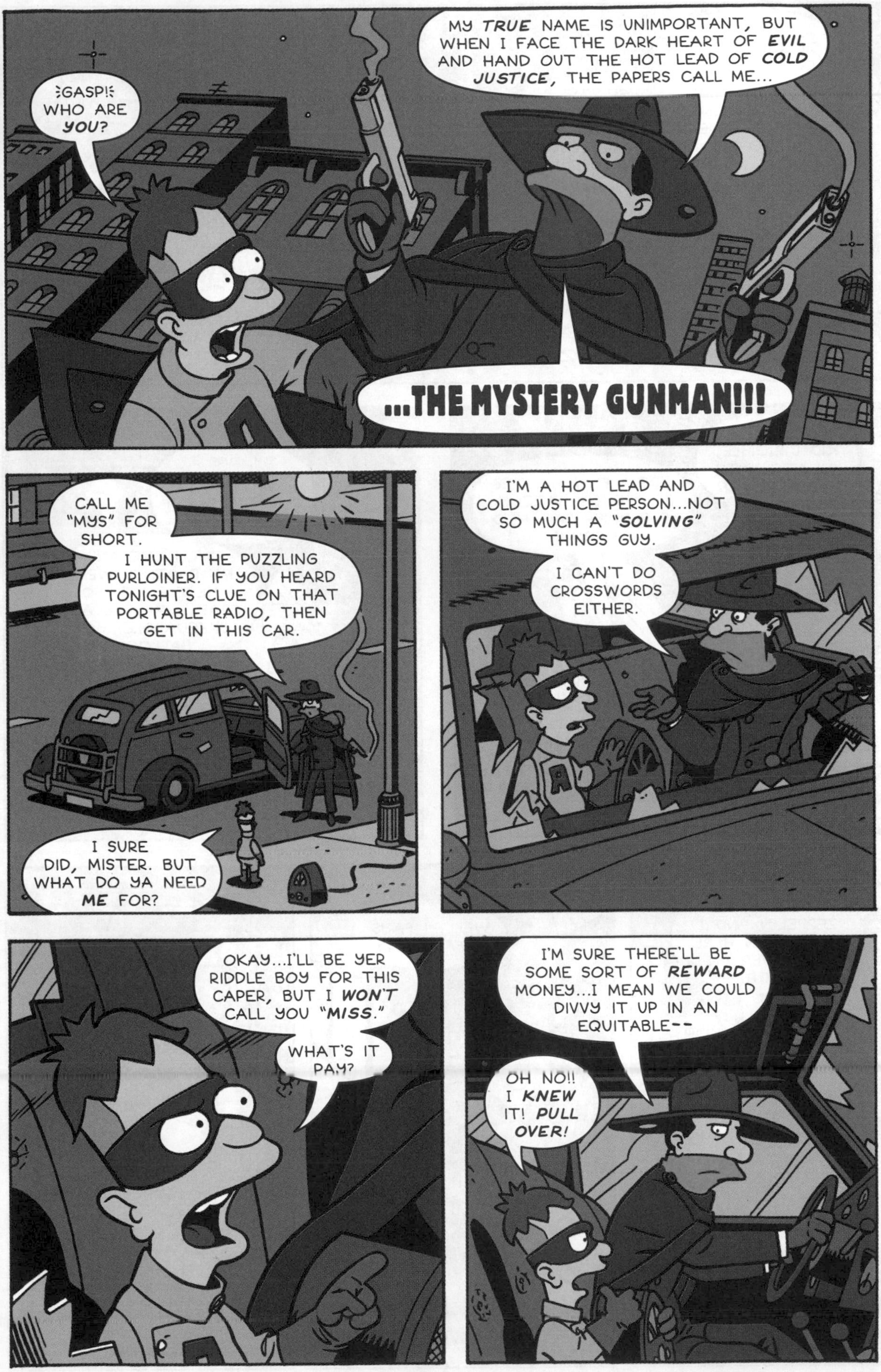

MY TRUE NAME IS UNIMPORTANT, BUT WHEN I FACE THE DARK HEART OF EVIL AND HAND OUT THE HOT LEAD OF COLD JUSTICE, THE PAPERS CALL ME...
GASP! WHO ARE YOU?
...THE MYSTERY GUNMAN!!!
CALL ME "MYS" FOR SHORT.
I HUNT THE PUZZLING PURLOINER. IF YOU HEARD TONIGHT'S CLUE ON THAT PORTABLE RADIO, THEN GET IN THIS CAR.
I SURE DID, MISTER. BUT WHAT DO YA NEED ME FOR?
I'M A HOT LEAD AND COLD JUSTICE PERSON...NOT SO MUCH A "SOLVING" THINGS GUY.
I CAN'T DO CROSSWORDS EITHER.
OKAY...I'LL BE YER RIDDLE BOY FOR THIS CAPER, BUT I WON'T CALL YOU "MISS."
WHAT'S IT PAY?
I'M SURE THERE'LL BE SOME SORT OF REWARD MONEY...I MEAN WE COULD DIVVY IT UP IN AN EQUITABLE--
OH NO!! I KNEW IT! PULL OVER!

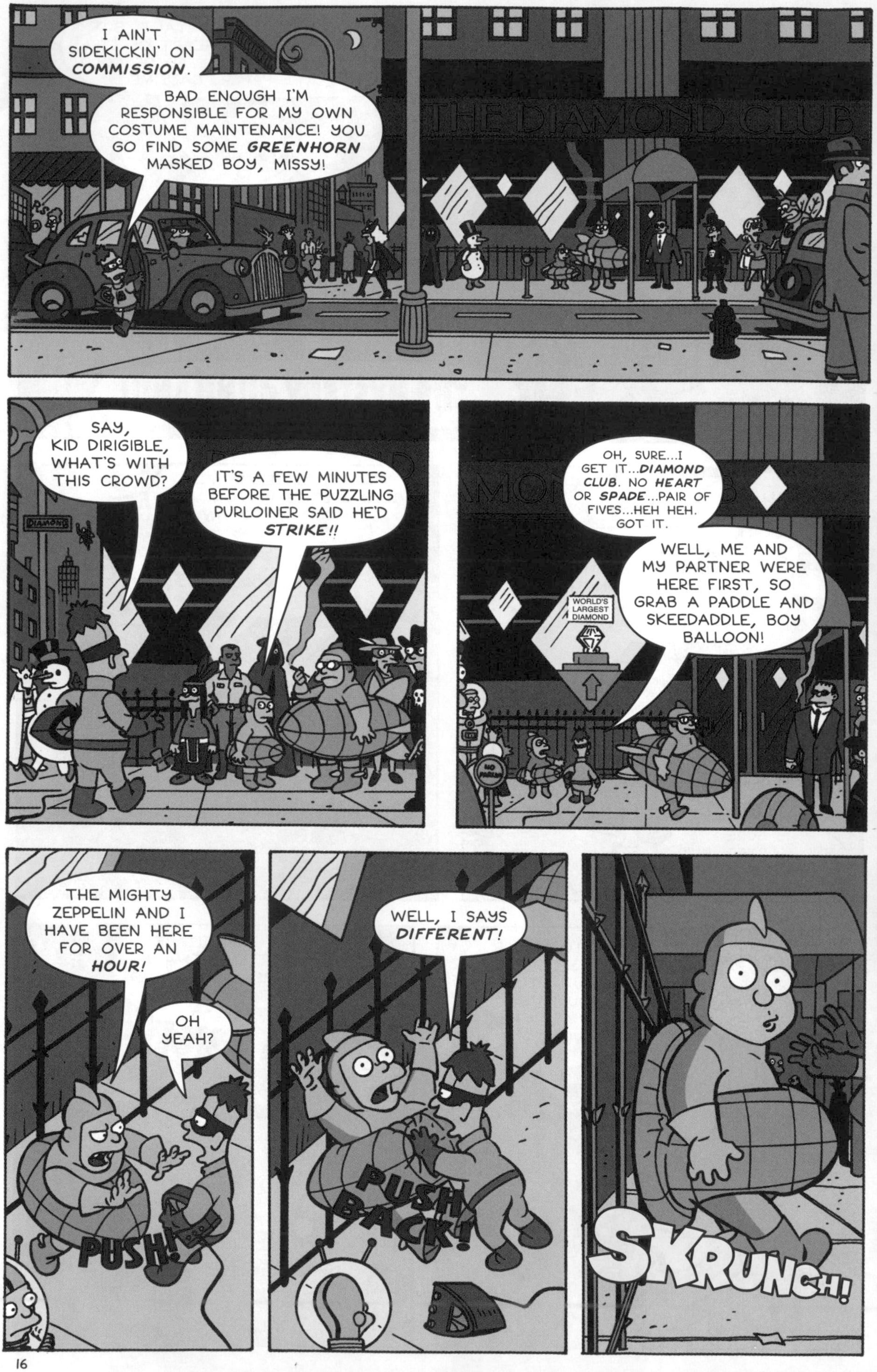

I AIN'T SIDEKICKIN' ON *COMMISSION*.
BAD ENOUGH I'M RESPONSIBLE FOR MY OWN COSTUME MAINTENANCE! YOU GO FIND SOME *GREENHORN* MASKED BOY, MISSY!
THE DIAMOND CLUB
SAY, KID DIRIGIBLE, WHAT'S WITH THIS CROWD?
IT'S A FEW MINUTES BEFORE THE PUZZLING PURLOINER SAID HE'D *STRIKE*!!
OH, SURE...I GET IT...*DIAMOND CLUB*. NO *HEART* OR *SPADE*...PAIR OF FIVES...HEH HEH. GOT IT.
WORLD'S LARGEST DIAMOND
WELL, ME AND MY PARTNER WERE HERE FIRST, SO GRAB A PADDLE AND SKEEDADDLE, BOY BALLOON!
THE MIGHTY ZEPPELIN AND I HAVE BEEN HERE FOR OVER AN *HOUR*!
OH YEAH?
PUSH!
WELL, I SAYS *DIFFERENT*!
PUSH BACK!
SKRUNCH!

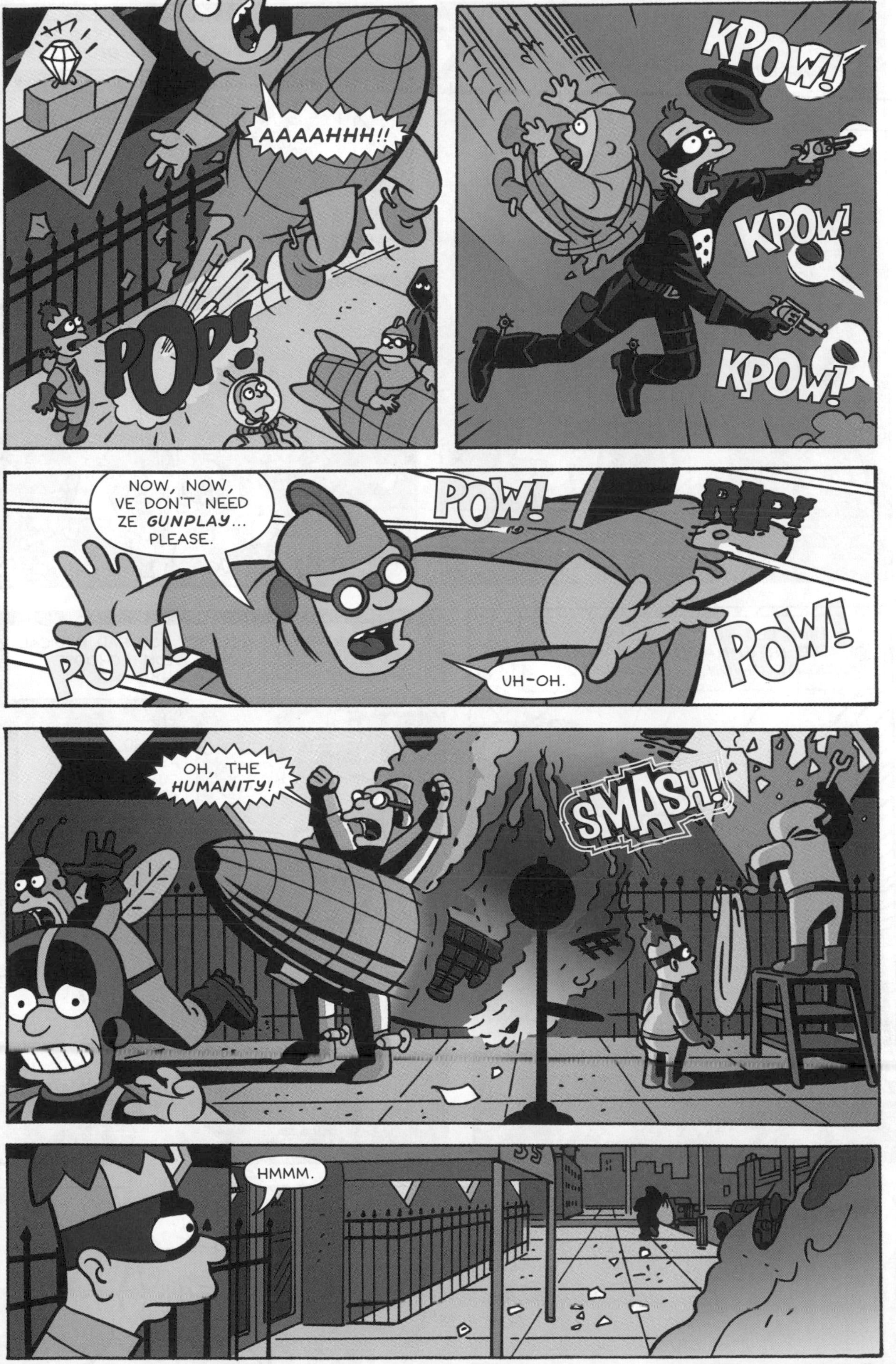
AAAAHHH!!
POP!
KPOW!
KPOW!
KPOW!
NOW, NOW, VE DON'T NEED ZE GUNPLAY... PLEASE.
POW!
RIP!
POW!
POW!
UH-OH.
OH, THE HUMANITY!
SMASH!
HMMM.

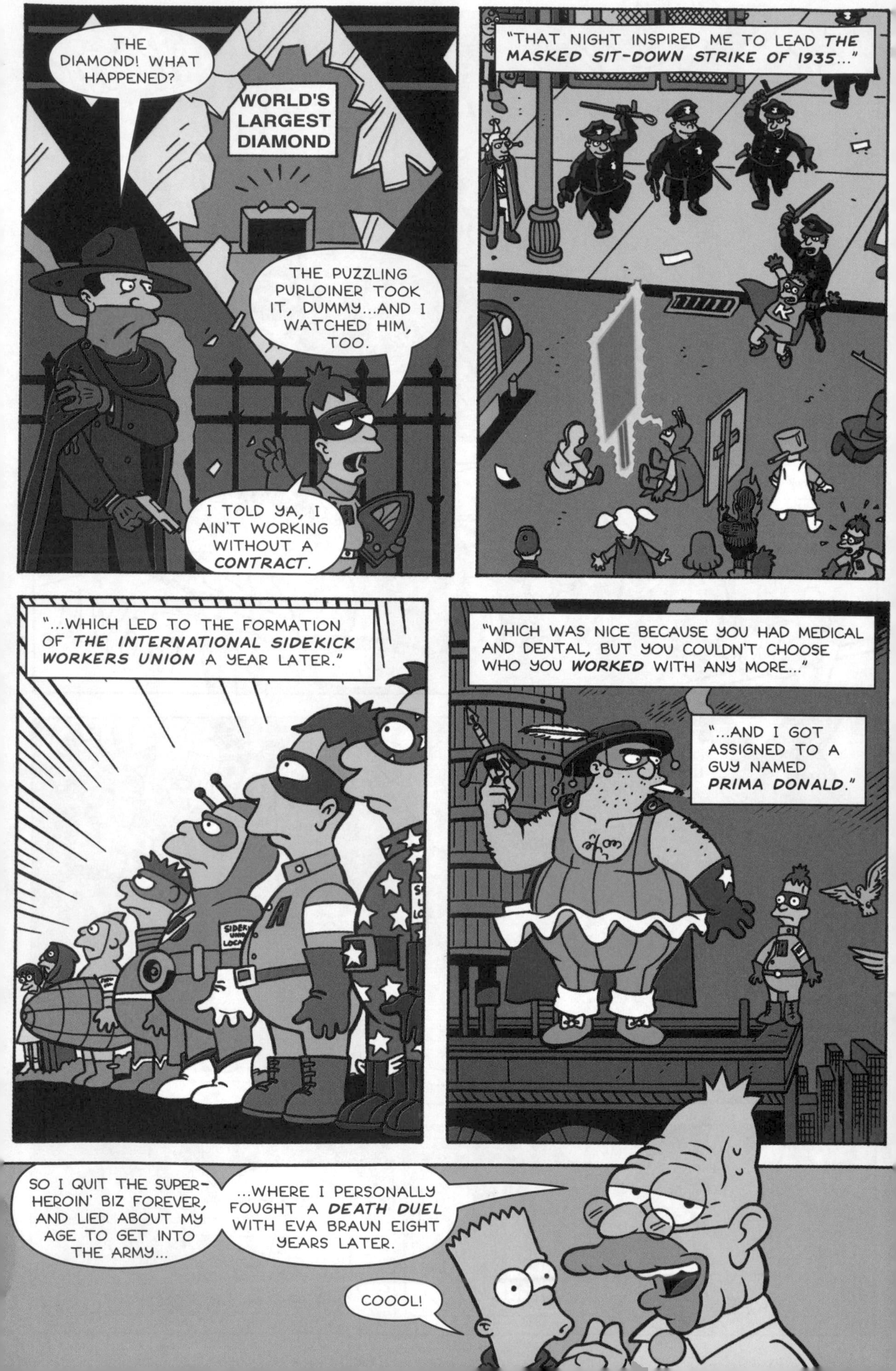
THE DIAMOND! WHAT HAPPENED?
WORLD'S LARGEST DIAMOND
THE PUZZLING PURLOINER TOOK IT, DUMMY...AND I WATCHED HIM, TOO.
I TOLD YA, I AIN'T WORKING WITHOUT A CONTRACT.
"THAT NIGHT INSPIRED ME TO LEAD THE MASKED SIT-DOWN STRIKE OF 1935..."
"...WHICH LED TO THE FORMATION OF THE INTERNATIONAL SIDEKICK WORKERS UNION A YEAR LATER."
"WHICH WAS NICE BECAUSE YOU HAD MEDICAL AND DENTAL, BUT YOU COULDN'T CHOOSE WHO YOU WORKED WITH ANY MORE..."
"...AND I GOT ASSIGNED TO A GUY NAMED PRIMA DONALD."
SO I QUIT THE SUPER-HEROIN' BIZ FOREVER, AND LIED ABOUT MY AGE TO GET INTO THE ARMY...
...WHERE I PERSONALLY FOUGHT A DEATH DUEL WITH EVA BRAUN EIGHT YEARS LATER.
COOOL!

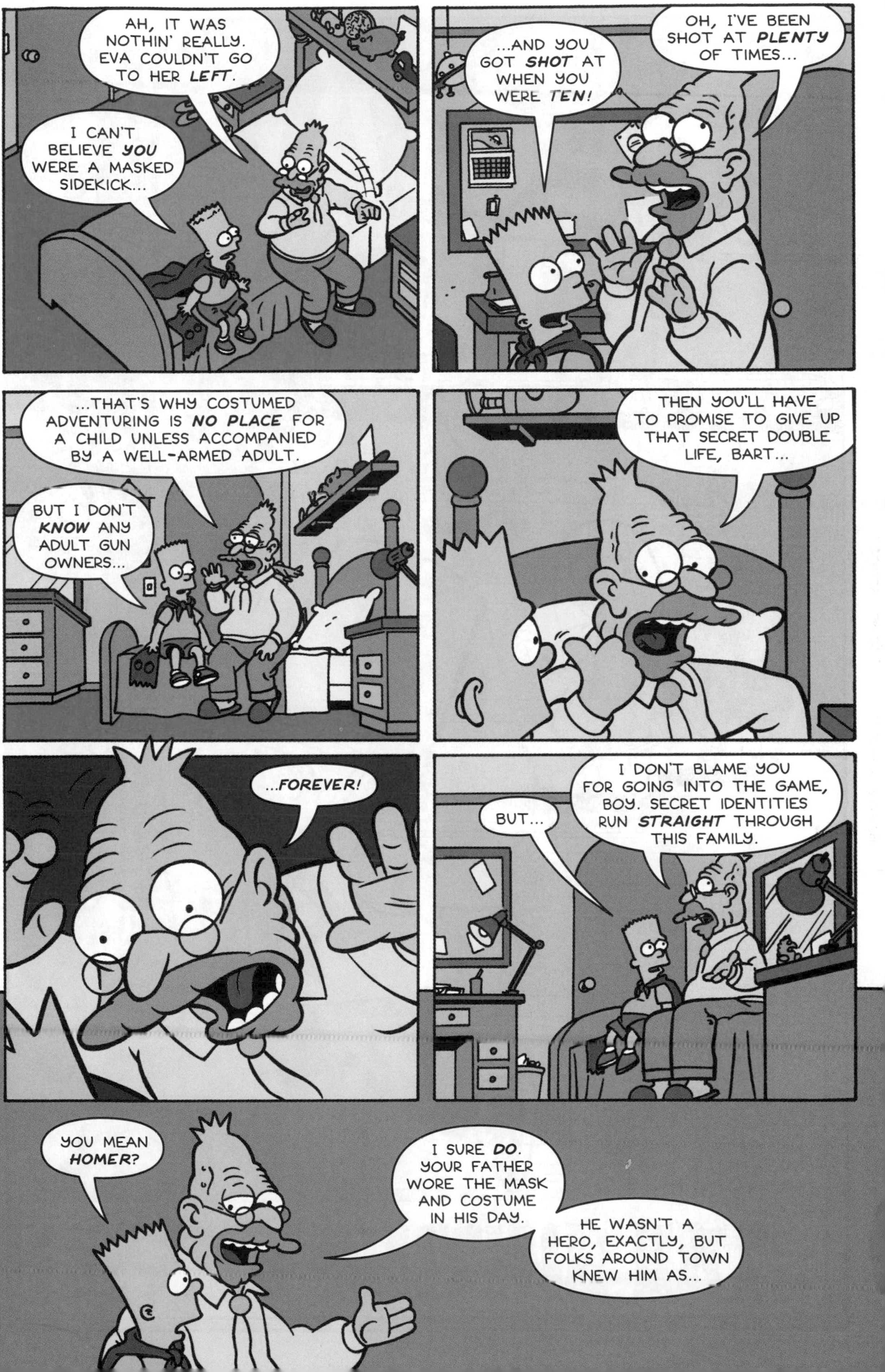
AH, IT WAS NOTHIN' REALLY. EVA COULDN'T GO TO HER *LEFT*.
I CAN'T BELIEVE *YOU* WERE A MASKED SIDEKICK...
...AND YOU GOT *SHOT* AT WHEN YOU WERE *TEN*!
OH, I'VE BEEN SHOT AT *PLENTY* OF TIMES...
...THAT'S WHY COSTUMED ADVENTURING IS *NO PLACE* FOR A CHILD UNLESS ACCOMPANIED BY A WELL-ARMED ADULT.
BUT I DON'T *KNOW* ANY ADULT GUN OWNERS...
THEN YOU'LL HAVE TO PROMISE TO GIVE UP THAT SECRET DOUBLE LIFE, BART...
...*FOREVER!*
BUT...
I DON'T BLAME YOU FOR GOING INTO THE GAME, BOY. SECRET IDENTITIES RUN *STRAIGHT* THROUGH THIS FAMILY.
YOU MEAN *HOMER*?
I SURE *DO*. YOUR FATHER WORE THE MASK AND COSTUME IN HIS DAY.
HE WASN'T A HERO, EXACTLY, BUT FOLKS AROUND TOWN KNEW HIM AS...

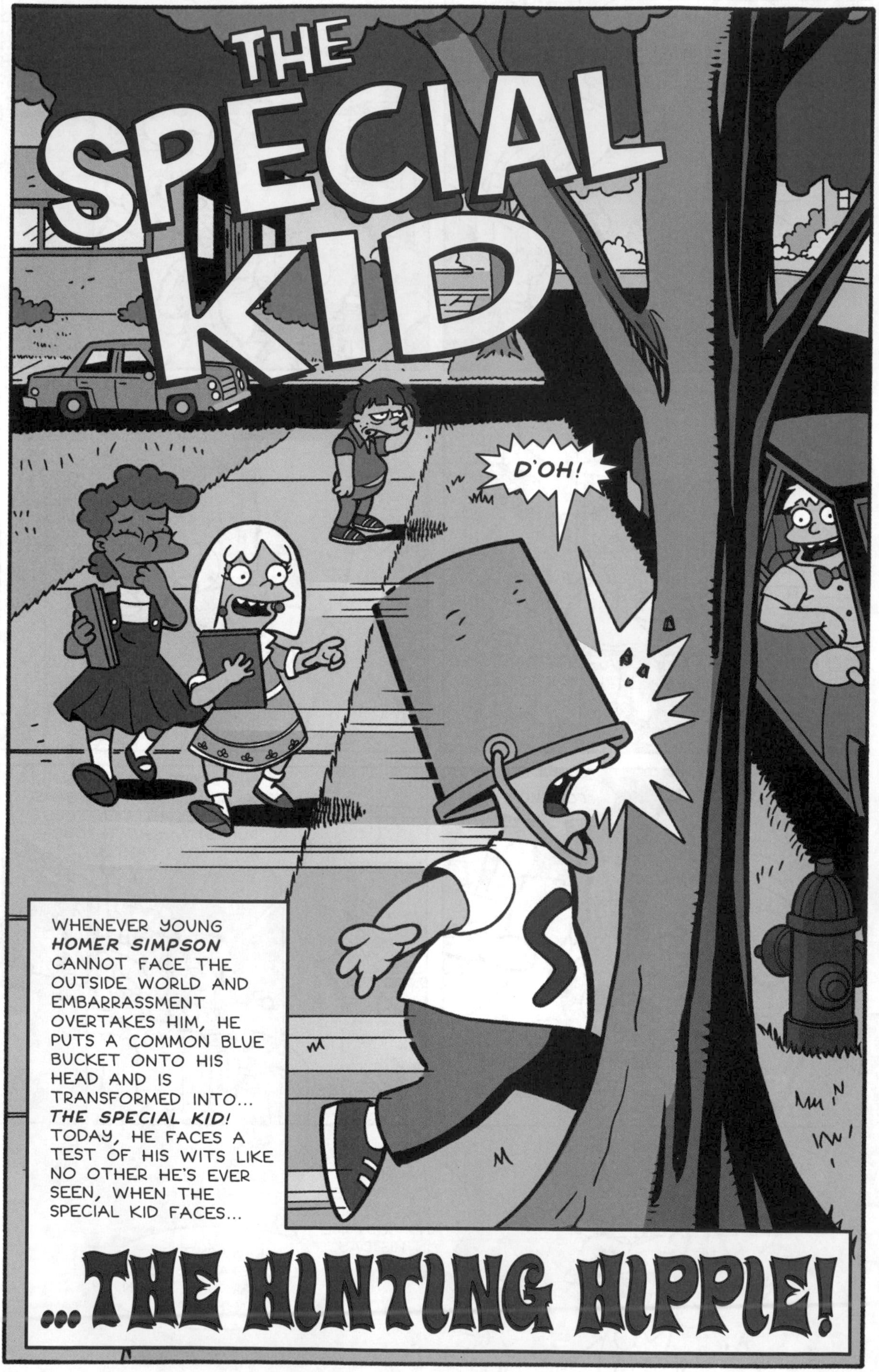
THE SPECIAL KID
D'OH!
WHENEVER YOUNG HOMER SIMPSON CANNOT FACE THE OUTSIDE WORLD AND EMBARRASSMENT OVERTAKES HIM, HE PUTS A COMMON BLUE BUCKET ONTO HIS HEAD AND IS TRANSFORMED INTO... THE SPECIAL KID! TODAY, HE FACES A TEST OF HIS WITS LIKE NO OTHER HE'S EVER SEEN, WHEN THE SPECIAL KID FACES...
...THE HINTING HIPPIE!

OUR STORY BEGINS ONE FINE DAY AS HOMER SIMPSON AND HIS BRAINY BUDDY, BARNEY, SPEND THE DAY WITH SCIENCE...

HEY, HOMER! THIS BOOK SAYS THAT LOWER LUNAR GRAVITY MIGHT RETARD THE HUMAN METABOLIC CLOCK AND LENGTHEN THE LIFESPAN OF MOON COLONISTS.

TAKE *THAT,* STUPID *MOON ROCKS!* UNGH! *UNGH!*

SMASH!

WE SHOULD GO BACK. THE SMELL FROM OUR EXPERIMENT SHOULDA CLEARED OUT OF YOUR HOUSE BY NOW.

I SURE HOPE MY *DAD* DOESN'T FIND OUT WHAT WE *DID!* HOMER *DEFEATS* THE *MOON ROCKS!*

HEY, DIDN'T I LEAVE THE FRONT DOOR *OPEN* WHEN WE LEFT THE HOUSE?

YEAH...AND SOMEONE'S MOVED THE BROKEN GLASS AROUND.

SOMETHING'S GOING ON...

HELLOO... ANYBODY HOME...?

AAAAAHH!

THE TV IS GONE! THE TV IS GONE! OUR NEW COLOR TV!!

SOMEONE BROKE IN OUR HOUSE...BUT HOW?

THERE'S A *NOTE*...

BUT IT'S IN SOME WEIRD *ALIEN* LANGUAGE...

OR IT'S UPSIDE DOWN.

Thanks fo letting me liberate your color tv. Stay groovy. Peace.

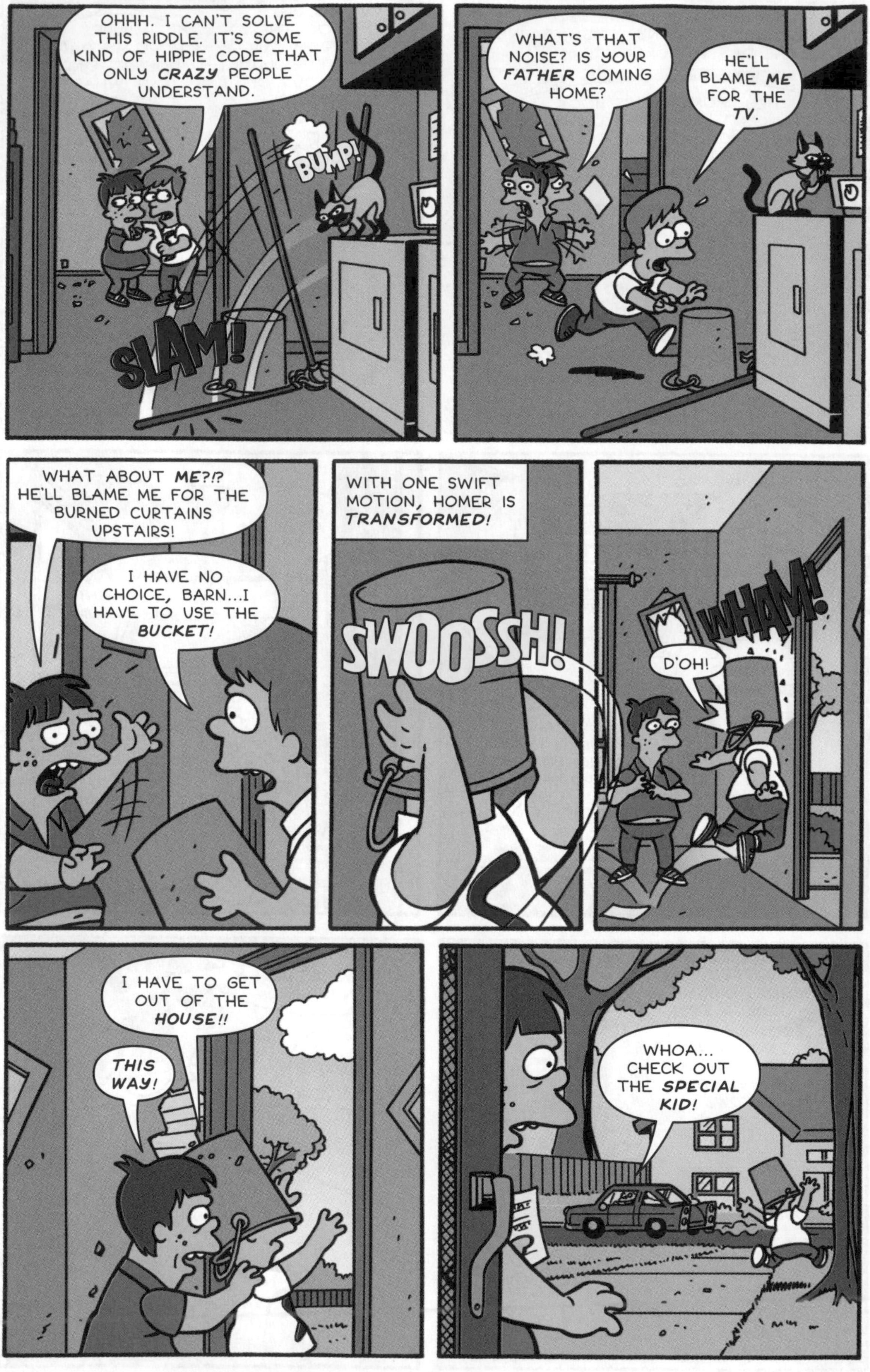
OHHH. I CAN'T SOLVE THIS RIDDLE. IT'S SOME KIND OF HIPPIE CODE THAT ONLY CRAZY PEOPLE UNDERSTAND.
BUMP!
SLAM!
WHAT'S THAT NOISE? IS YOUR FATHER COMING HOME?
HE'LL BLAME ME FOR THE TV.
WHAT ABOUT ME?!? HE'LL BLAME ME FOR THE BURNED CURTAINS UPSTAIRS!
I HAVE NO CHOICE, BARN...I HAVE TO USE THE BUCKET!
WITH ONE SWIFT MOTION, HOMER IS TRANSFORMED!
SWOOSSH!
WHAM!
D'OH!
I HAVE TO GET OUT OF THE HOUSE!!
THIS WAY!
WHOA... CHECK OUT THE SPECIAL KID!

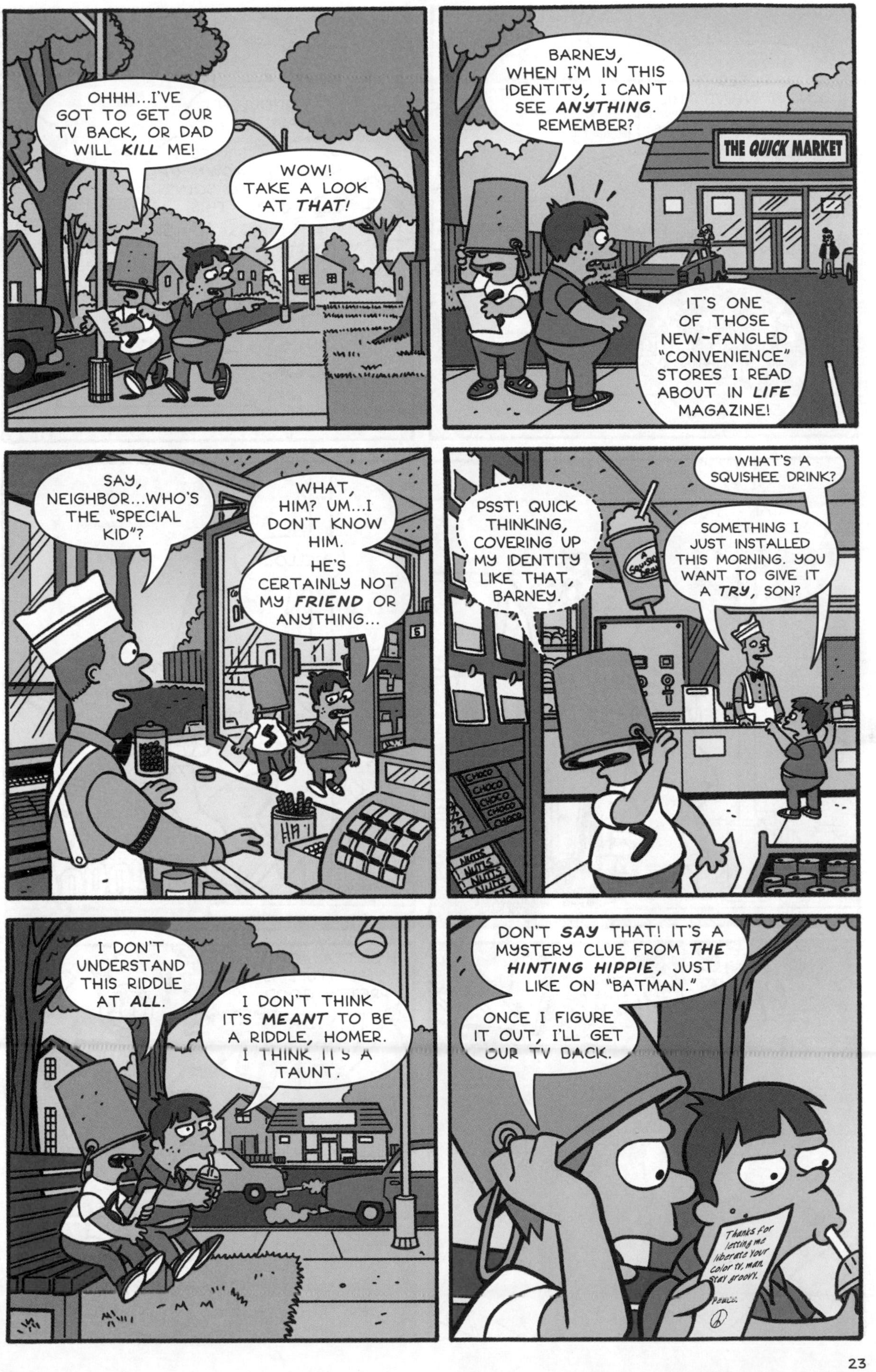
OHHH...I'VE GOT TO GET OUR TV BACK, OR DAD WILL KILL ME!
WOW! TAKE A LOOK AT THAT!
BARNEY, WHEN I'M IN THIS IDENTITY, I CAN'T SEE ANYTHING. REMEMBER?
THE QUICK MARKET
IT'S ONE OF THOSE NEW-FANGLED "CONVENIENCE" STORES I READ ABOUT IN LIFE MAGAZINE!
SAY, NEIGHBOR...WHO'S THE "SPECIAL KID"?
WHAT, HIM? UM...I DON'T KNOW HIM.
HE'S CERTAINLY NOT MY FRIEND OR ANYTHING...
PSST! QUICK THINKING, COVERING UP MY IDENTITY LIKE THAT, BARNEY.
WHAT'S A SQUISHEE DRINK?
SOMETHING I JUST INSTALLED THIS MORNING. YOU WANT TO GIVE IT A TRY, SON?
I DON'T UNDERSTAND THIS RIDDLE AT ALL.
I DON'T THINK IT'S MEANT TO BE A RIDDLE, HOMER. I THINK IT'S A TAUNT.
DON'T SAY THAT! IT'S A MYSTERY CLUE FROM THE HINTING HIPPIE, JUST LIKE ON "BATMAN."
ONCE I FIGURE IT OUT, I'LL GET OUR TV BACK.
Thanks for letting me liberate Your color tv, man. Stay groovy.
Peace.

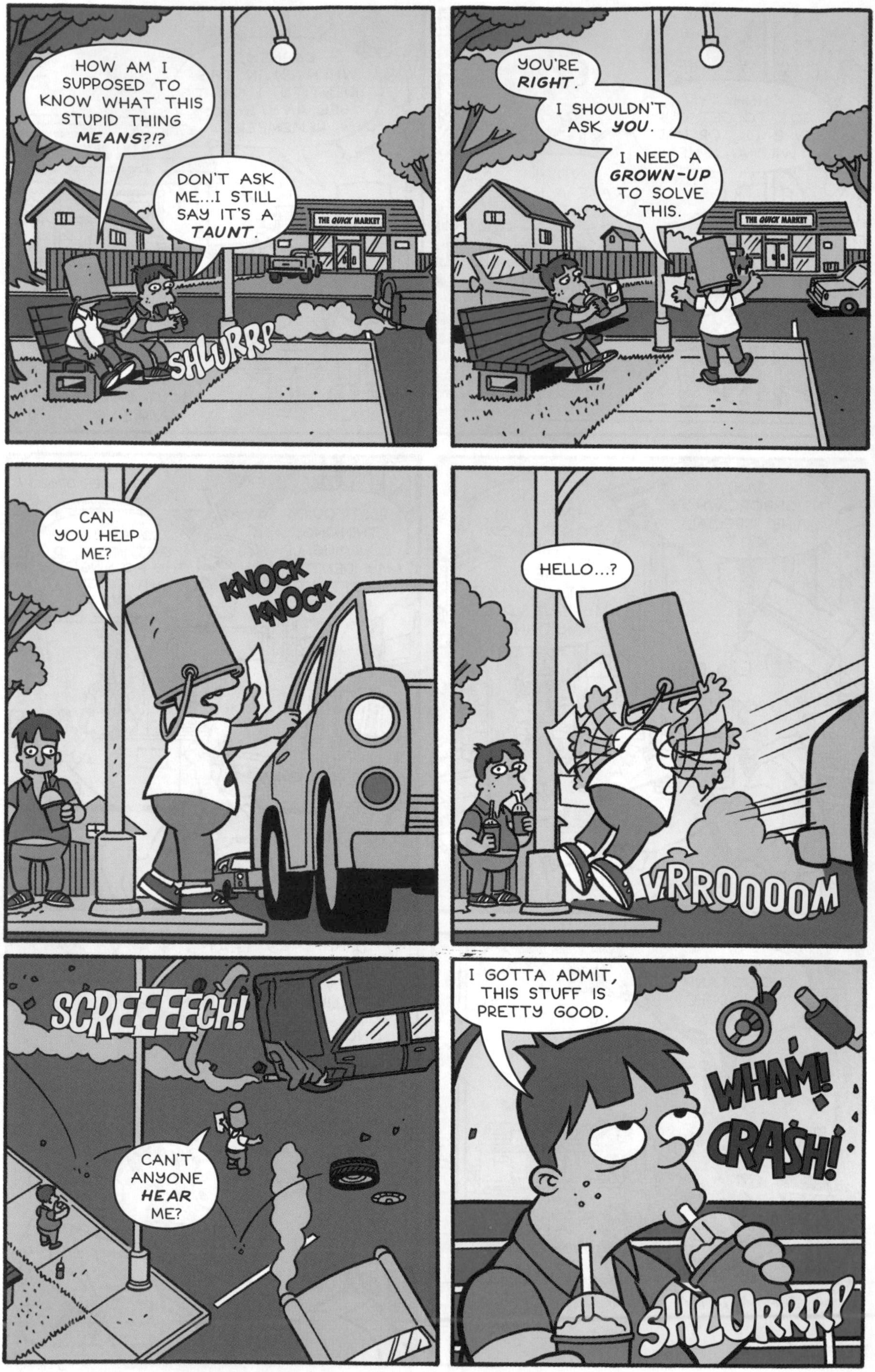
HOW AM I SUPPOSED TO KNOW WHAT THIS STUPID THING MEANS?!?
DON'T ASK ME...I STILL SAY IT'S A TAUNT.
THE QUICK MARKET
SHLURRP
YOU'RE RIGHT.
I SHOULDN'T ASK YOU.
I NEED A GROWN-UP TO SOLVE THIS.
THE QUICK MARKET
CAN YOU HELP ME?
KNOCK KNOCK
HELLO...?
VRROOOOOM
SCREEEEECH!
CAN'T ANYONE HEAR ME?
I GOTTA ADMIT, THIS STUFF IS PRETTY GOOD.
WHAM!
CRASH!
SHLURRRP

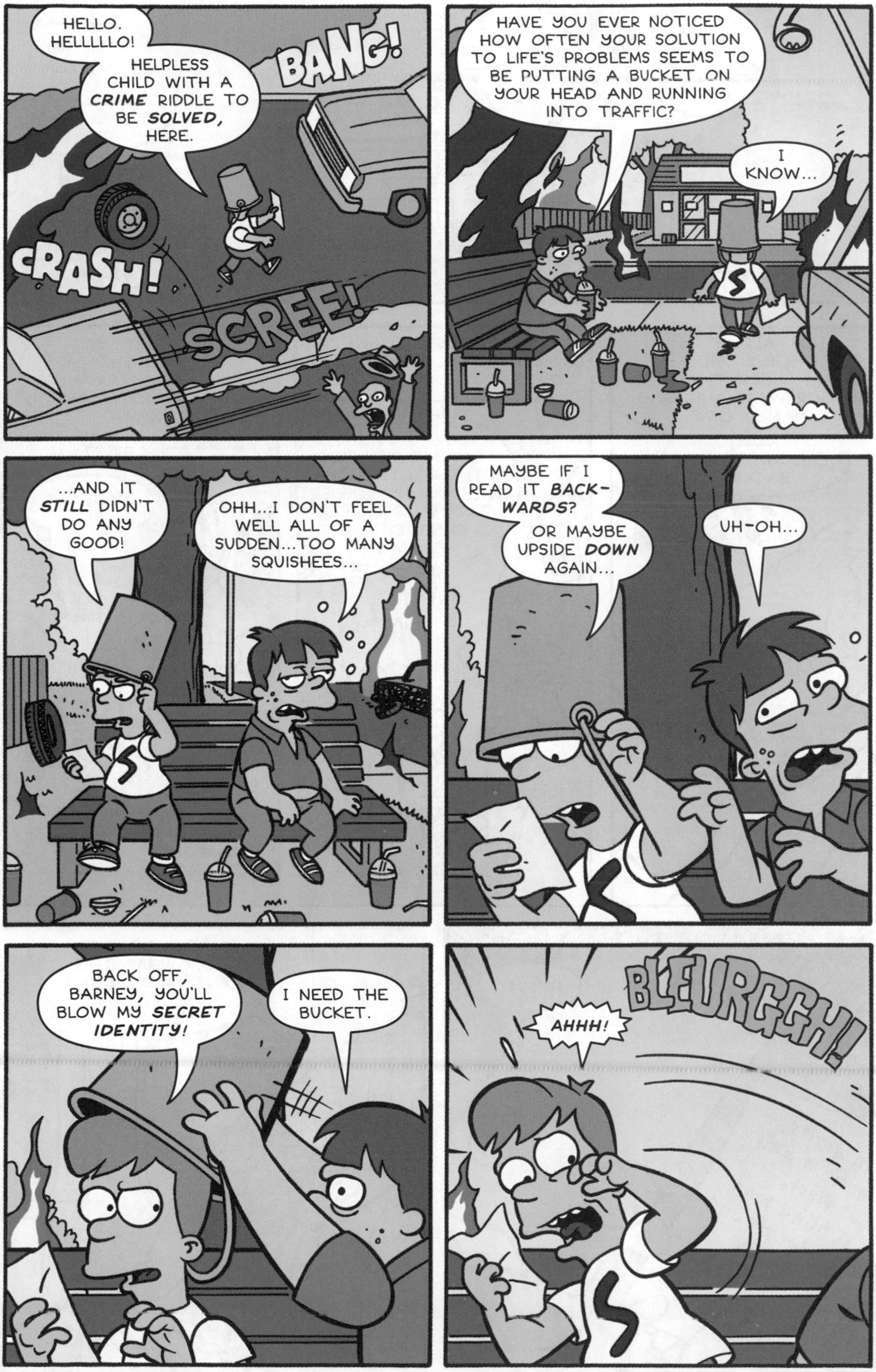
HELLO. HELLLLLO!
HELPLESS CHILD WITH A *CRIME* RIDDLE TO BE *SOLVED,* HERE.
BANG!
CRASH!
SCREE!
HAVE YOU EVER NOTICED HOW OFTEN YOUR SOLUTION TO LIFE'S PROBLEMS SEEMS TO BE PUTTING A BUCKET ON YOUR HEAD AND RUNNING INTO TRAFFIC?
I KNOW...
...AND IT *STILL* DIDN'T DO ANY GOOD!
OHH...I DON'T FEEL WELL ALL OF A SUDDEN...TOO MANY SQUISHEES...
MAYBE IF I READ IT *BACK-WARDS*?
OR MAYBE UPSIDE *DOWN* AGAIN...
UH-OH...
BACK OFF, BARNEY, YOU'LL BLOW MY *SECRET IDENTITY*!
I NEED THE BUCKET.
BLEURGGH!
AHHH!

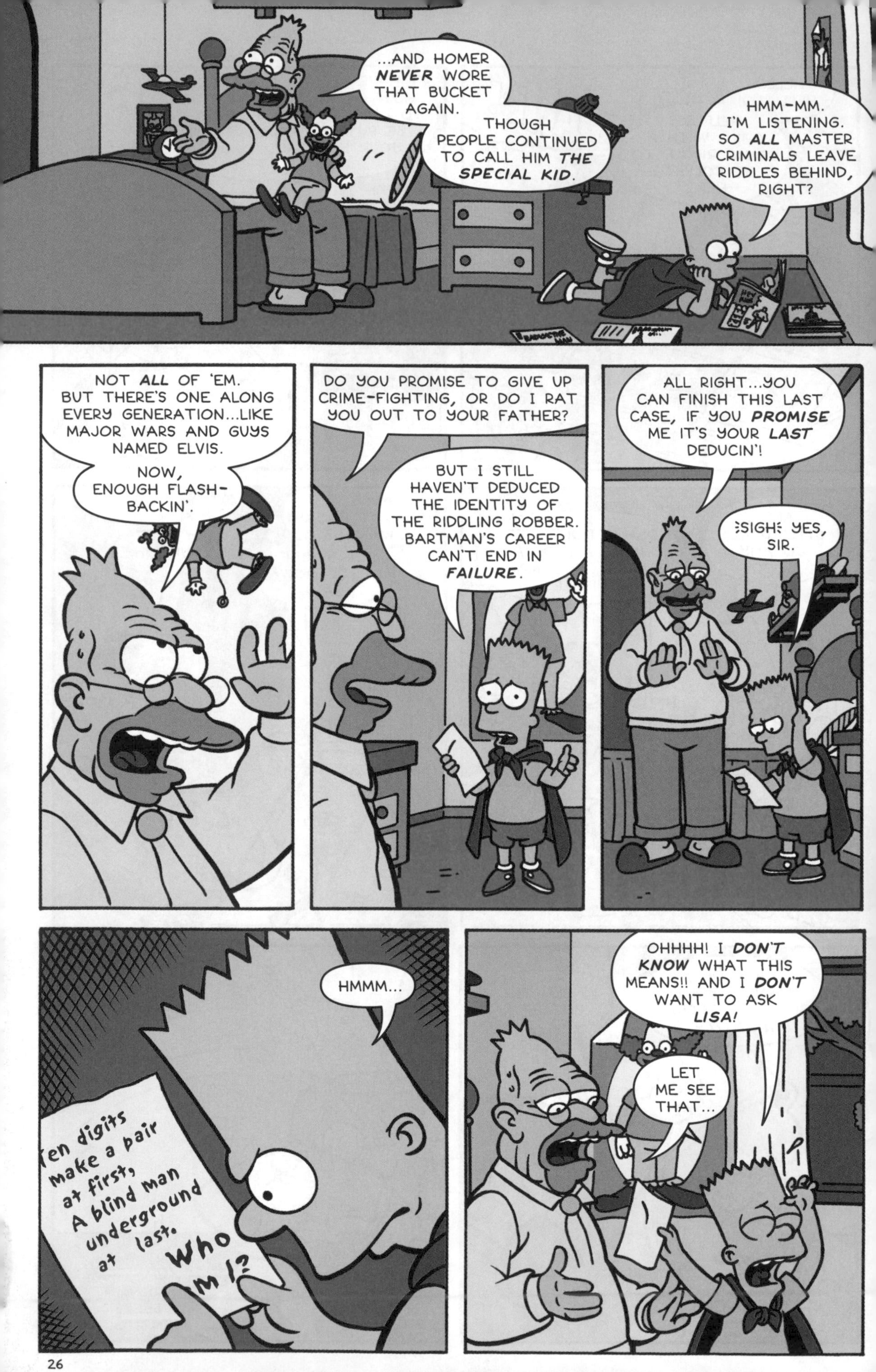
...AND HOMER NEVER WORE THAT BUCKET AGAIN.
THOUGH PEOPLE CONTINUED TO CALL HIM THE SPECIAL KID.
HMM-MM. I'M LISTENING. SO ALL MASTER CRIMINALS LEAVE RIDDLES BEHIND, RIGHT?
NOT ALL OF 'EM. BUT THERE'S ONE ALONG EVERY GENERATION...LIKE MAJOR WARS AND GUYS NAMED ELVIS.
NOW, ENOUGH FLASH-BACKIN'.
DO YOU PROMISE TO GIVE UP CRIME-FIGHTING, OR DO I RAT YOU OUT TO YOUR FATHER?
BUT I STILL HAVEN'T DEDUCED THE IDENTITY OF THE RIDDLING ROBBER. BARTMAN'S CAREER CAN'T END IN FAILURE.
ALL RIGHT...YOU CAN FINISH THIS LAST CASE, IF YOU PROMISE ME IT'S YOUR LAST DEDUCIN'!
SIGH YES, SIR.
HMMM...
Ten digits make a pair at first, A blind man underground at last. Who m I?
OHHHH! I DON'T KNOW WHAT THIS MEANS!! AND I DON'T WANT TO ASK LISA!
LET ME SEE THAT...

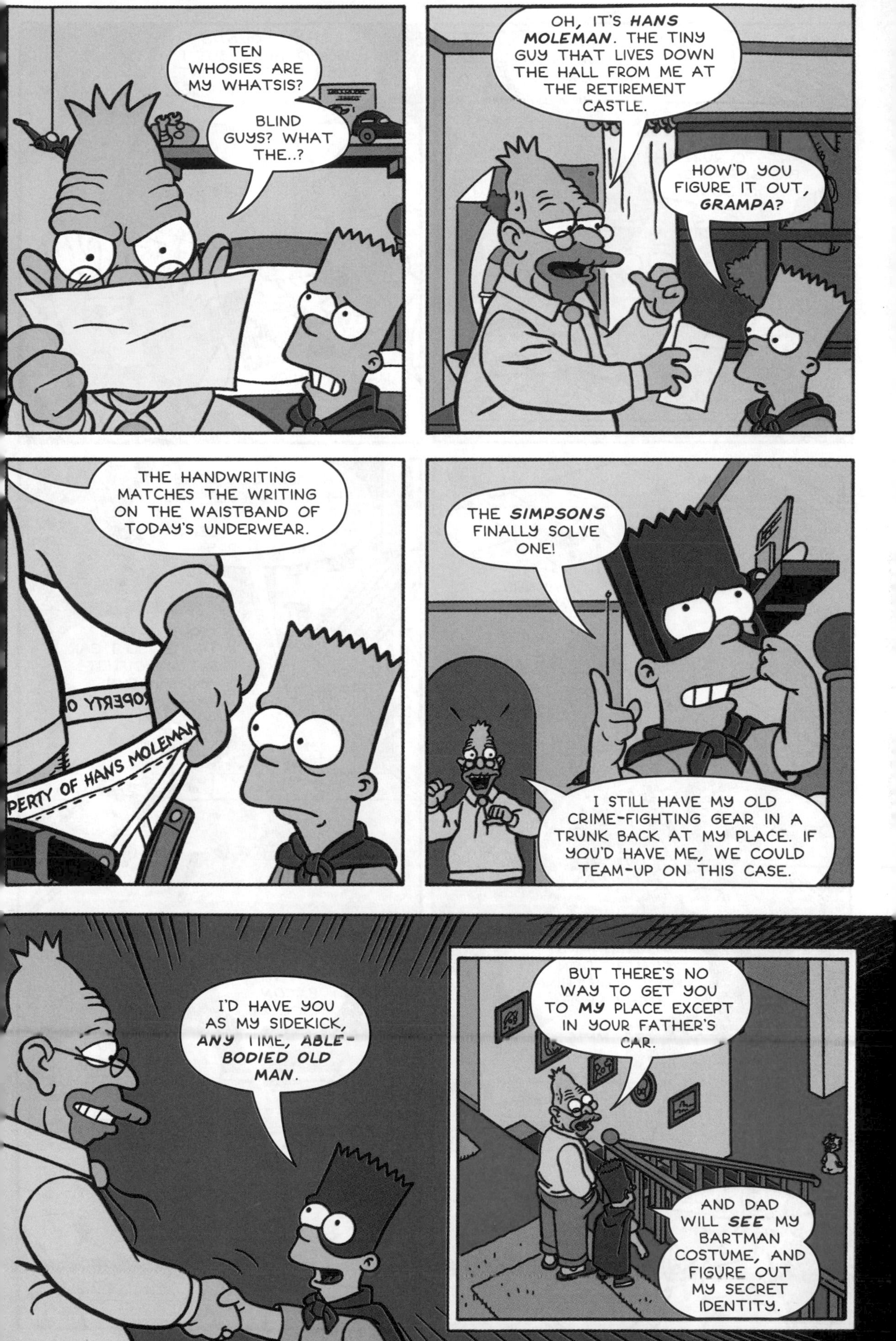
TEN WHOSIES ARE MY WHATSIS?
BLIND GUYS? WHAT THE..?
OH, IT'S HANS MOLEMAN. THE TINY GUY THAT LIVES DOWN THE HALL FROM ME AT THE RETIREMENT CASTLE.
HOW'D YOU FIGURE IT OUT, GRAMPA?
THE HANDWRITING MATCHES THE WRITING ON THE WAISTBAND OF TODAY'S UNDERWEAR.
PERTY OF HANS MOLEMAN
THE SIMPSONS FINALLY SOLVE ONE!
I STILL HAVE MY OLD CRIME-FIGHTING GEAR IN A TRUNK BACK AT MY PLACE. IF YOU'D HAVE ME, WE COULD TEAM-UP ON THIS CASE.
I'D HAVE YOU AS MY SIDEKICK, ANY TIME, ABLE-BODIED OLD MAN.
BUT THERE'S NO WAY TO GET YOU TO MY PLACE EXCEPT IN YOUR FATHER'S CAR.
AND DAD WILL SEE MY BARTMAN COSTUME, AND FIGURE OUT MY SECRET IDENTITY.

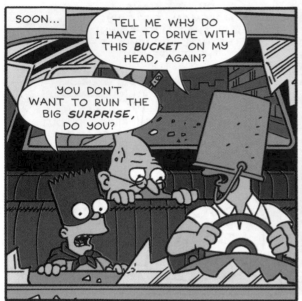

SOON...

TELL ME WHY DO I HAVE TO DRIVE WITH THIS *BUCKET* ON MY HEAD, AGAIN?

YOU DON'T WANT TO RUIN THE BIG *SURPRISE*, DO YOU?

THAT *SOUNDS* REASONABLE...BUT I NEED ANOTHER HINT. DOES THE SURPRISE INCLUDE *BACON*?

MAKE A QUICK LEFT IF YOU DON'T WANT TO HIT THE STOP SIGN.

ANNNND... WE'RE HERE! *HIT THE BRAKES!*

SCREEEECH!

WAM!

HOMER, YOU STAY HERE AND KEEP THE MOTOR RUNNING IN CASE WE HAVE TO LEAVE IN A HURRY.

BART, WAIT WITH ME, SO I CAN GET MY OUTFIT AND MY GUNS.

OUTFIT AND *GUNS*? I DON'T KNOW...SOMETHING'S *FISHY* HERE...

MMM... FISH.

FISH WITH *BACON*... OOOOH.

CAN *YOU* DRIVE ME *HOME*, MR. ROBOT MAN?

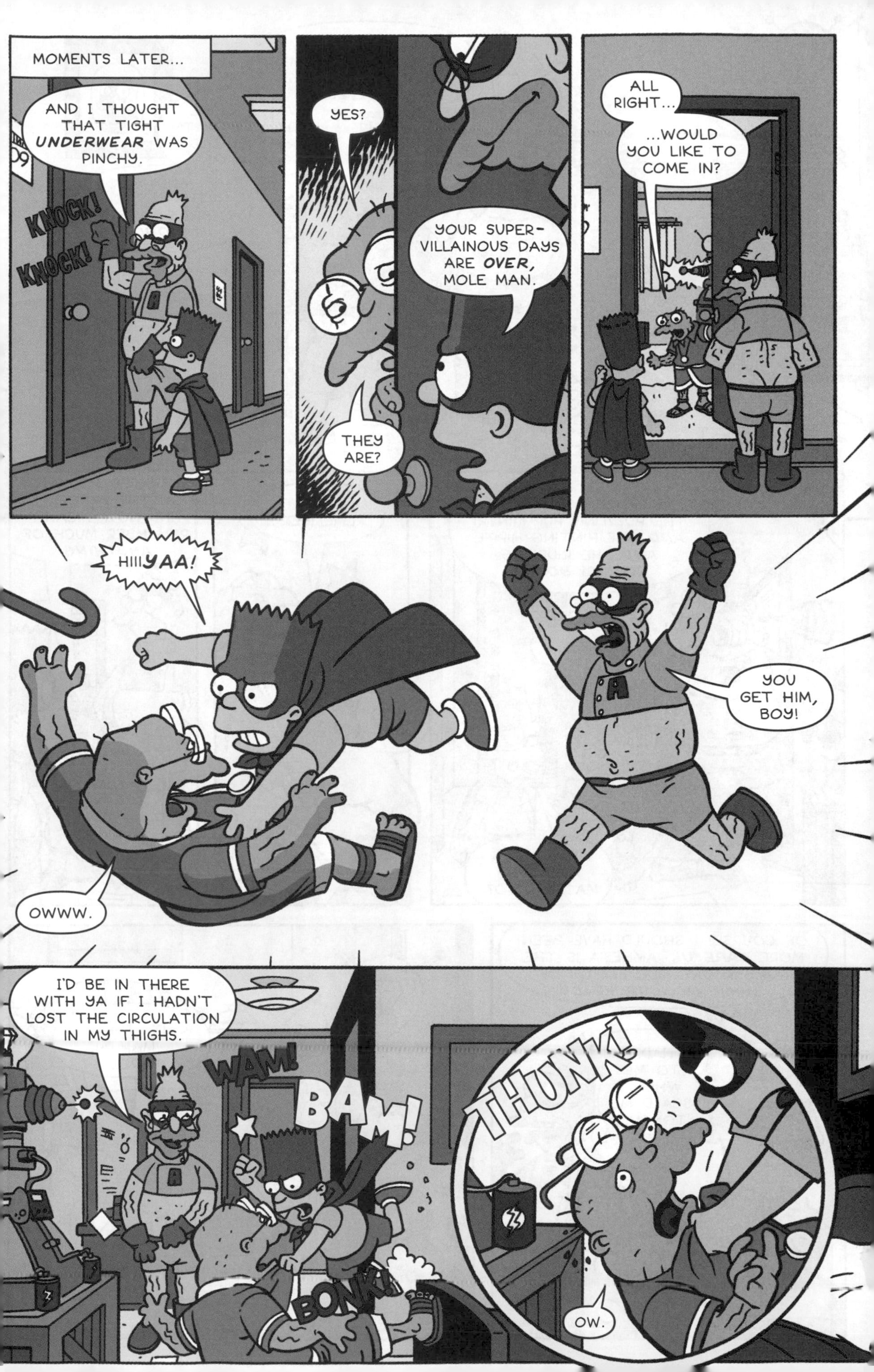
MOMENTS LATER...
AND I THOUGHT THAT TIGHT UNDERWEAR WAS PINCHY.
KNOCK! KNOCK!
YES?
YOUR SUPER-VILLAINOUS DAYS ARE OVER, MOLE MAN.
THEY ARE?
ALL RIGHT...
...WOULD YOU LIKE TO COME IN?
HIIIYAA!
YOU GET HIM, BOY!
OWWW.
I'D BE IN THERE WITH YA IF I HADN'T LOST THE CIRCULATION IN MY THIGHS.
WAM!
BAM!
BONK!
THUNK!
OW.

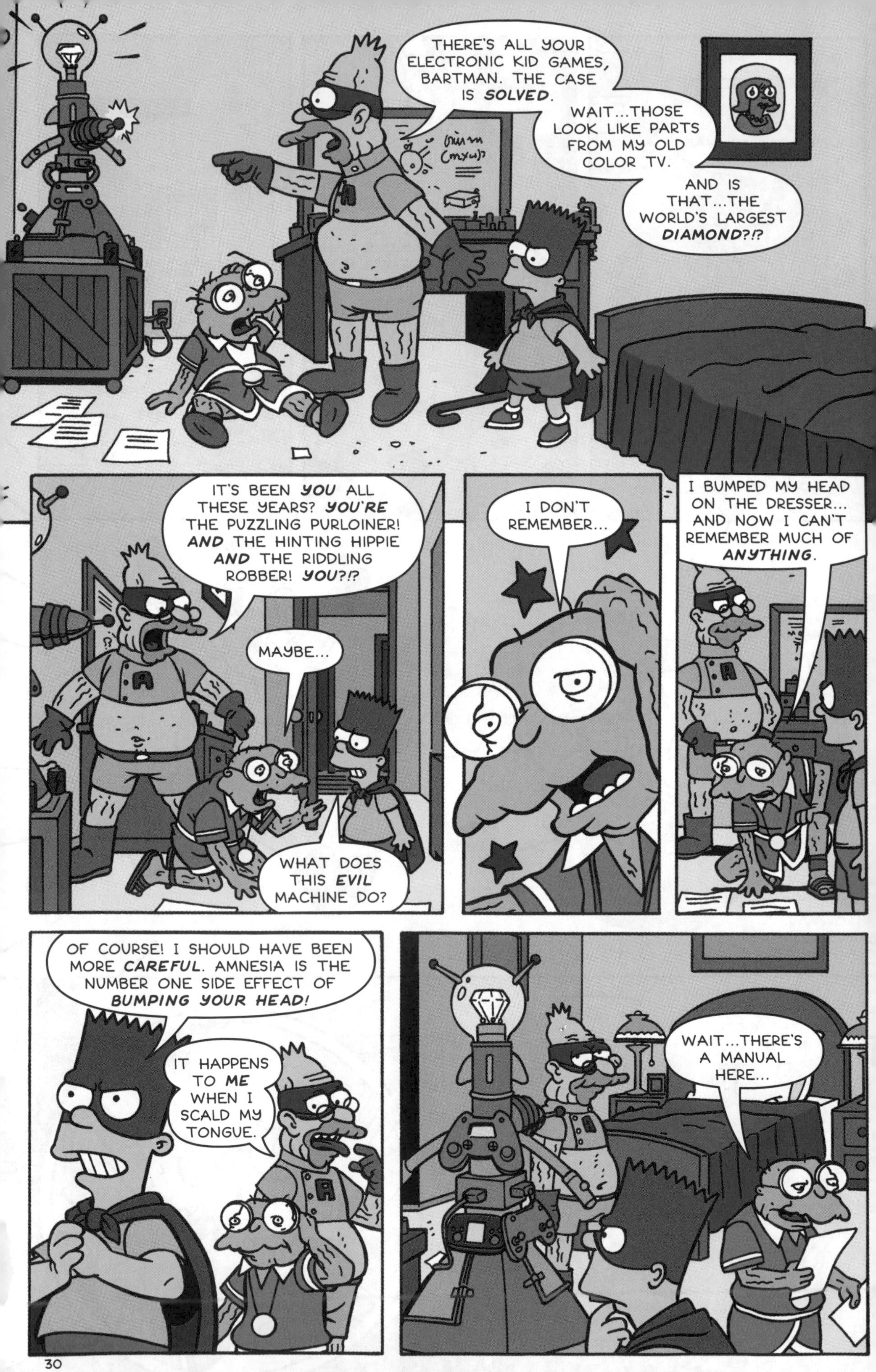
THERE'S ALL YOUR ELECTRONIC KID GAMES, BARTMAN. THE CASE IS *SOLVED*.
WAIT...THOSE LOOK LIKE PARTS FROM MY OLD COLOR TV.
AND IS THAT...THE WORLD'S LARGEST *DIAMOND*?!?
IT'S BEEN *YOU* ALL THESE YEARS? *YOU'RE* THE PUZZLING PURLOINER! *AND* THE HINTING HIPPIE *AND* THE RIDDLING ROBBER! *YOU*?!?
MAYBE...
WHAT DOES THIS *EVIL* MACHINE DO?
I DON'T REMEMBER...
I BUMPED MY HEAD ON THE DRESSER... AND NOW I CAN'T REMEMBER MUCH OF *ANYTHING*.
OF COURSE! I SHOULD HAVE BEEN MORE *CAREFUL*. AMNESIA IS THE NUMBER ONE SIDE EFFECT OF *BUMPING YOUR HEAD*!
IT HAPPENS TO *ME* WHEN I SCALD MY TONGUE.
WAIT...THERE'S A MANUAL HERE...

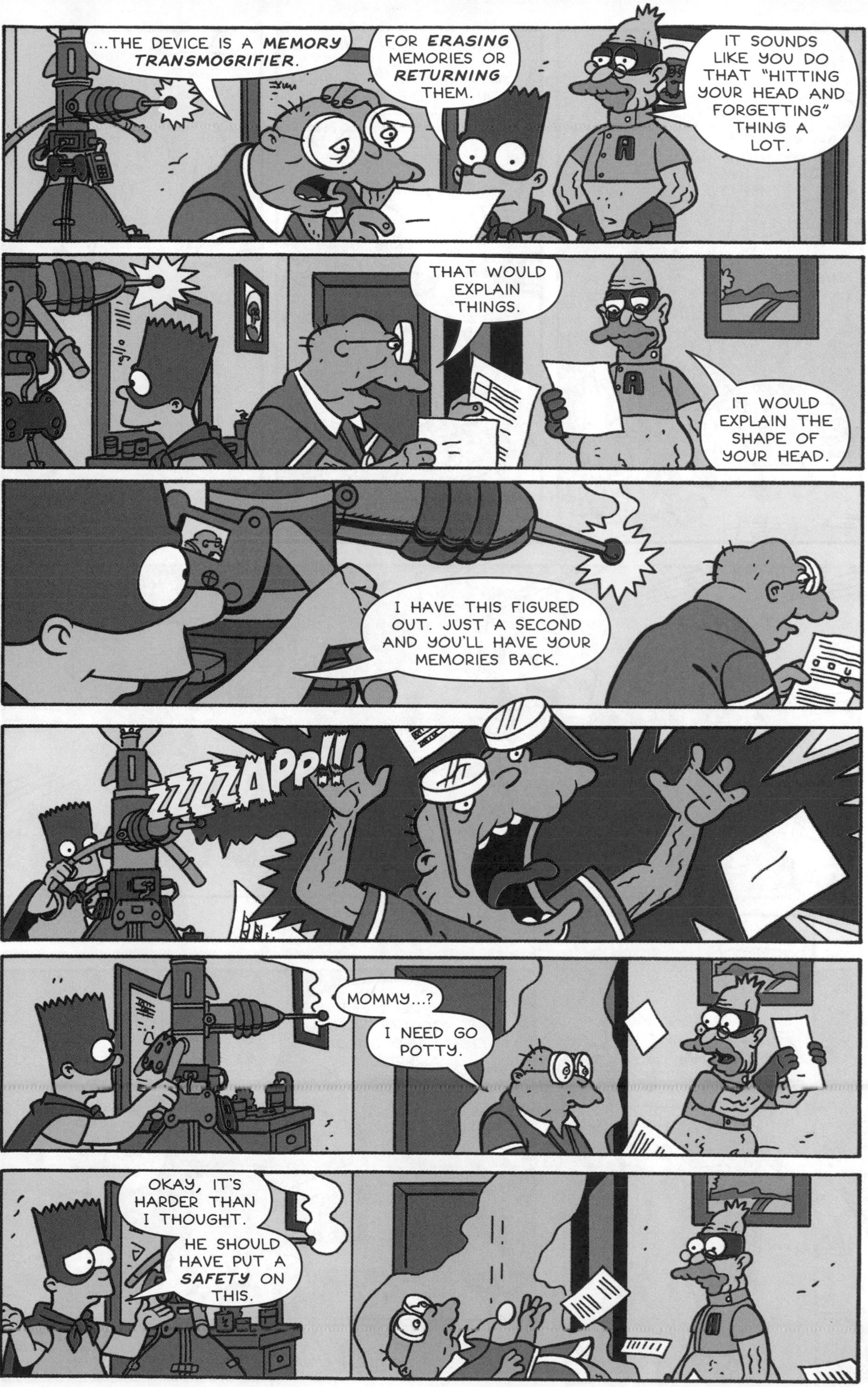
...THE DEVICE IS A MEMORY TRANSMOGRIFIER.
FOR ERASING MEMORIES OR RETURNING THEM.
IT SOUNDS LIKE YOU DO THAT "HITTING YOUR HEAD AND FORGETTING" THING A LOT.
THAT WOULD EXPLAIN THINGS.
IT WOULD EXPLAIN THE SHAPE OF YOUR HEAD.
I HAVE THIS FIGURED OUT. JUST A SECOND AND YOU'LL HAVE YOUR MEMORIES BACK.
ZZZZAPP!!
MOMMY...?
I NEED GO POTTY.
OKAY, IT'S HARDER THAN I THOUGHT.
HE SHOULD HAVE PUT A SAFETY ON THIS.

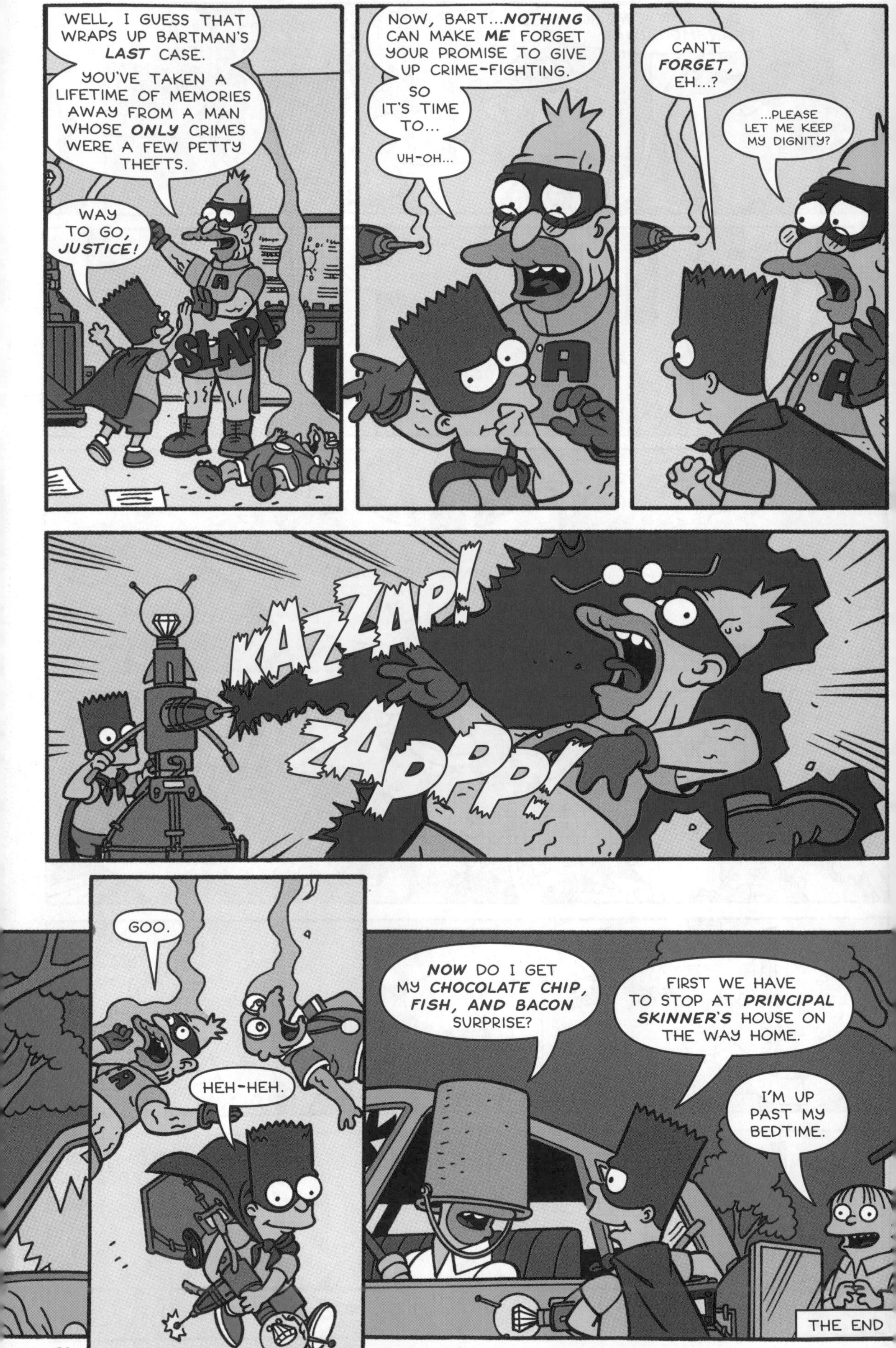
WELL, I GUESS THAT WRAPS UP BARTMAN'S LAST CASE.
YOU'VE TAKEN A LIFETIME OF MEMORIES AWAY FROM A MAN WHOSE ONLY CRIMES WERE A FEW PETTY THEFTS.
WAY TO GO, JUSTICE!
SLAP!
NOW, BART...NOTHING CAN MAKE ME FORGET YOUR PROMISE TO GIVE UP CRIME-FIGHTING.
SO IT'S TIME TO...
UH-OH...
CAN'T FORGET, EH...?
...PLEASE LET ME KEEP MY DIGNITY?
KAZZAP!
ZAPPP!
GOO.
HEH-HEH.
NOW DO I GET MY CHOCOLATE CHIP, FISH, AND BACON SURPRISE?
FIRST WE HAVE TO STOP AT PRINCIPAL SKINNER'S HOUSE ON THE WAY HOME.
I'M UP PAST MY BEDTIME.
THE END

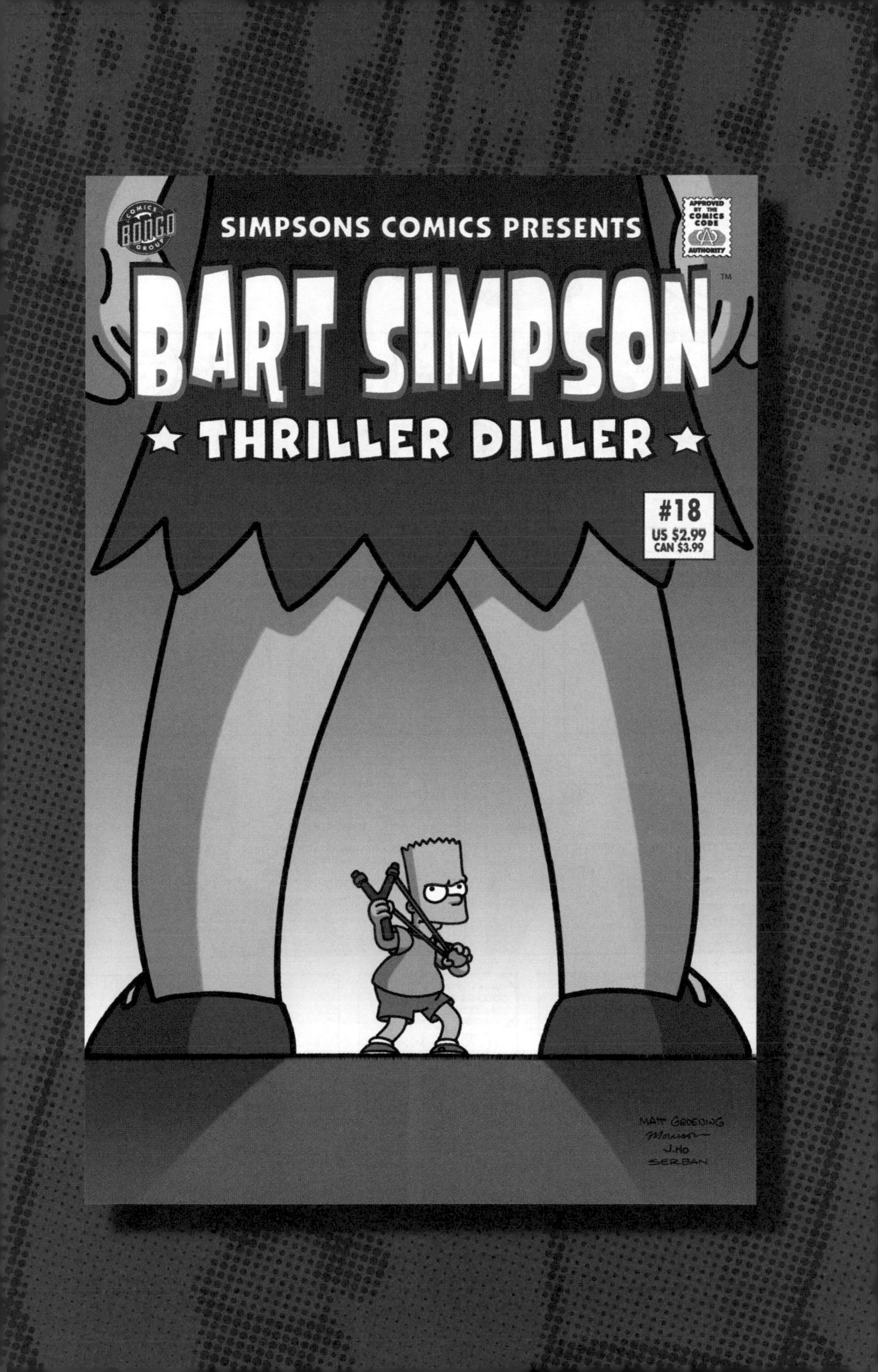
COMICS BONGO GROUP
SIMPSONS COMICS PRESENTS
APPROVED BY THE COMICS CODE AUTHORITY
BART SIMPSON™
THRILLER DILLER
#18
US $2.99
CAN $3.99
MATT GROENING
J.HO
SERBAN

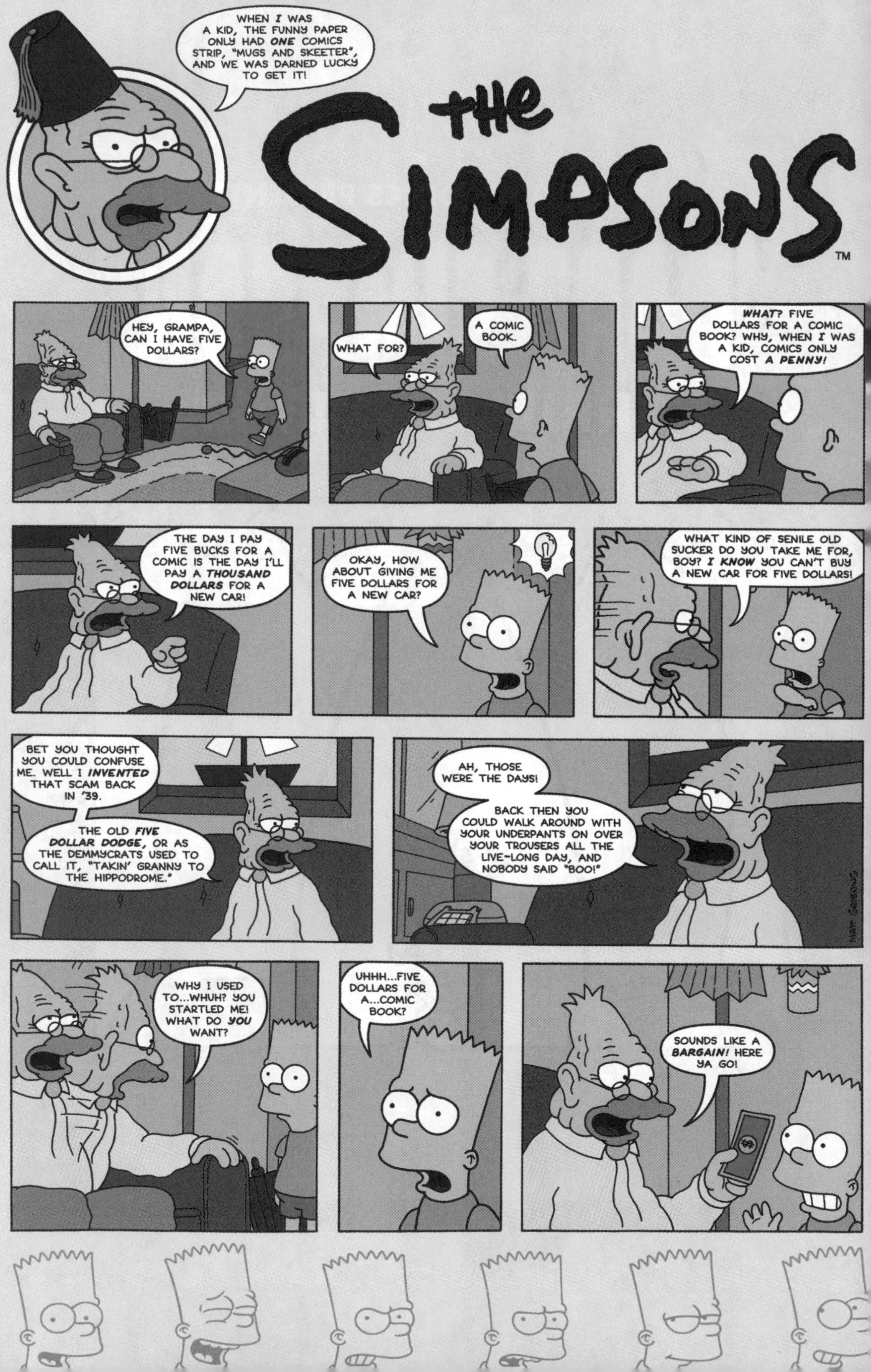

WHEN I WAS A KID, THE FUNNY PAPER ONLY HAD ONE COMICS STRIP, "MUGS AND SKEETER", AND WE WAS DARNED LUCKY TO GET IT!
THE SIMPSONS™
HEY, GRAMPA, CAN I HAVE FIVE DOLLARS?
WHAT FOR?
A COMIC BOOK.
WHAT? FIVE DOLLARS FOR A COMIC BOOK? WHY, WHEN I WAS A KID, COMICS ONLY COST A PENNY!
THE DAY I PAY FIVE BUCKS FOR A COMIC IS THE DAY I'LL PAY A THOUSAND DOLLARS FOR A NEW CAR!
OKAY, HOW ABOUT GIVING ME FIVE DOLLARS FOR A NEW CAR?
WHAT KIND OF SENILE OLD SUCKER DO YOU TAKE ME FOR, BOY? I KNOW YOU CAN'T BUY A NEW CAR FOR FIVE DOLLARS!
BET YOU THOUGHT YOU COULD CONFUSE ME. WELL I INVENTED THAT SCAM BACK IN '39.
THE OLD FIVE DOLLAR DODGE, OR AS THE DEMMYCRATS USED TO CALL IT, "TAKIN' GRANNY TO THE HIPPODROME."
AH, THOSE WERE THE DAYS!
BACK THEN YOU COULD WALK AROUND WITH YOUR UNDERPANTS ON OVER YOUR TROUSERS ALL THE LIVE-LONG DAY, AND NOBODY SAID "BOO!"
MATT GROENING
WHY I USED TO...WHUH? YOU STARTLED ME! WHAT DO YOU WANT?
UHHH...FIVE DOLLARS FOR A...COMIC BOOK?
SOUNDS LIKE A BARGAIN! HERE YA GO!

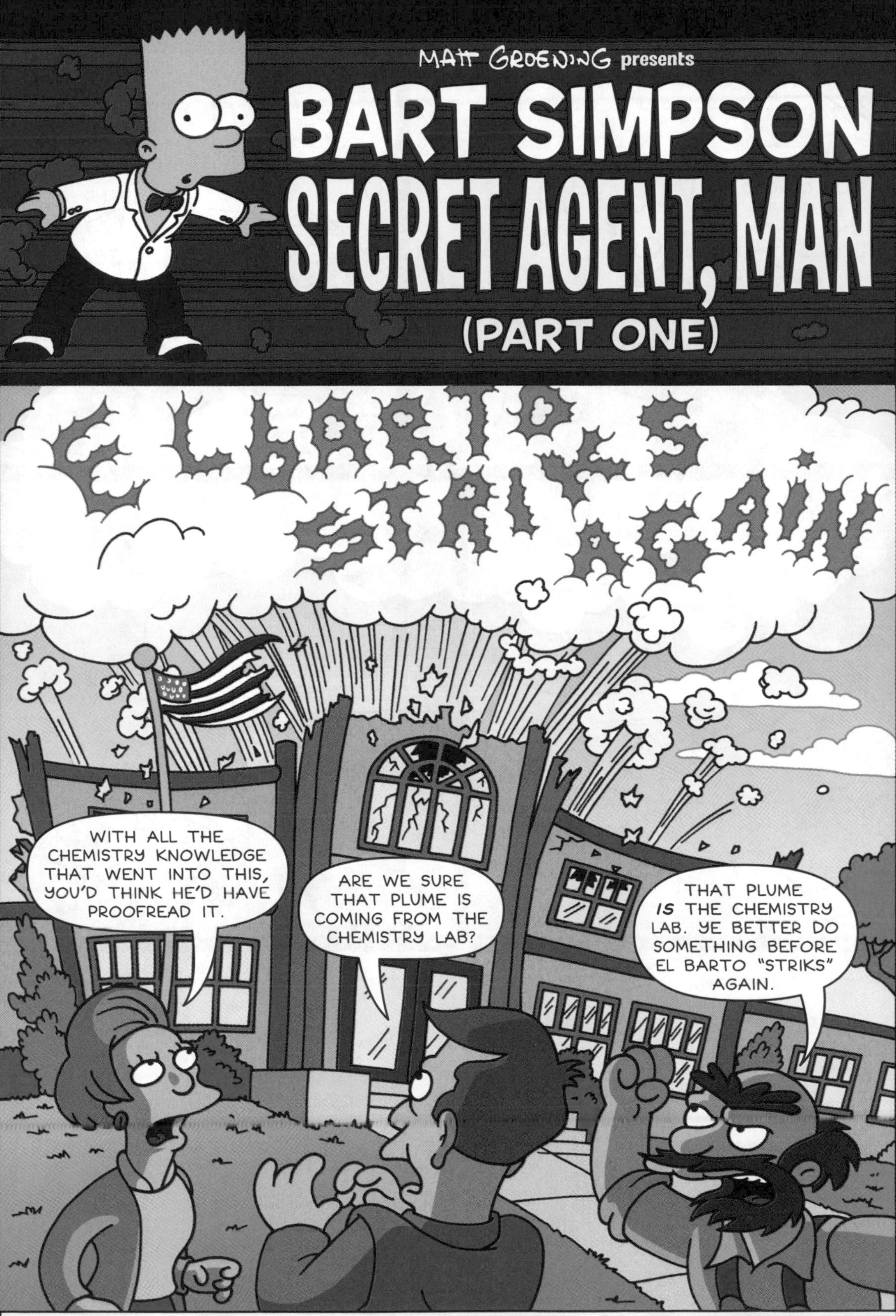
MATT GROENING presents
BART SIMPSON
SECRET AGENT, MAN
(PART ONE)
EL BARTO STRIKS AGAIN
WITH ALL THE CHEMISTRY KNOWLEDGE THAT WENT INTO THIS, YOU'D THINK HE'D HAVE PROOFREAD IT.
ARE WE SURE THAT PLUME IS COMING FROM THE CHEMISTRY LAB?
THAT PLUME *IS* THE CHEMISTRY LAB. YE BETTER DO SOMETHING BEFORE EL BARTO "STRIKS" AGAIN.

PATRIC VERRONE SCRIPT
RYAN RIVETTE PENCILS
PATRICK OWSLEY INKS
ART VILLANUEVA COLORS
KAREN BATES LETTERS
BILL MORRISON EDITOR

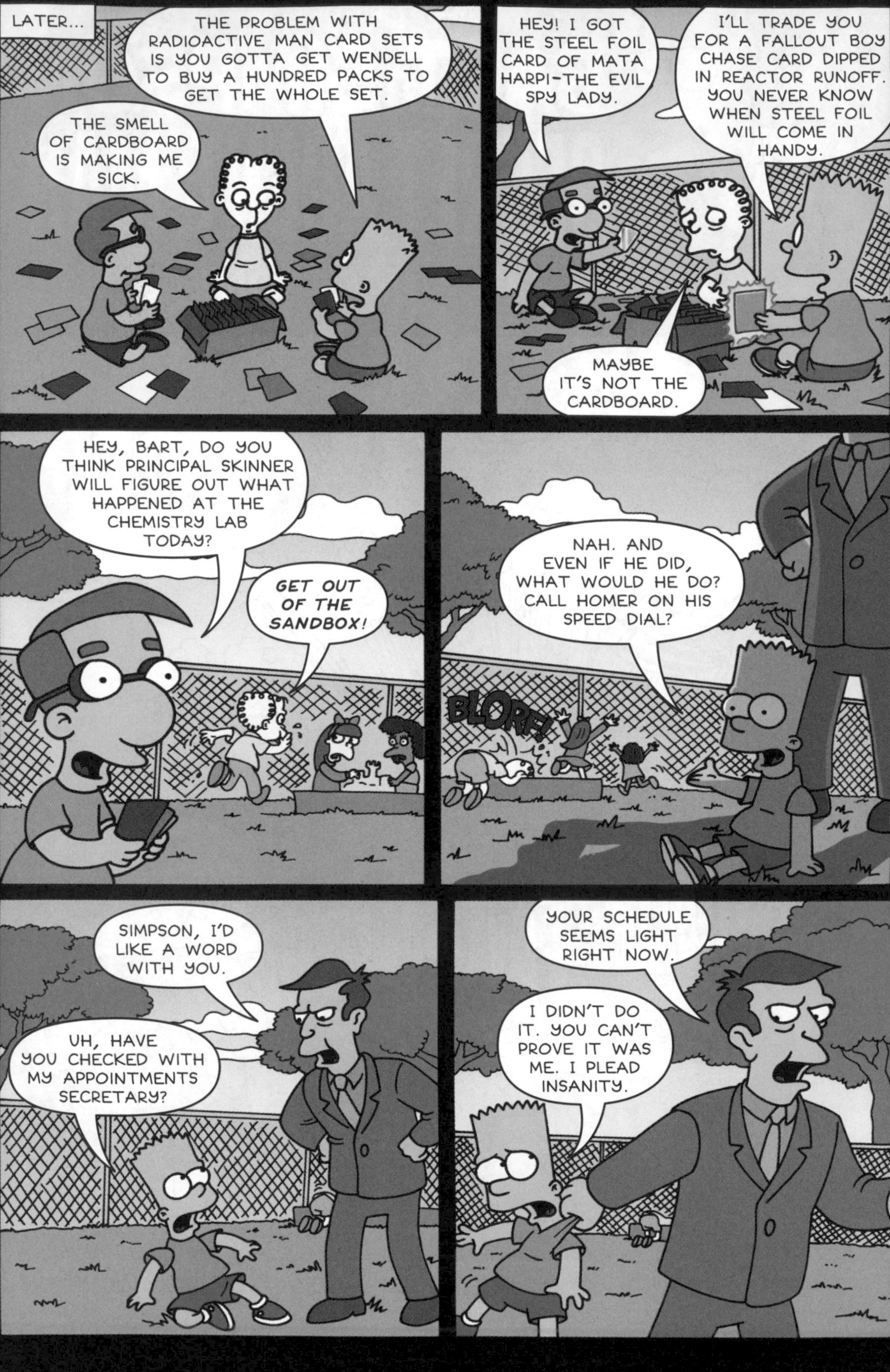
LATER...
THE PROBLEM WITH RADIOACTIVE MAN CARD SETS IS YOU GOTTA GET WENDELL TO BUY A HUNDRED PACKS TO GET THE WHOLE SET.
THE SMELL OF CARDBOARD IS MAKING ME SICK.
HEY! I GOT THE STEEL FOIL CARD OF MATA HARPI—THE EVIL SPY LADY.
I'LL TRADE YOU FOR A FALLOUT BOY CHASE CARD DIPPED IN REACTOR RUNOFF. YOU NEVER KNOW WHEN STEEL FOIL WILL COME IN HANDY.
MAYBE IT'S NOT THE CARDBOARD.
HEY, BART, DO YOU THINK PRINCIPAL SKINNER WILL FIGURE OUT WHAT HAPPENED AT THE CHEMISTRY LAB TODAY?
GET OUT OF THE SANDBOX!
NAH. AND EVEN IF HE DID, WHAT WOULD HE DO? CALL HOMER ON HIS SPEED DIAL?
BLORF!
SIMPSON, I'D LIKE A WORD WITH YOU.
UH, HAVE YOU CHECKED WITH MY APPOINTMENTS SECRETARY?
YOUR SCHEDULE SEEMS LIGHT RIGHT NOW.
I DIDN'T DO IT. YOU CAN'T PROVE IT WAS ME. I PLEAD INSANITY.

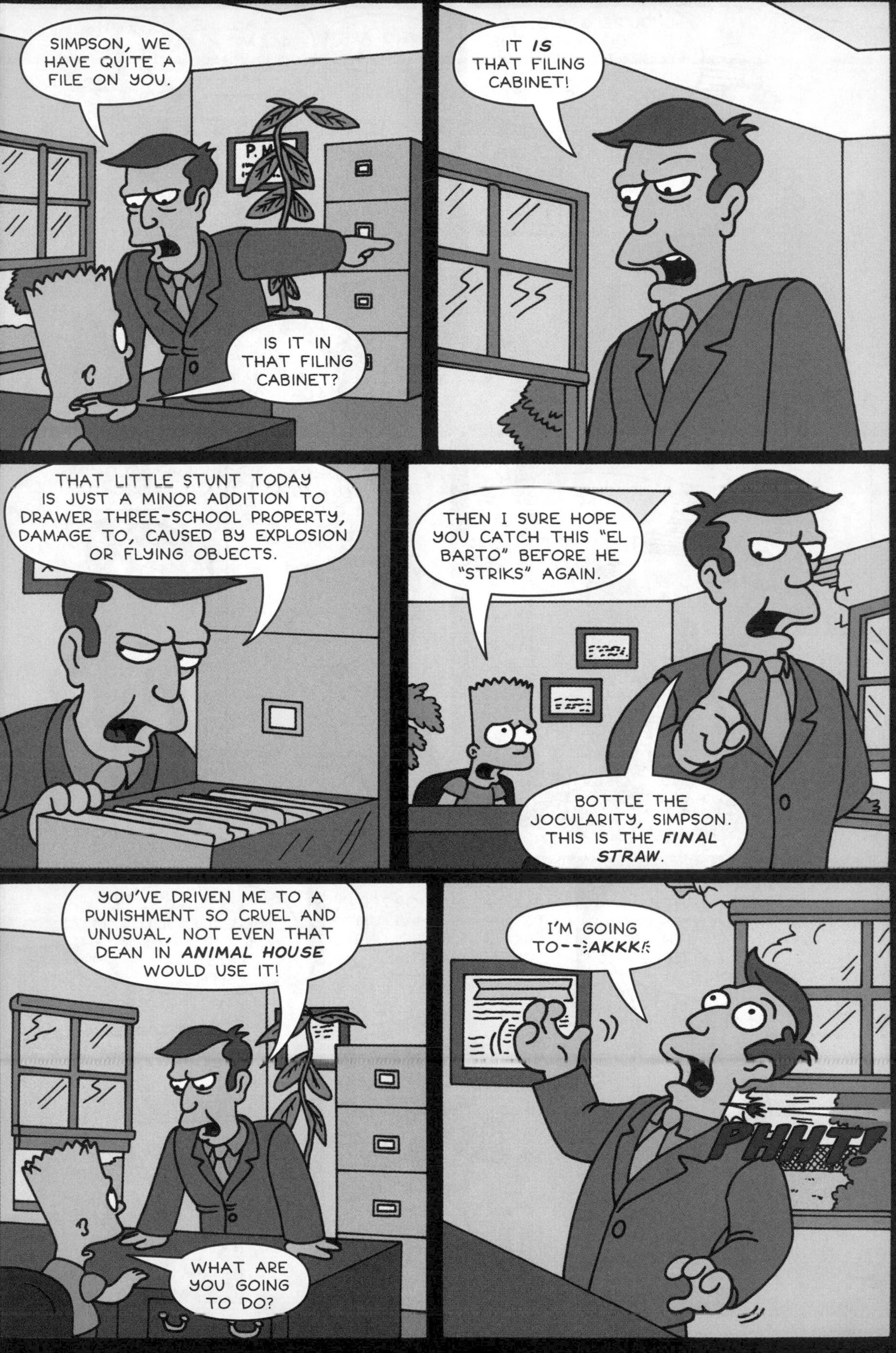
SIMPSON, WE HAVE QUITE A FILE ON YOU.
IS IT IN THAT FILING CABINET?
IT *IS* THAT FILING CABINET!
THAT LITTLE STUNT TODAY IS JUST A MINOR ADDITION TO DRAWER THREE-SCHOOL PROPERTY, DAMAGE TO, CAUSED BY EXPLOSION OR FLYING OBJECTS.
THEN I SURE HOPE YOU CATCH THIS "EL BARTO" BEFORE HE "STRIKS" AGAIN.
BOTTLE THE JOCULARITY, SIMPSON. THIS IS THE *FINAL STRAW*.
YOU'VE DRIVEN ME TO A PUNISHMENT SO CRUEL AND UNUSUAL, NOT EVEN THAT DEAN IN *ANIMAL HOUSE* WOULD USE IT!
WHAT ARE YOU GOING TO DO?
I'M GOING TO--*AKKK*
PHHT!

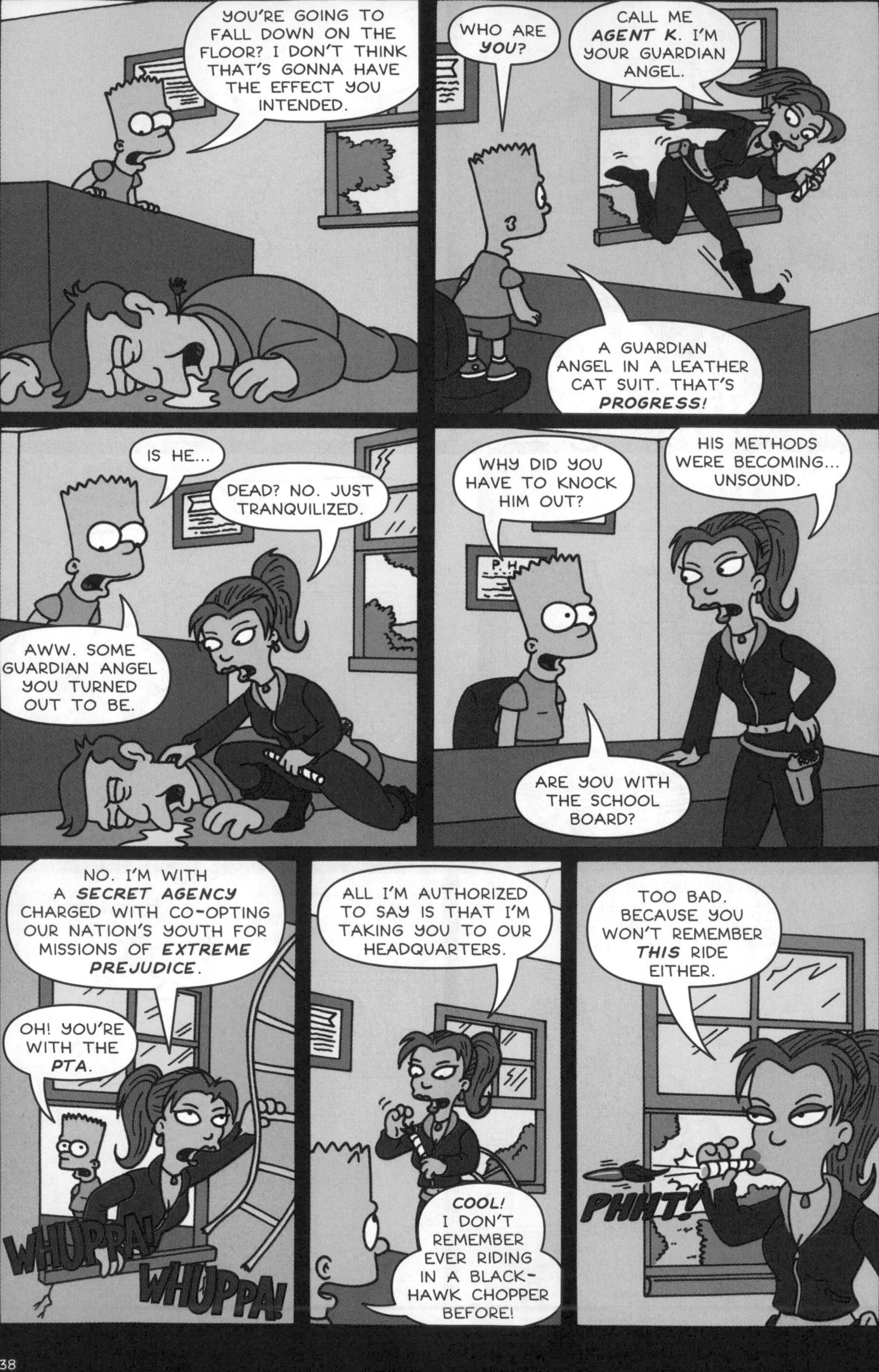
YOU'RE GOING TO FALL DOWN ON THE FLOOR? I DON'T THINK THAT'S GONNA HAVE THE EFFECT YOU INTENDED.
WHO ARE *YOU*?
CALL ME ***AGENT K***. I'M YOUR GUARDIAN ANGEL.
A GUARDIAN ANGEL IN A LEATHER CAT SUIT. THAT'S ***PROGRESS***!
IS HE...
DEAD? NO. JUST TRANQUILIZED.
AWW. SOME GUARDIAN ANGEL YOU TURNED OUT TO BE.
WHY DID YOU HAVE TO KNOCK HIM OUT?
HIS METHODS WERE BECOMING... UNSOUND.
ARE YOU WITH THE SCHOOL BOARD?
NO. I'M WITH A ***SECRET AGENCY*** CHARGED WITH CO-OPTING OUR NATION'S YOUTH FOR MISSIONS OF ***EXTREME PREJUDICE***.
OH! YOU'RE WITH THE ***PTA***.
WHUPPA!
WHUPPA!
ALL I'M AUTHORIZED TO SAY IS THAT I'M TAKING YOU TO OUR HEADQUARTERS.
COOL! I DON'T REMEMBER EVER RIDING IN A BLACK-HAWK CHOPPER BEFORE!
TOO BAD. BECAUSE YOU WON'T REMEMBER ***THIS*** RIDE EITHER.
PHHT!

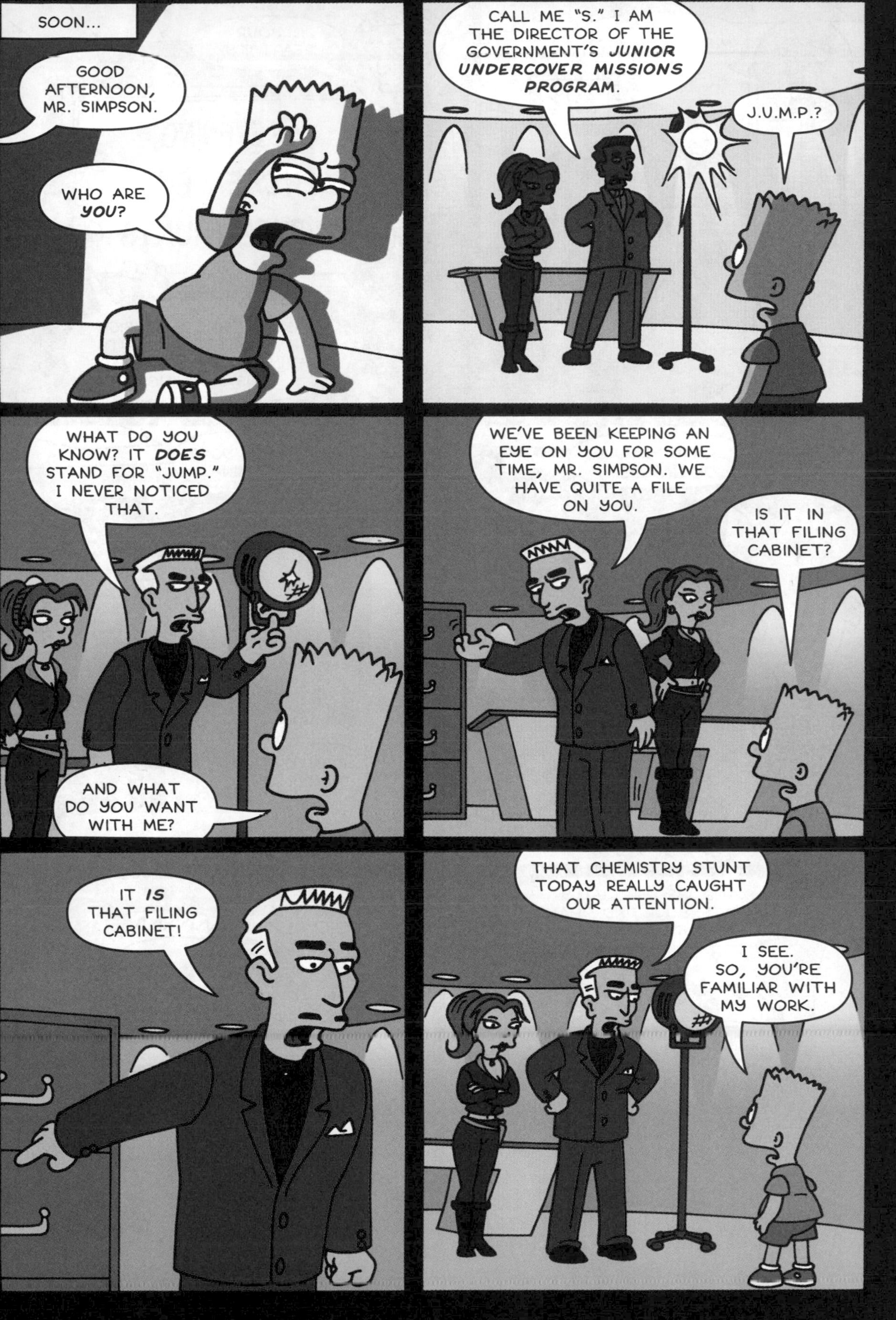
SOON...
GOOD AFTERNOON, MR. SIMPSON.
WHO ARE *YOU*?
CALL ME "S." I AM THE DIRECTOR OF THE GOVERNMENT'S ***JUNIOR UNDERCOVER MISSIONS PROGRAM***.
J.U.M.P.?
WHAT DO YOU KNOW? IT ***DOES*** STAND FOR "JUMP." I NEVER NOTICED THAT.
AND WHAT DO YOU WANT WITH ME?
WE'VE BEEN KEEPING AN EYE ON YOU FOR SOME TIME, MR. SIMPSON. WE HAVE QUITE A FILE ON YOU.
IS IT IN THAT FILING CABINET?
IT ***IS*** THAT FILING CABINET!
THAT CHEMISTRY STUNT TODAY REALLY CAUGHT OUR ATTENTION.
I SEE. SO, YOU'RE FAMILIAR WITH MY WORK.

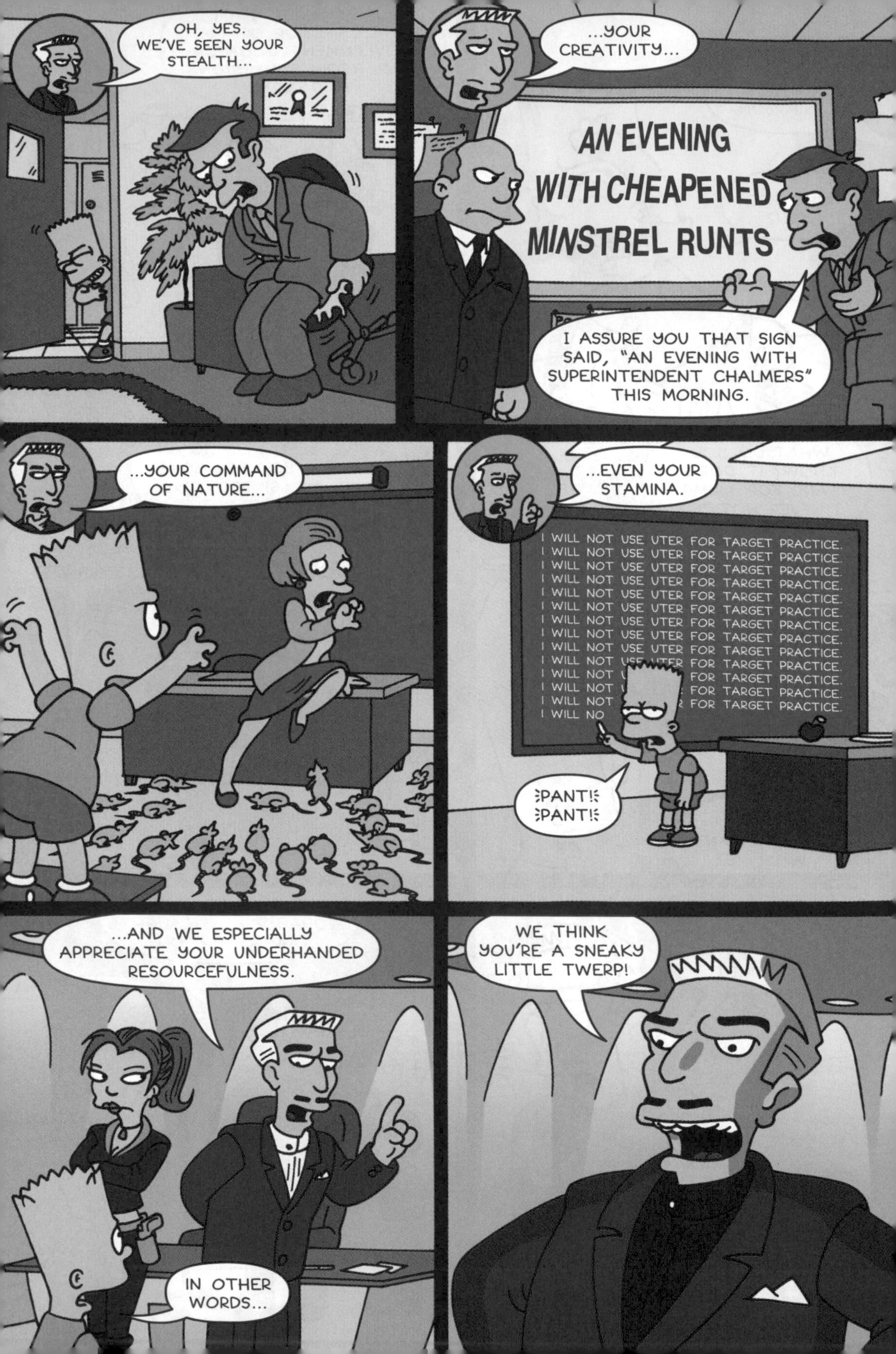
OH, YES. WE'VE SEEN YOUR STEALTH...
...YOUR CREATIVITY...
AN EVENING WITH CHEAPENED MINSTREL RUNTS
I ASSURE YOU THAT SIGN SAID, "AN EVENING WITH SUPERINTENDENT CHALMERS" THIS MORNING.
...YOUR COMMAND OF NATURE...
...EVEN YOUR STAMINA.
I WILL NOT USE UTER FOR TARGET PRACTICE.
I WILL NO
PANT! PANT!
...AND WE ESPECIALLY APPRECIATE YOUR UNDERHANDED RESOURCEFULNESS.
IN OTHER WORDS...
WE THINK YOU'RE A SNEAKY LITTLE TWERP!

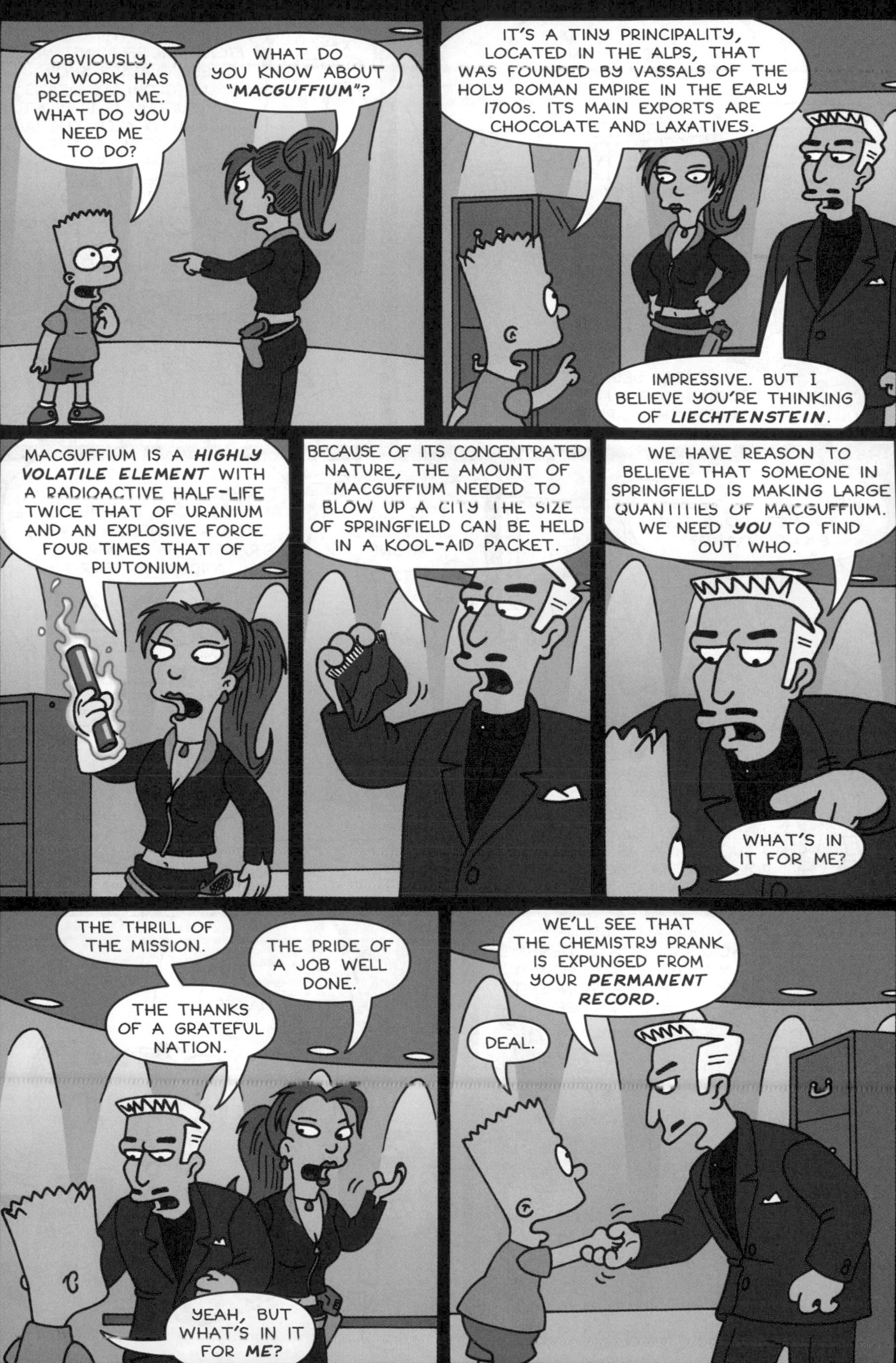
OBVIOUSLY, MY WORK HAS PRECEDED ME. WHAT DO YOU NEED ME TO DO?
WHAT DO YOU KNOW ABOUT "MACGUFFIUM"?
IT'S A TINY PRINCIPALITY, LOCATED IN THE ALPS, THAT WAS FOUNDED BY VASSALS OF THE HOLY ROMAN EMPIRE IN THE EARLY 1700s. ITS MAIN EXPORTS ARE CHOCOLATE AND LAXATIVES.
IMPRESSIVE. BUT I BELIEVE YOU'RE THINKING OF LIECHTENSTEIN.
MACGUFFIUM IS A HIGHLY VOLATILE ELEMENT WITH A RADIOACTIVE HALF-LIFE TWICE THAT OF URANIUM AND AN EXPLOSIVE FORCE FOUR TIMES THAT OF PLUTONIUM.
BECAUSE OF ITS CONCENTRATED NATURE, THE AMOUNT OF MACGUFFIUM NEEDED TO BLOW UP A CITY THE SIZE OF SPRINGFIELD CAN BE HELD IN A KOOL-AID PACKET.
WE HAVE REASON TO BELIEVE THAT SOMEONE IN SPRINGFIELD IS MAKING LARGE QUANTITIES OF MACGUFFIUM. WE NEED YOU TO FIND OUT WHO.
WHAT'S IN IT FOR ME?
THE THRILL OF THE MISSION.
THE PRIDE OF A JOB WELL DONE.
THE THANKS OF A GRATEFUL NATION.
YEAH, BUT WHAT'S IN IT FOR ME?
WE'LL SEE THAT THE CHEMISTRY PRANK IS EXPUNGED FROM YOUR PERMANENT RECORD.
DEAL.

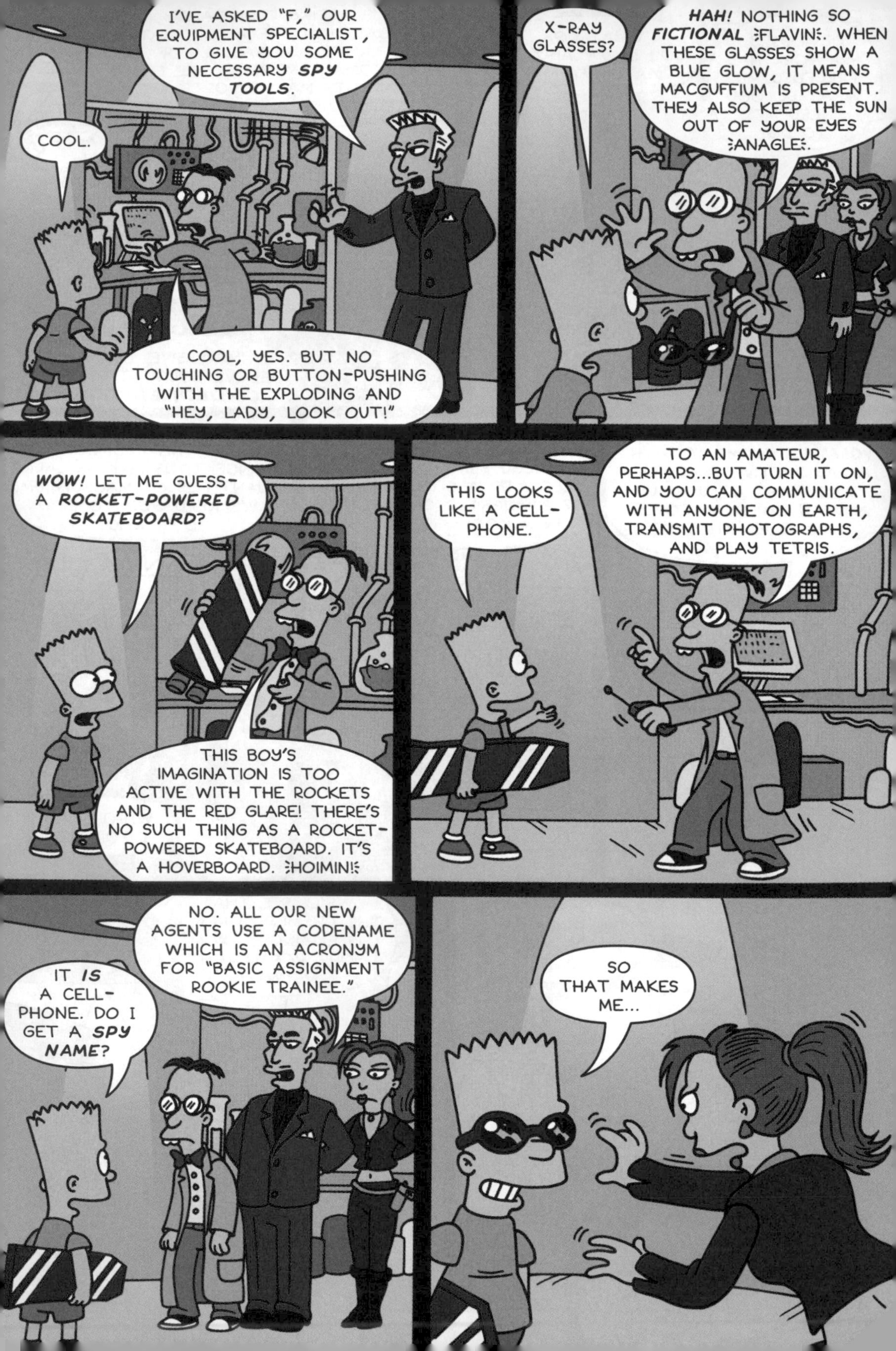
I'VE ASKED "F," OUR EQUIPMENT SPECIALIST, TO GIVE YOU SOME NECESSARY SPY TOOLS.
COOL.
COOL, YES. BUT NO TOUCHING OR BUTTON-PUSHING WITH THE EXPLODING AND "HEY, LADY, LOOK OUT!"
X-RAY GLASSES?
HAH! NOTHING SO FICTIONAL ⁝FLAVIN⁝. WHEN THESE GLASSES SHOW A BLUE GLOW, IT MEANS MACGUFFIUM IS PRESENT. THEY ALSO KEEP THE SUN OUT OF YOUR EYES ⁝ANAGLE⁝.
WOW! LET ME GUESS- A ROCKET-POWERED SKATEBOARD?
THIS BOY'S IMAGINATION IS TOO ACTIVE WITH THE ROCKETS AND THE RED GLARE! THERE'S NO SUCH THING AS A ROCKET-POWERED SKATEBOARD. IT'S A HOVERBOARD. ⁝HOIMIN!⁝
THIS LOOKS LIKE A CELL-PHONE.
TO AN AMATEUR, PERHAPS...BUT TURN IT ON, AND YOU CAN COMMUNICATE WITH ANYONE ON EARTH, TRANSMIT PHOTOGRAPHS, AND PLAY TETRIS.
IT IS A CELL-PHONE. DO I GET A SPY NAME?
NO. ALL OUR NEW AGENTS USE A CODENAME WHICH IS AN ACRONYM FOR "BASIC ASSIGNMENT ROOKIE TRAINEE."
SO THAT MAKES ME...

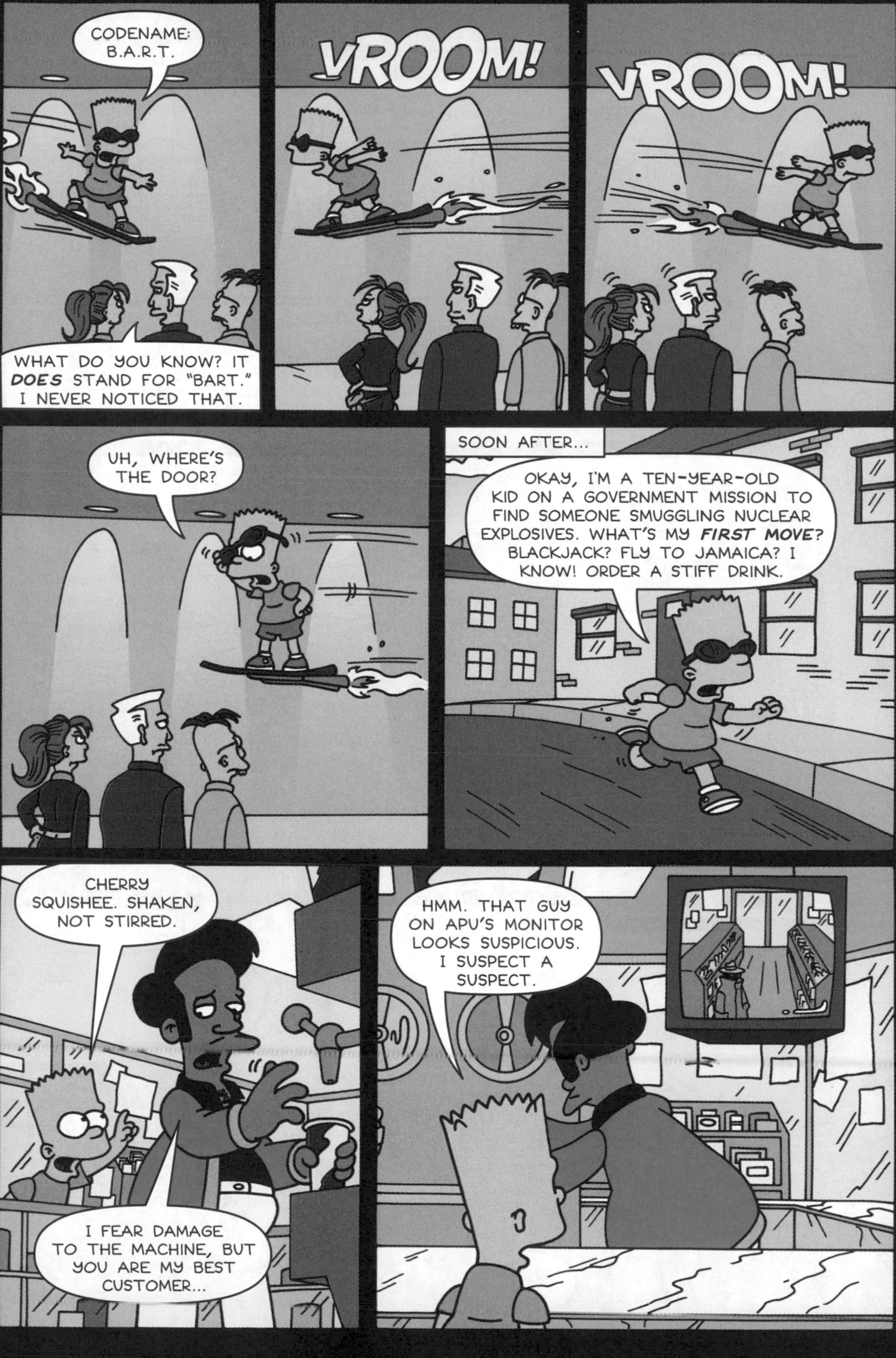
CODENAME: B.A.R.T.
WHAT DO YOU KNOW? IT *DOES* STAND FOR "BART." I NEVER NOTICED THAT.
VROOM!
VROOM!
UH, WHERE'S THE DOOR?
SOON AFTER...
OKAY, I'M A TEN-YEAR-OLD KID ON A GOVERNMENT MISSION TO FIND SOMEONE SMUGGLING NUCLEAR EXPLOSIVES. WHAT'S MY *FIRST MOVE*? BLACKJACK? FLY TO JAMAICA? I KNOW! ORDER A STIFF DRINK.
CHERRY SQUISHEE. SHAKEN, NOT STIRRED.
I FEAR DAMAGE TO THE MACHINE, BUT YOU ARE MY BEST CUSTOMER...
HMM. THAT GUY ON APU'S MONITOR LOOKS SUSPICIOUS. I SUSPECT A SUSPECT.

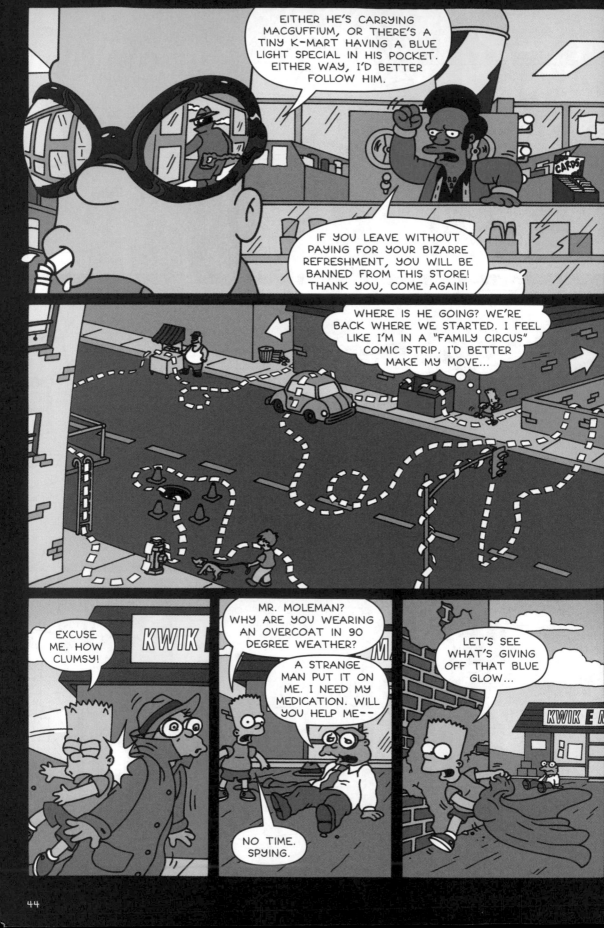

EITHER HE'S CARRYING MACGUFFIUM, OR THERE'S A TINY K-MART HAVING A BLUE LIGHT SPECIAL IN HIS POCKET. EITHER WAY, I'D BETTER FOLLOW HIM.

IF YOU LEAVE WITHOUT PAYING FOR YOUR BIZARRE REFRESHMENT, YOU WILL BE BANNED FROM THIS STORE! THANK YOU, COME AGAIN!

WHERE IS HE GOING? WE'RE BACK WHERE WE STARTED. I FEEL LIKE I'M IN A "FAMILY CIRCUS" COMIC STRIP. I'D BETTER MAKE MY MOVE...

EXCUSE ME. HOW CLUMSY!

MR. MOLEMAN? WHY ARE YOU WEARING AN OVERCOAT IN 90 DEGREE WEATHER?

A STRANGE MAN PUT IT ON ME. I NEED MY MEDICATION. WILL YOU HELP ME--

NO TIME. SPYING.

LET'S SEE WHAT'S GIVING OFF THAT BLUE GLOW...

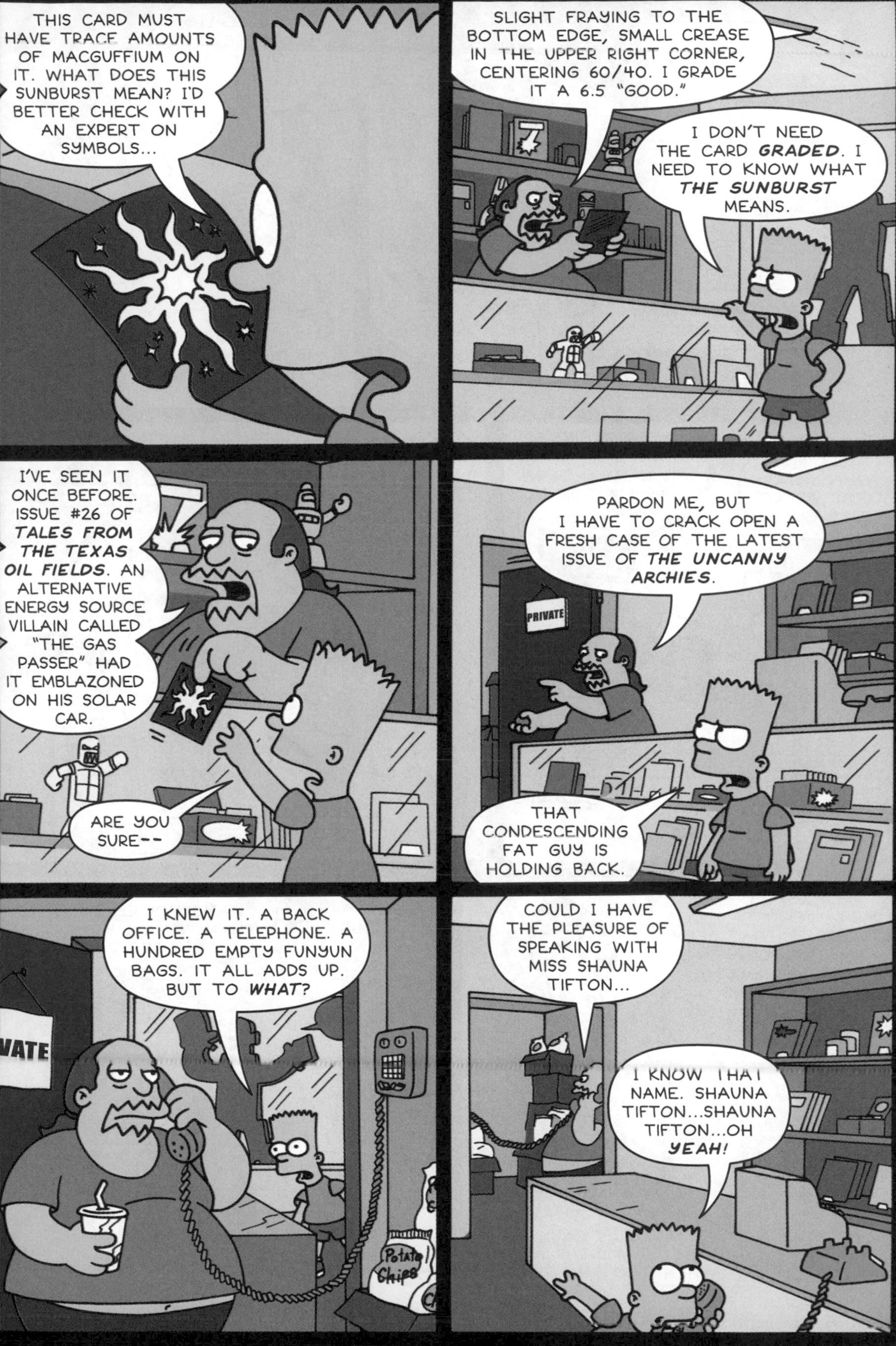
THIS CARD MUST HAVE TRACE AMOUNTS OF MACGUFFIUM ON IT. WHAT DOES THIS SUNBURST MEAN? I'D BETTER CHECK WITH AN EXPERT ON SYMBOLS...
SLIGHT FRAYING TO THE BOTTOM EDGE, SMALL CREASE IN THE UPPER RIGHT CORNER, CENTERING 60/40. I GRADE IT A 6.5 "GOOD."
I DON'T NEED THE CARD GRADED. I NEED TO KNOW WHAT THE SUNBURST MEANS.
I'VE SEEN IT ONCE BEFORE. ISSUE #26 OF TALES FROM THE TEXAS OIL FIELDS. AN ALTERNATIVE ENERGY SOURCE VILLAIN CALLED "THE GAS PASSER" HAD IT EMBLAZONED ON HIS SOLAR CAR.
ARE YOU SURE--
PARDON ME, BUT I HAVE TO CRACK OPEN A FRESH CASE OF THE LATEST ISSUE OF THE UNCANNY ARCHIES.
PRIVATE
THAT CONDESCENDING FAT GUY IS HOLDING BACK.
I KNEW IT. A BACK OFFICE. A TELEPHONE. A HUNDRED EMPTY FUNYUN BAGS. IT ALL ADDS UP. BUT TO WHAT?
VATE
Potato Chips
COULD I HAVE THE PLEASURE OF SPEAKING WITH MISS SHAUNA TIFTON...
I KNOW THAT NAME. SHAUNA TIFTON...SHAUNA TIFTON...OH YEAH!

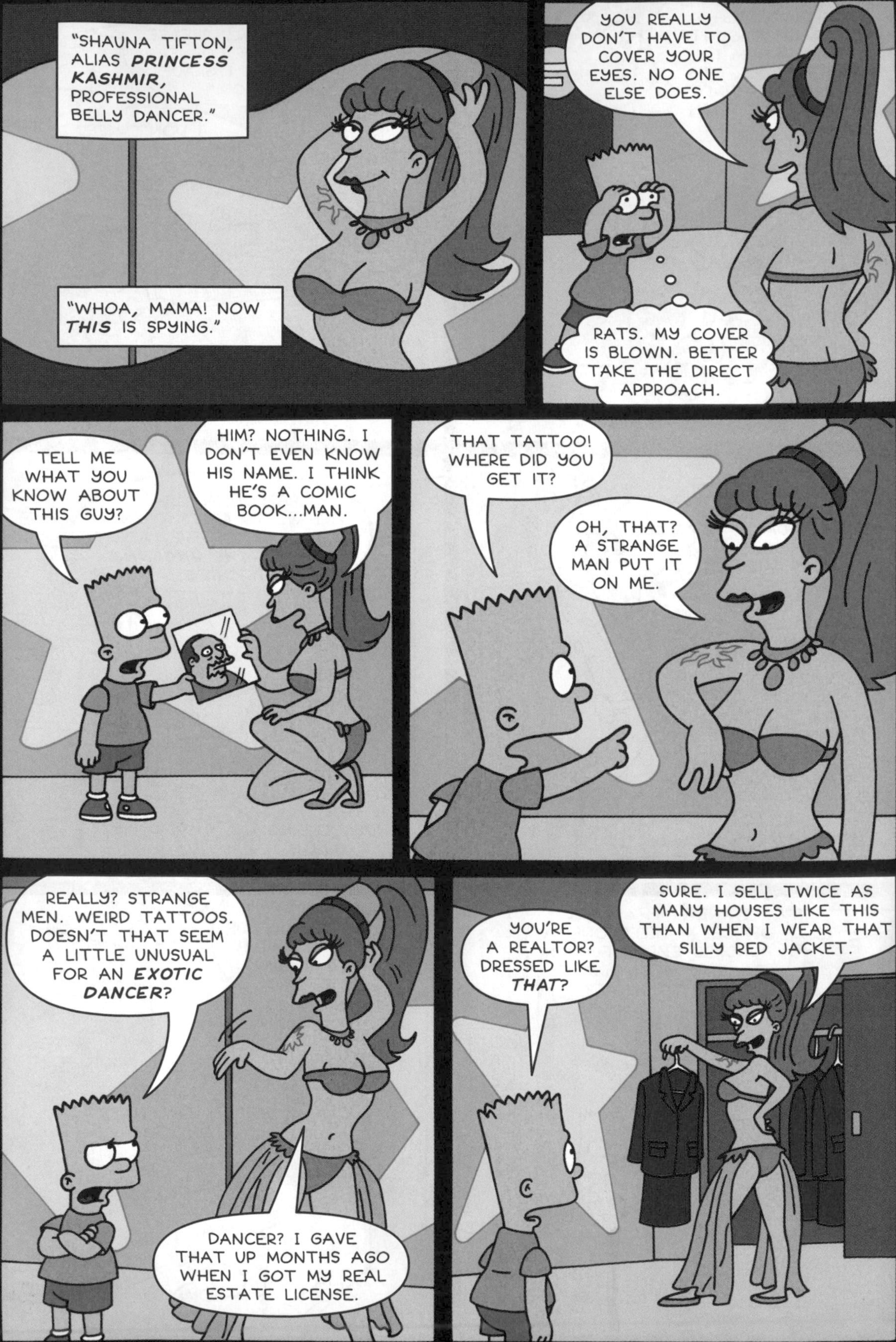
"SHAUNA TIFTON, ALIAS **PRINCESS KASHMIR,** PROFESSIONAL BELLY DANCER."
"WHOA, MAMA! NOW **THIS** IS SPYING."
YOU REALLY DON'T HAVE TO COVER YOUR EYES. NO ONE ELSE DOES.
RATS. MY COVER IS BLOWN. BETTER TAKE THE DIRECT APPROACH.
TELL ME WHAT YOU KNOW ABOUT THIS GUY?
HIM? NOTHING. I DON'T EVEN KNOW HIS NAME. I THINK HE'S A COMIC BOOK...MAN.
THAT TATTOO! WHERE DID YOU GET IT?
OH, THAT? A STRANGE MAN PUT IT ON ME.
REALLY? STRANGE MEN. WEIRD TATTOOS. DOESN'T THAT SEEM A LITTLE UNUSUAL FOR AN **EXOTIC DANCER**?
DANCER? I GAVE THAT UP MONTHS AGO WHEN I GOT MY REAL ESTATE LICENSE.
YOU'RE A REALTOR? DRESSED LIKE **THAT**?
SURE. I SELL TWICE AS MANY HOUSES LIKE THIS THAN WHEN I WEAR THAT SILLY RED JACKET.

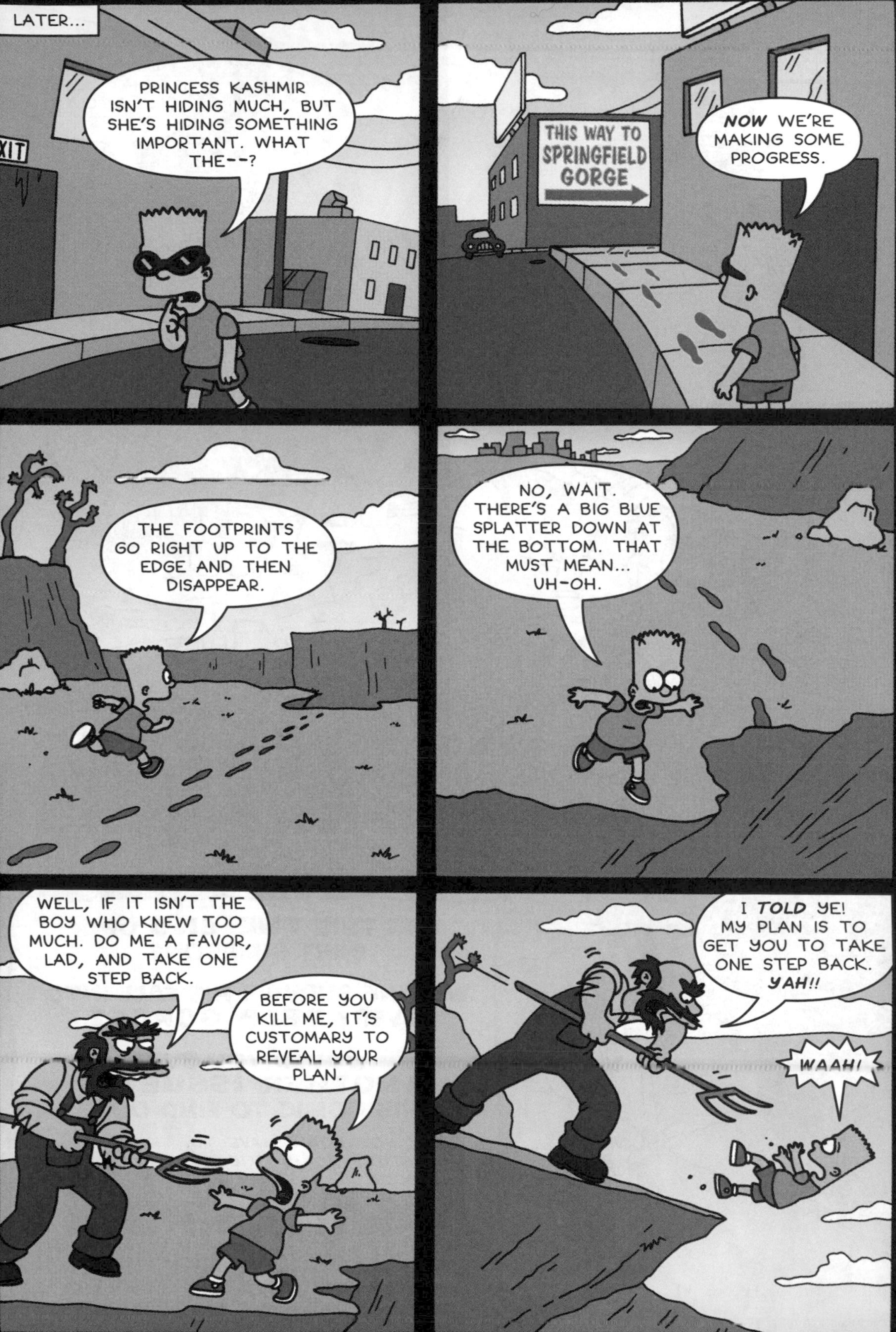

LATER...
PRINCESS KASHMIR ISN'T HIDING MUCH, BUT SHE'S HIDING SOMETHING IMPORTANT. WHAT THE--?
EXIT
THIS WAY TO SPRINGFIELD GORGE
NOW WE'RE MAKING SOME PROGRESS.
THE FOOTPRINTS GO RIGHT UP TO THE EDGE AND THEN DISAPPEAR.
NO, WAIT. THERE'S A BIG BLUE SPLATTER DOWN AT THE BOTTOM. THAT MUST MEAN... UH-OH.
WELL, IF IT ISN'T THE BOY WHO KNEW TOO MUCH. DO ME A FAVOR, LAD, AND TAKE ONE STEP BACK.
BEFORE YOU KILL ME, IT'S CUSTOMARY TO REVEAL YOUR PLAN.
I TOLD YE! MY PLAN IS TO GET YOU TO TAKE ONE STEP BACK. YAH!!
WAAH!

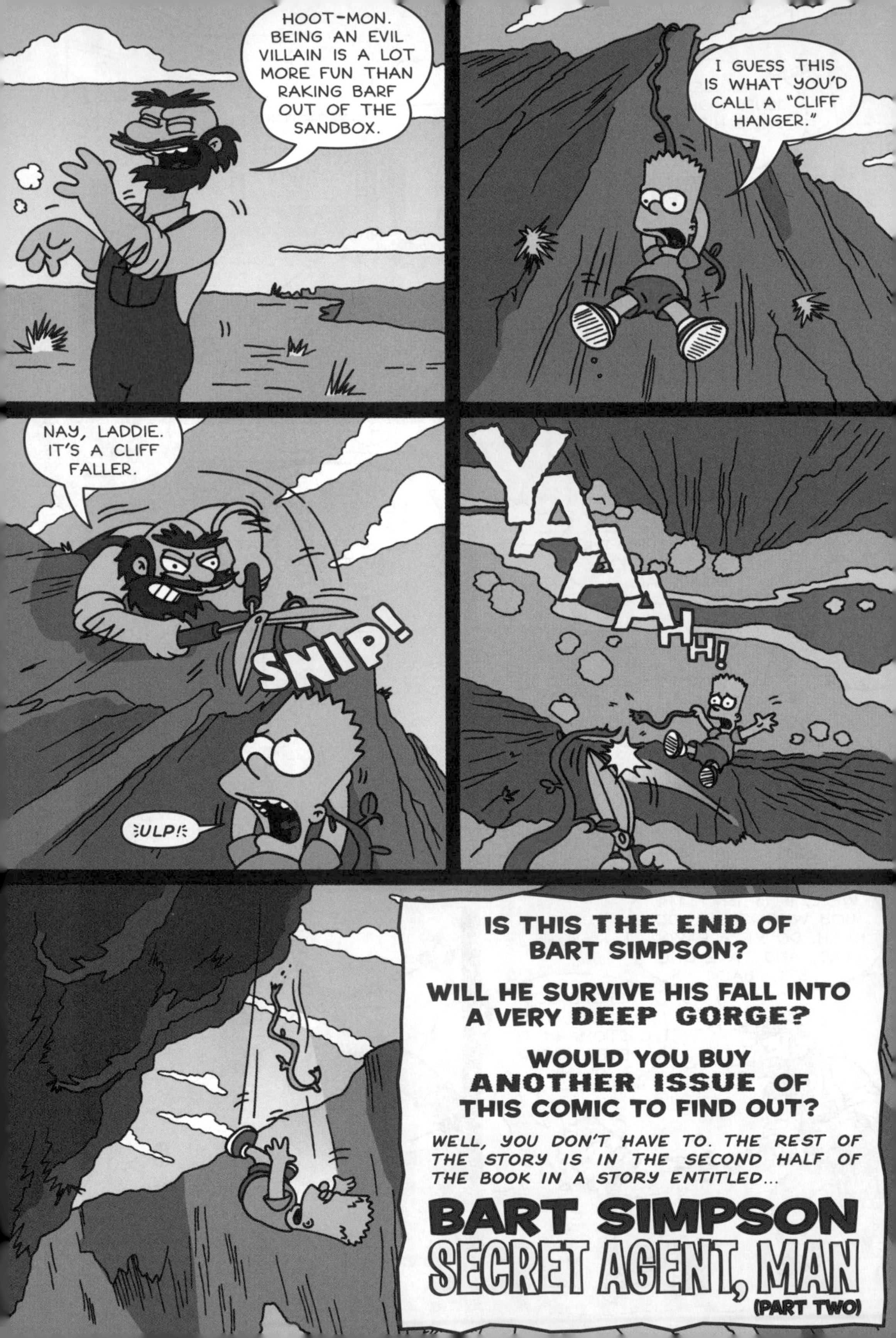

HOOT-MON. BEING AN EVIL VILLAIN IS A LOT MORE FUN THAN RAKING BARF OUT OF THE SANDBOX.
I GUESS THIS IS WHAT YOU'D CALL A "CLIFF HANGER."
NAY, LADDIE. IT'S A CLIFF FALLER.
SNIP!
ULP!
YAAAHH!
IS THIS THE END OF BART SIMPSON?
WILL HE SURVIVE HIS FALL INTO A VERY DEEP GORGE?
WOULD YOU BUY ANOTHER ISSUE OF THIS COMIC TO FIND OUT?
WELL, YOU DON'T HAVE TO. THE REST OF THE STORY IS IN THE SECOND HALF OF THE BOOK IN A STORY ENTITLED...
BART SIMPSON
SECRET AGENT, MAN
(PART TWO)

ITCHY & SCRATCHY in THE TRUTH ABOUT CATS AND MICE

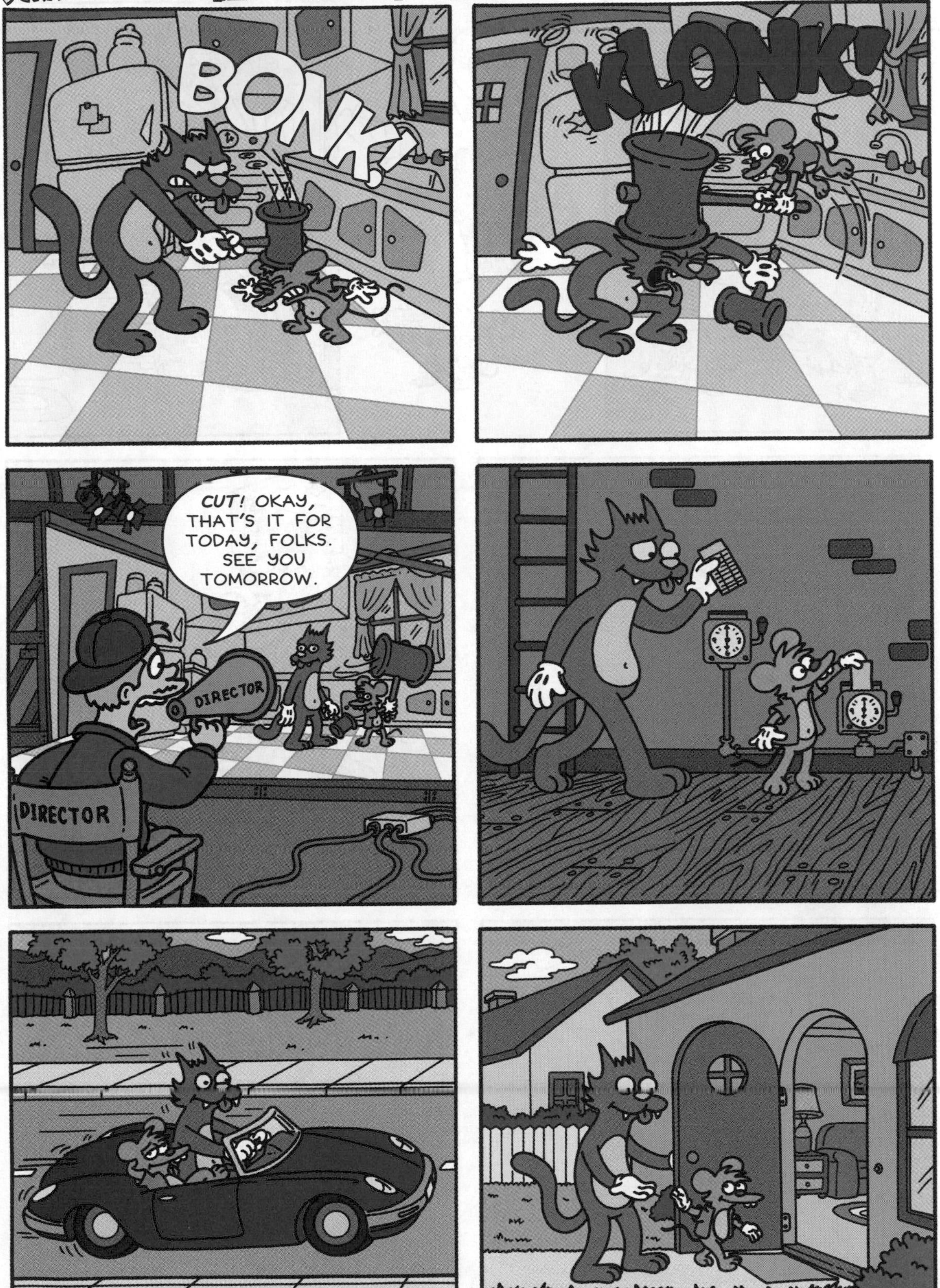
BONK!
KLONK!
CUT! OKAY, THAT'S IT FOR TODAY, FOLKS. SEE YOU TOMORROW.
DIRECTOR
DIRECTOR

PATRIC VERRONE SCRIPT
MARK ERVIN PENCILS
JASON HO INKS
ROBERT STANLEY COLORS
KAREN BATES LETTERS
BILL MORRISON EDITOR

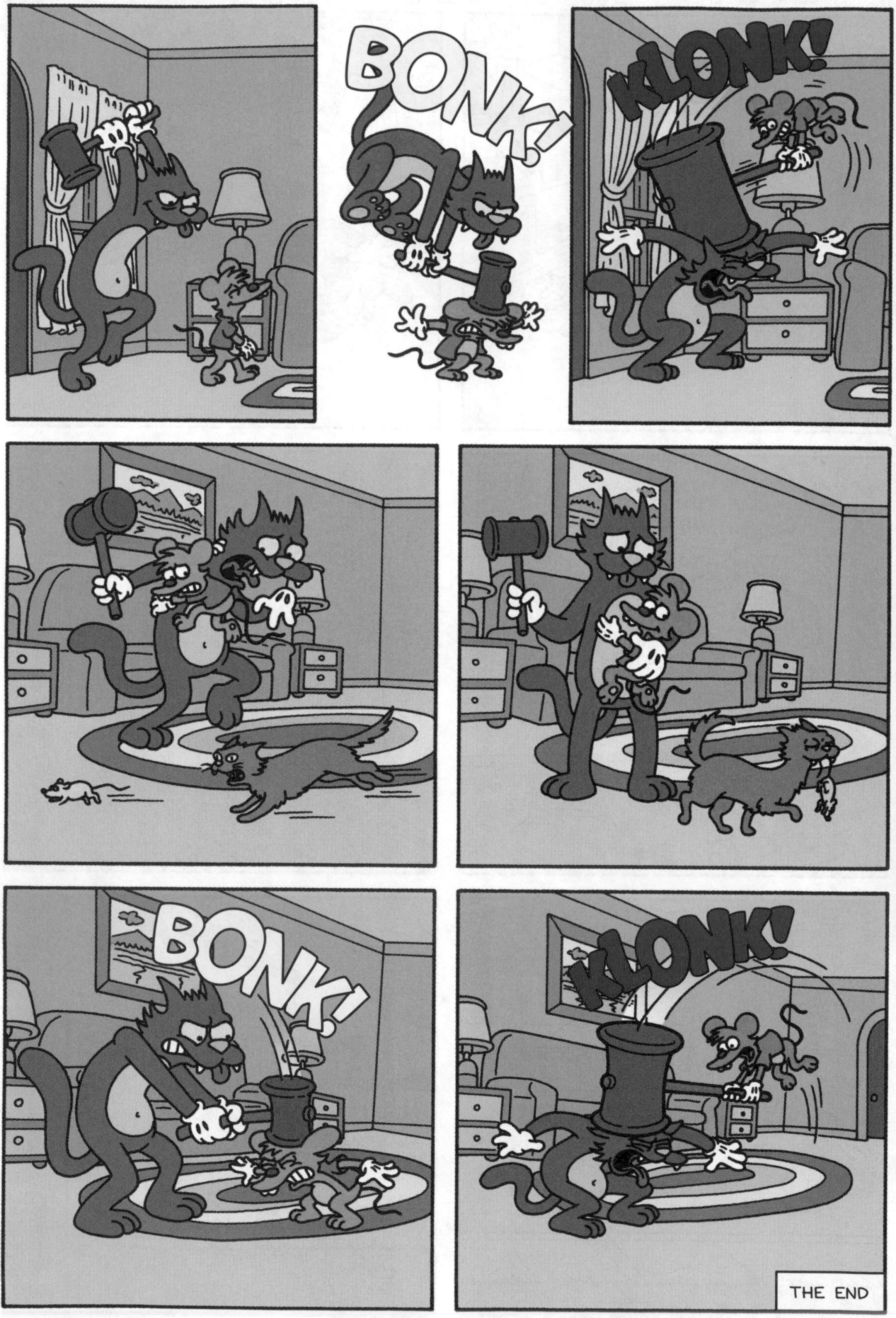
BONK!
KLONK!
BONK!
KLONK!
THE END

BART SIMPSON SECRET AGENT, MAN (PART TWO)

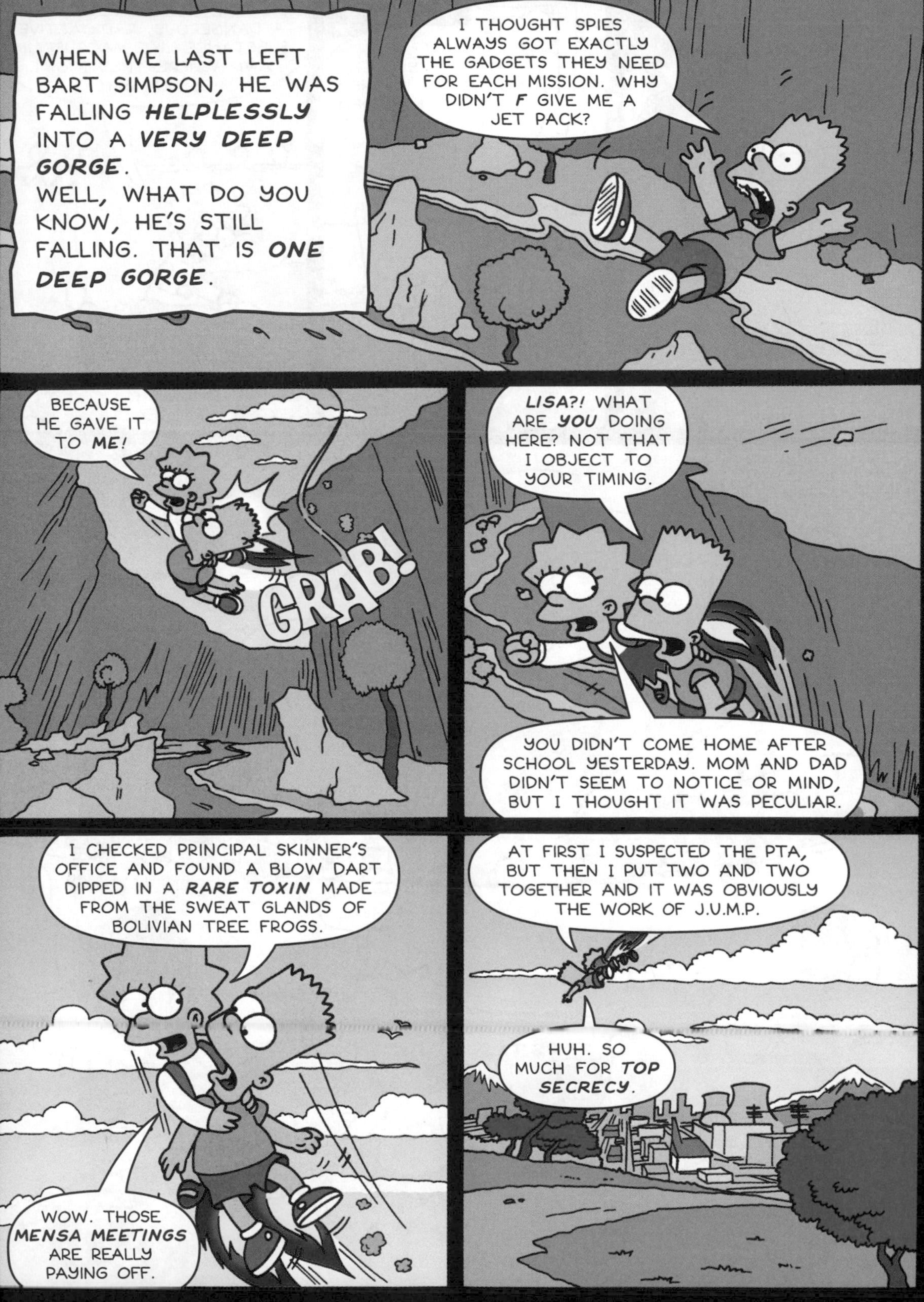
WHEN WE LAST LEFT BART SIMPSON, HE WAS FALLING ***HELPLESSLY*** INTO A ***VERY DEEP GORGE***.
WELL, WHAT DO YOU KNOW, HE'S STILL FALLING. THAT IS ***ONE DEEP GORGE***.
I THOUGHT SPIES ALWAYS GOT EXACTLY THE GADGETS THEY NEED FOR EACH MISSION. WHY DIDN'T ***F*** GIVE ME A JET PACK?
BECAUSE HE GAVE IT TO ***ME***!
GRAB!
LISA?! WHAT ARE ***YOU*** DOING HERE? NOT THAT I OBJECT TO YOUR TIMING.
YOU DIDN'T COME HOME AFTER SCHOOL YESTERDAY. MOM AND DAD DIDN'T SEEM TO NOTICE OR MIND, BUT I THOUGHT IT WAS PECULIAR.
I CHECKED PRINCIPAL SKINNER'S OFFICE AND FOUND A BLOW DART DIPPED IN A ***RARE TOXIN*** MADE FROM THE SWEAT GLANDS OF BOLIVIAN TREE FROGS.
WOW. THOSE ***MENSA MEETINGS*** ARE REALLY PAYING OFF.
AT FIRST I SUSPECTED THE PTA, BUT THEN I PUT TWO AND TWO TOGETHER AND IT WAS OBVIOUSLY THE WORK OF J.U.M.P.
HUH. SO MUCH FOR ***TOP SECRECY***.

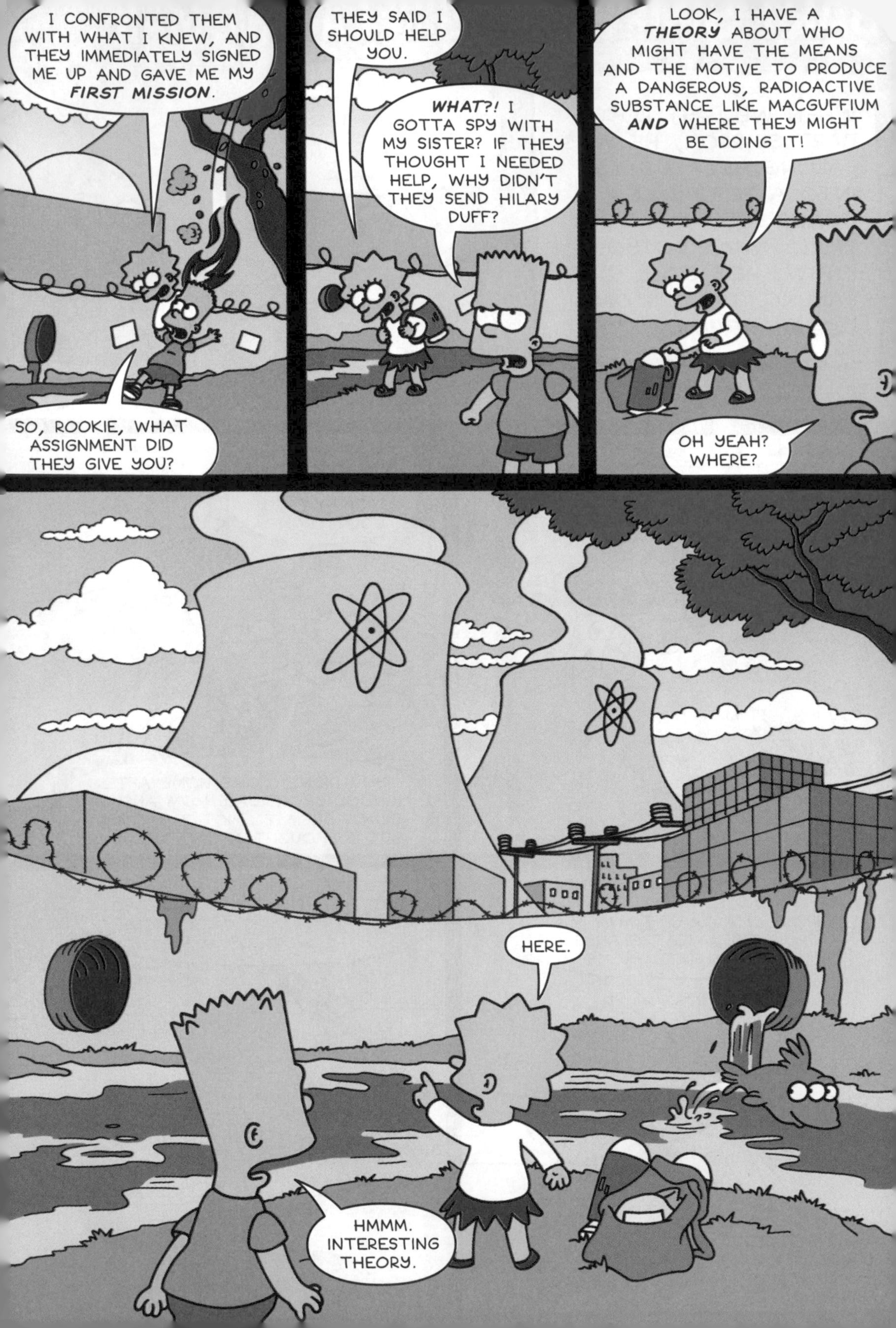

I CONFRONTED THEM WITH WHAT I KNEW, AND THEY IMMEDIATELY SIGNED ME UP AND GAVE ME MY FIRST MISSION.
SO, ROOKIE, WHAT ASSIGNMENT DID THEY GIVE YOU?
THEY SAID I SHOULD HELP YOU.
WHAT?! I GOTTA SPY WITH MY SISTER? IF THEY THOUGHT I NEEDED HELP, WHY DIDN'T THEY SEND HILARY DUFF?
LOOK, I HAVE A THEORY ABOUT WHO MIGHT HAVE THE MEANS AND THE MOTIVE TO PRODUCE A DANGEROUS, RADIOACTIVE SUBSTANCE LIKE MACGUFFIUM AND WHERE THEY MIGHT BE DOING IT!
OH YEAH? WHERE?
HERE.
HMMM. INTERESTING THEORY.

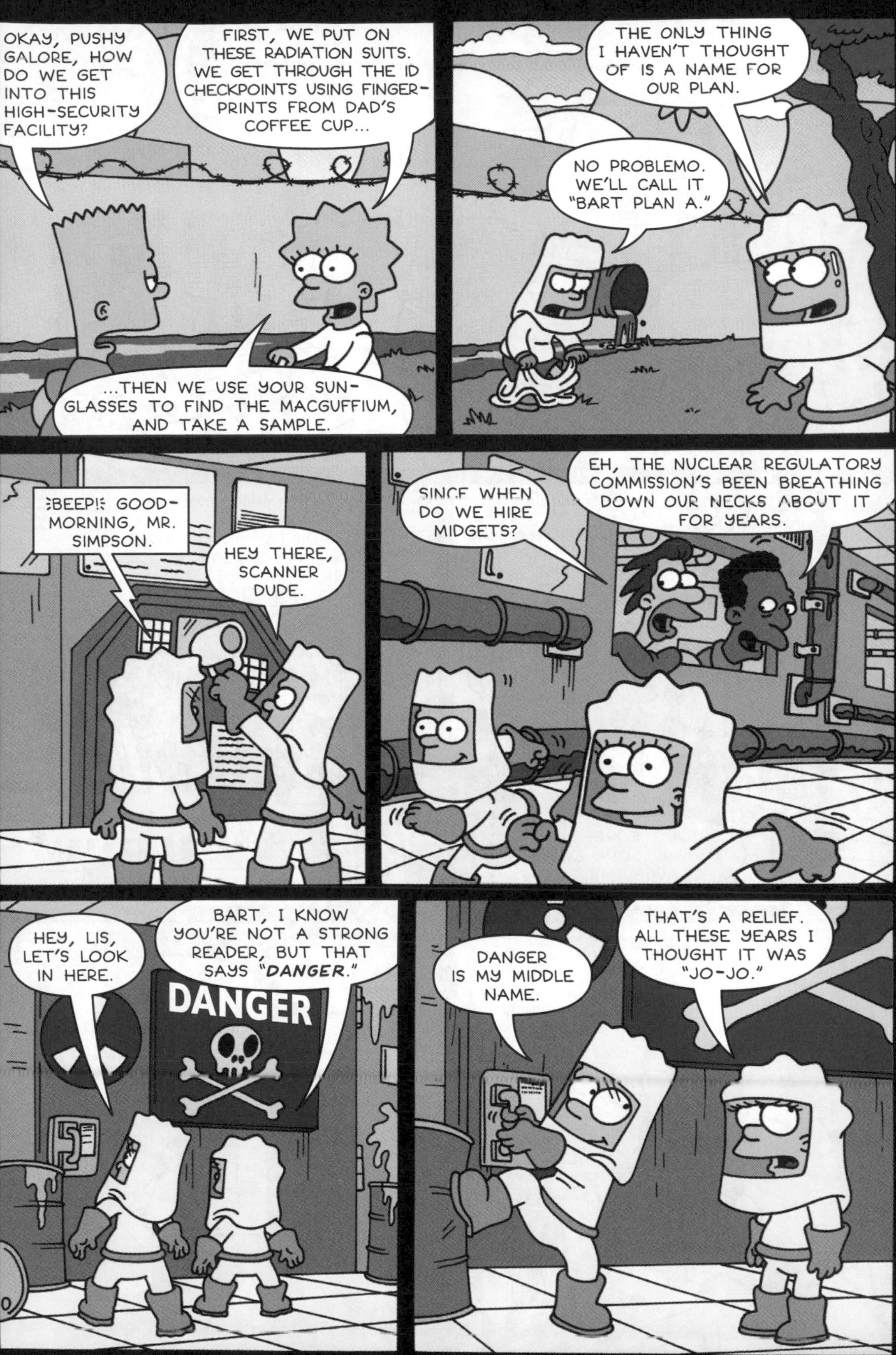
OKAY, PUSHY GALORE, HOW DO WE GET INTO THIS HIGH-SECURITY FACILITY?
FIRST, WE PUT ON THESE RADIATION SUITS. WE GET THROUGH THE ID CHECKPOINTS USING FINGER-PRINTS FROM DAD'S COFFEE CUP...
...THEN WE USE YOUR SUN-GLASSES TO FIND THE MACGUFFIUM, AND TAKE A SAMPLE.
THE ONLY THING I HAVEN'T THOUGHT OF IS A NAME FOR OUR PLAN.
NO PROBLEMO. WE'LL CALL IT "BART PLAN A."
BEEP! GOOD-MORNING, MR. SIMPSON.
HEY THERE, SCANNER DUDE.
SINCE WHEN DO WE HIRE MIDGETS?
EH, THE NUCLEAR REGULATORY COMMISSION'S BEEN BREATHING DOWN OUR NECKS ABOUT IT FOR YEARS.
HEY, LIS, LET'S LOOK IN HERE.
BART, I KNOW YOU'RE NOT A STRONG READER, BUT THAT SAYS "DANGER."
DANGER
DANGER IS MY MIDDLE NAME.
THAT'S A RELIEF. ALL THESE YEARS I THOUGHT IT WAS "JO-JO."

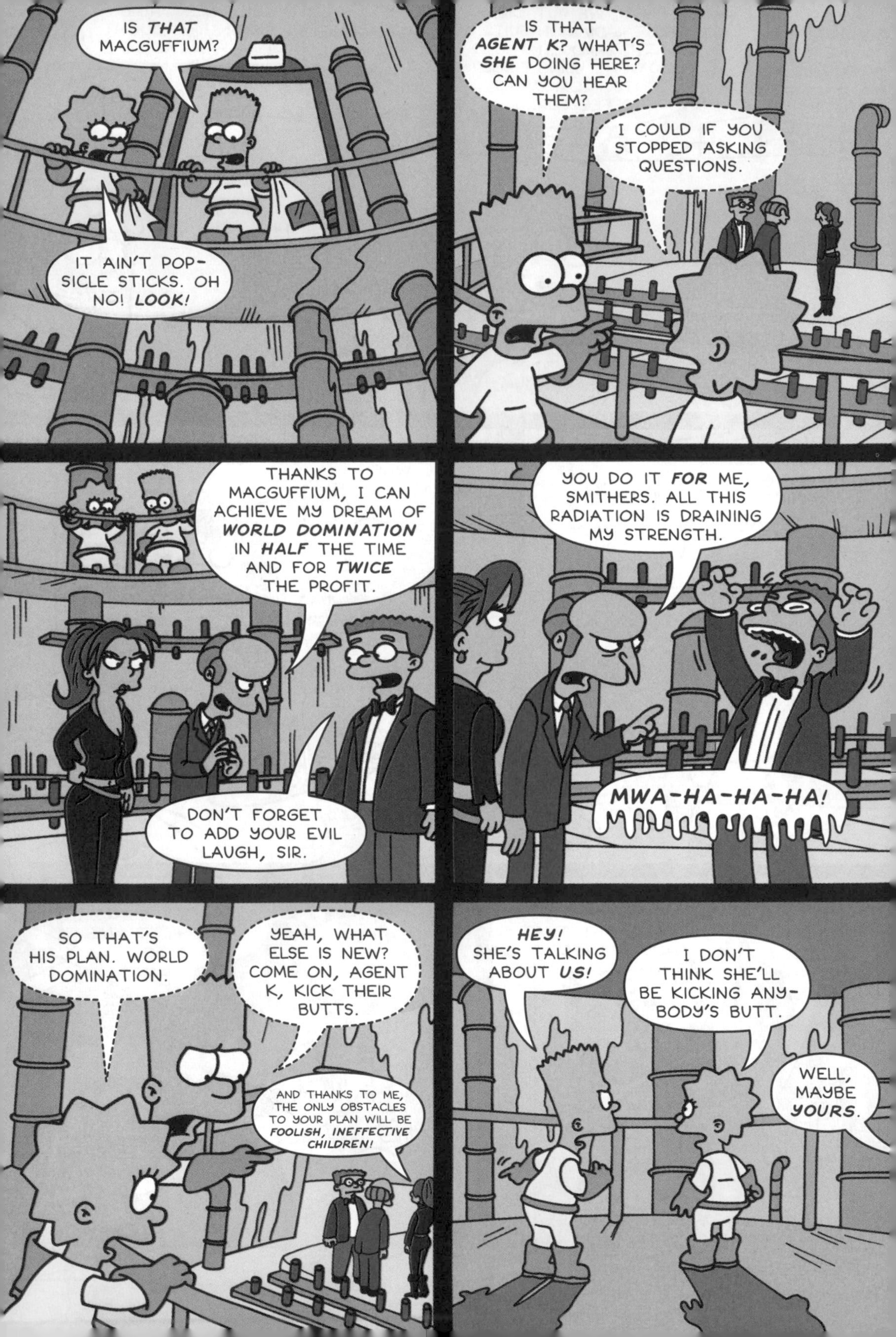
IS THAT MACGUFFIUM?
IT AIN'T POPSICLE STICKS. OH NO! LOOK!
IS THAT AGENT K? WHAT'S SHE DOING HERE? CAN YOU HEAR THEM?
I COULD IF YOU STOPPED ASKING QUESTIONS.
THANKS TO MACGUFFIUM, I CAN ACHIEVE MY DREAM OF WORLD DOMINATION IN HALF THE TIME AND FOR TWICE THE PROFIT.
DON'T FORGET TO ADD YOUR EVIL LAUGH, SIR.
YOU DO IT FOR ME, SMITHERS. ALL THIS RADIATION IS DRAINING MY STRENGTH.
MWA-HA-HA-HA!
SO THAT'S HIS PLAN. WORLD DOMINATION.
YEAH, WHAT ELSE IS NEW? COME ON, AGENT K, KICK THEIR BUTTS.
AND THANKS TO ME, THE ONLY OBSTACLES TO YOUR PLAN WILL BE FOOLISH, INEFFECTIVE CHILDREN!
HEY! SHE'S TALKING ABOUT US!
I DON'T THINK SHE'LL BE KICKING ANYBODY'S BUTT.
WELL, MAYBE YOURS.

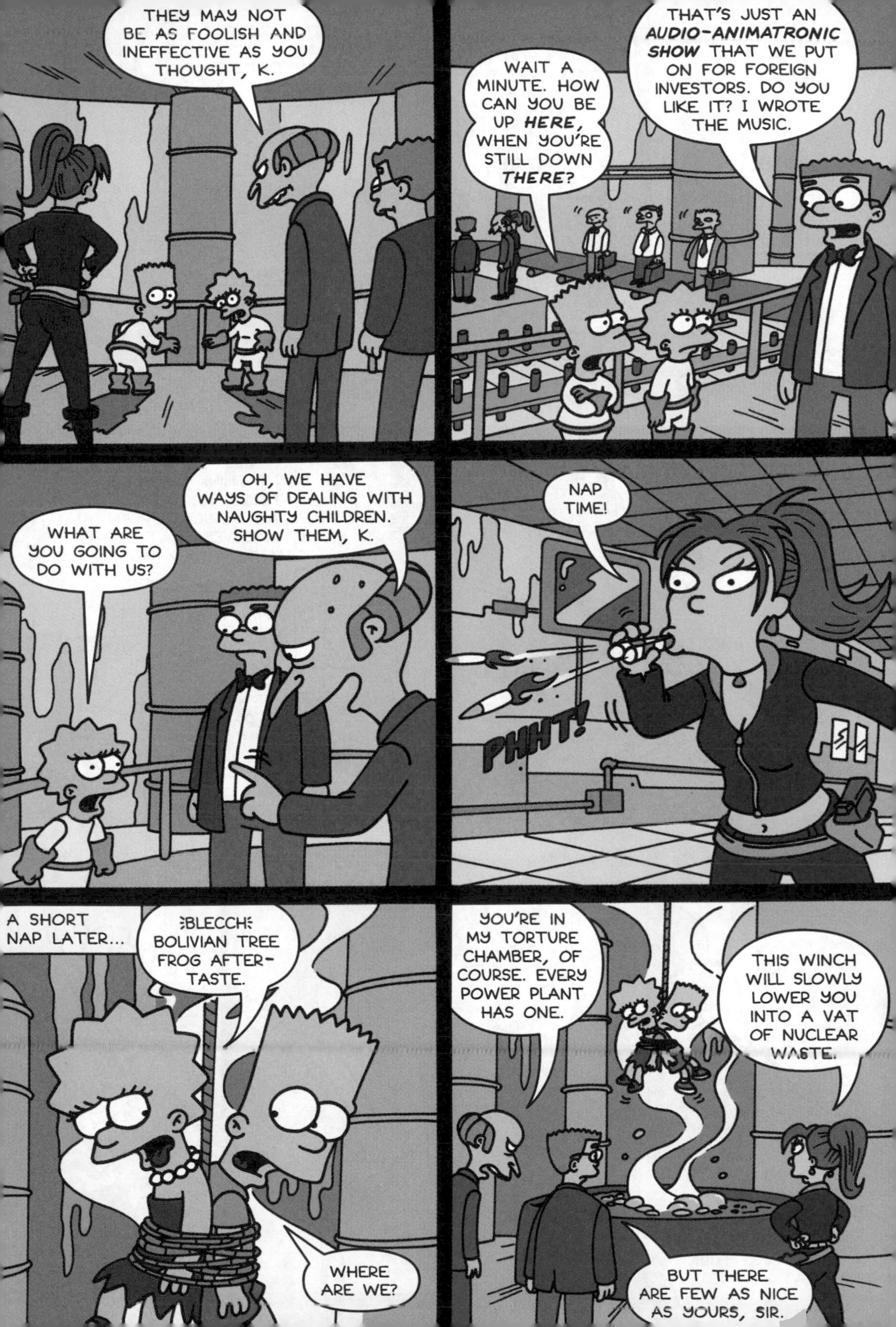
THEY MAY NOT BE AS FOOLISH AND INEFFECTIVE AS YOU THOUGHT, K.
WAIT A MINUTE. HOW CAN YOU BE UP **HERE,** WHEN YOU'RE STILL DOWN **THERE?**
THAT'S JUST AN **AUDIO-ANIMATRONIC SHOW** THAT WE PUT ON FOR FOREIGN INVESTORS. DO YOU LIKE IT? I WROTE THE MUSIC.
WHAT ARE YOU GOING TO DO WITH US?
OH, WE HAVE WAYS OF DEALING WITH NAUGHTY CHILDREN. SHOW THEM, K.
NAP TIME!
PHHT!
A SHORT NAP LATER...
BLECCH BOLIVIAN TREE FROG AFTER-TASTE.
WHERE ARE WE?
YOU'RE IN MY TORTURE CHAMBER, OF COURSE. EVERY POWER PLANT HAS ONE.
THIS WINCH WILL SLOWLY LOWER YOU INTO A VAT OF NUCLEAR WASTE.
BUT THERE ARE FEW AS NICE AS YOURS, SIR.

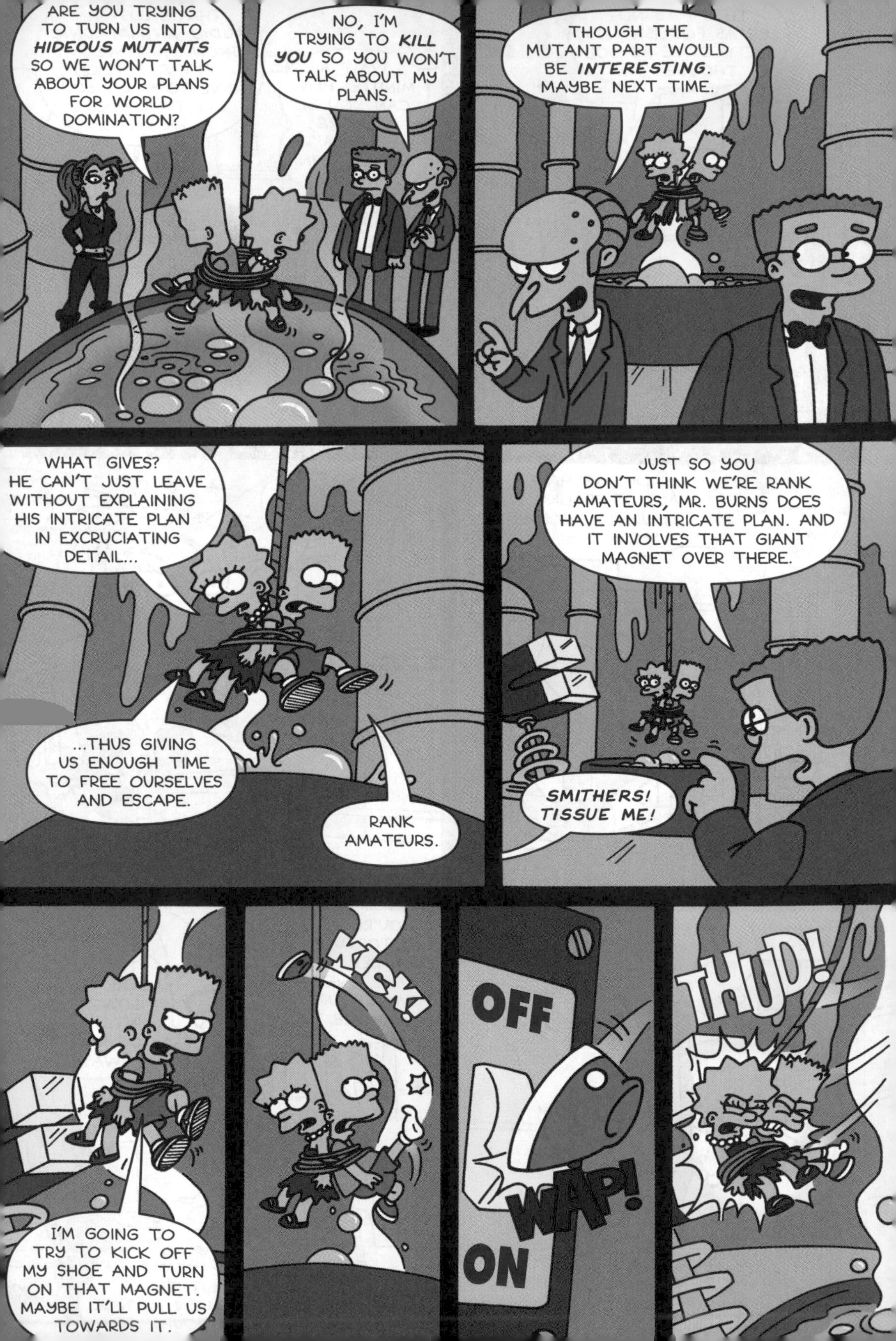
ARE YOU TRYING TO TURN US INTO HIDEOUS MUTANTS SO WE WON'T TALK ABOUT YOUR PLANS FOR WORLD DOMINATION?
NO, I'M TRYING TO KILL YOU SO YOU WON'T TALK ABOUT MY PLANS.
THOUGH THE MUTANT PART WOULD BE INTERESTING. MAYBE NEXT TIME.
WHAT GIVES? HE CAN'T JUST LEAVE WITHOUT EXPLAINING HIS INTRICATE PLAN IN EXCRUCIATING DETAIL...
...THUS GIVING US ENOUGH TIME TO FREE OURSELVES AND ESCAPE.
RANK AMATEURS.
JUST SO YOU DON'T THINK WE'RE RANK AMATEURS, MR. BURNS DOES HAVE AN INTRICATE PLAN. AND IT INVOLVES THAT GIANT MAGNET OVER THERE.
SMITHERS! TISSUE ME!
I'M GOING TO TRY TO KICK OFF MY SHOE AND TURN ON THAT MAGNET. MAYBE IT'LL PULL US TOWARDS IT.
KICK!
OFF
WAP!
ON
THUD!

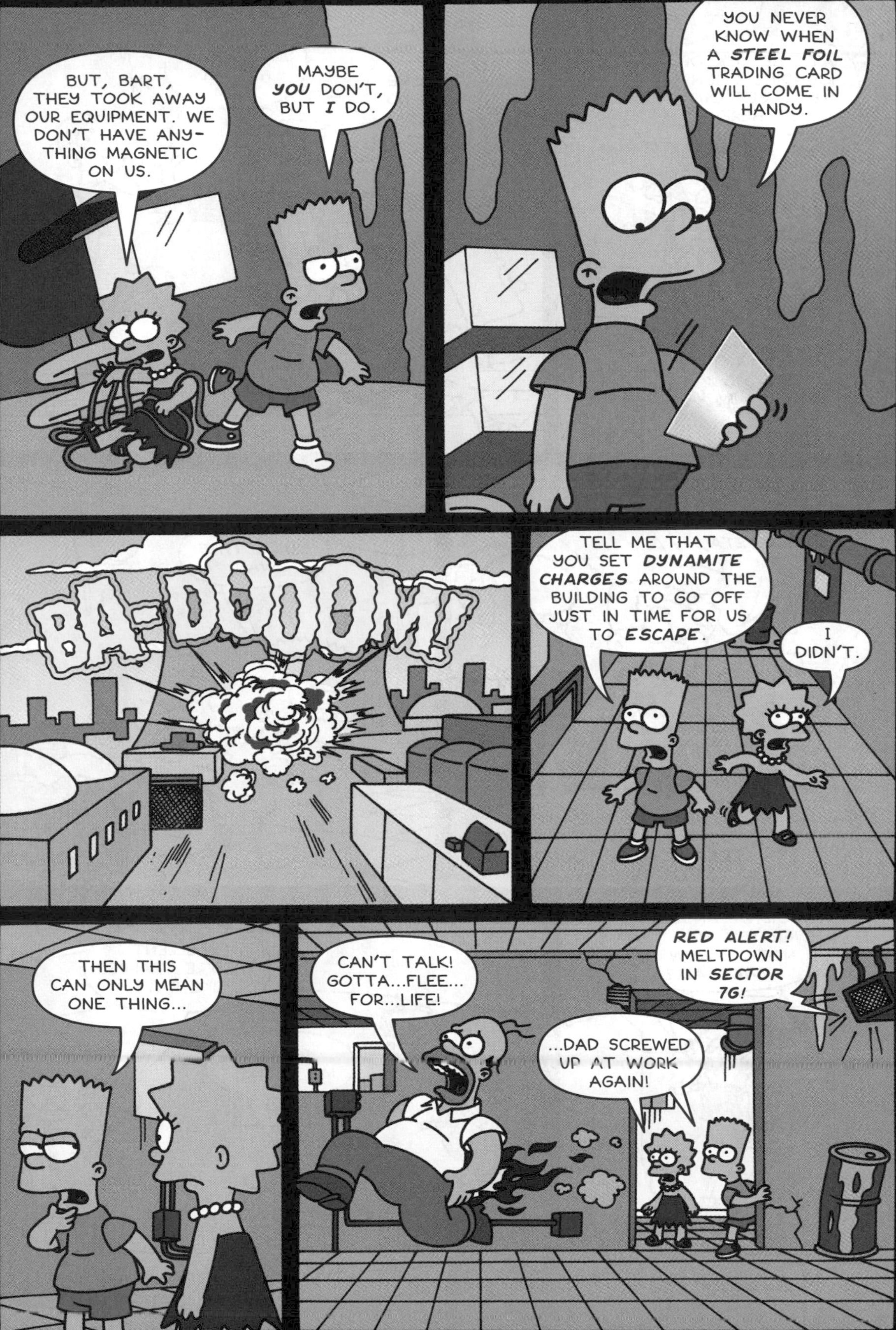
BUT, BART, THEY TOOK AWAY OUR EQUIPMENT. WE DON'T HAVE ANY-THING MAGNETIC ON US.
MAYBE YOU DON'T, BUT I DO.
YOU NEVER KNOW WHEN A STEEL FOIL TRADING CARD WILL COME IN HANDY.
BA-DOOOM!
TELL ME THAT YOU SET DYNAMITE CHARGES AROUND THE BUILDING TO GO OFF JUST IN TIME FOR US TO ESCAPE.
I DIDN'T.
THEN THIS CAN ONLY MEAN ONE THING...
CAN'T TALK! GOTTA...FLEE... FOR...LIFE!
RED ALERT! MELTDOWN IN SECTOR 7G!
...DAD SCREWED UP AT WORK AGAIN!

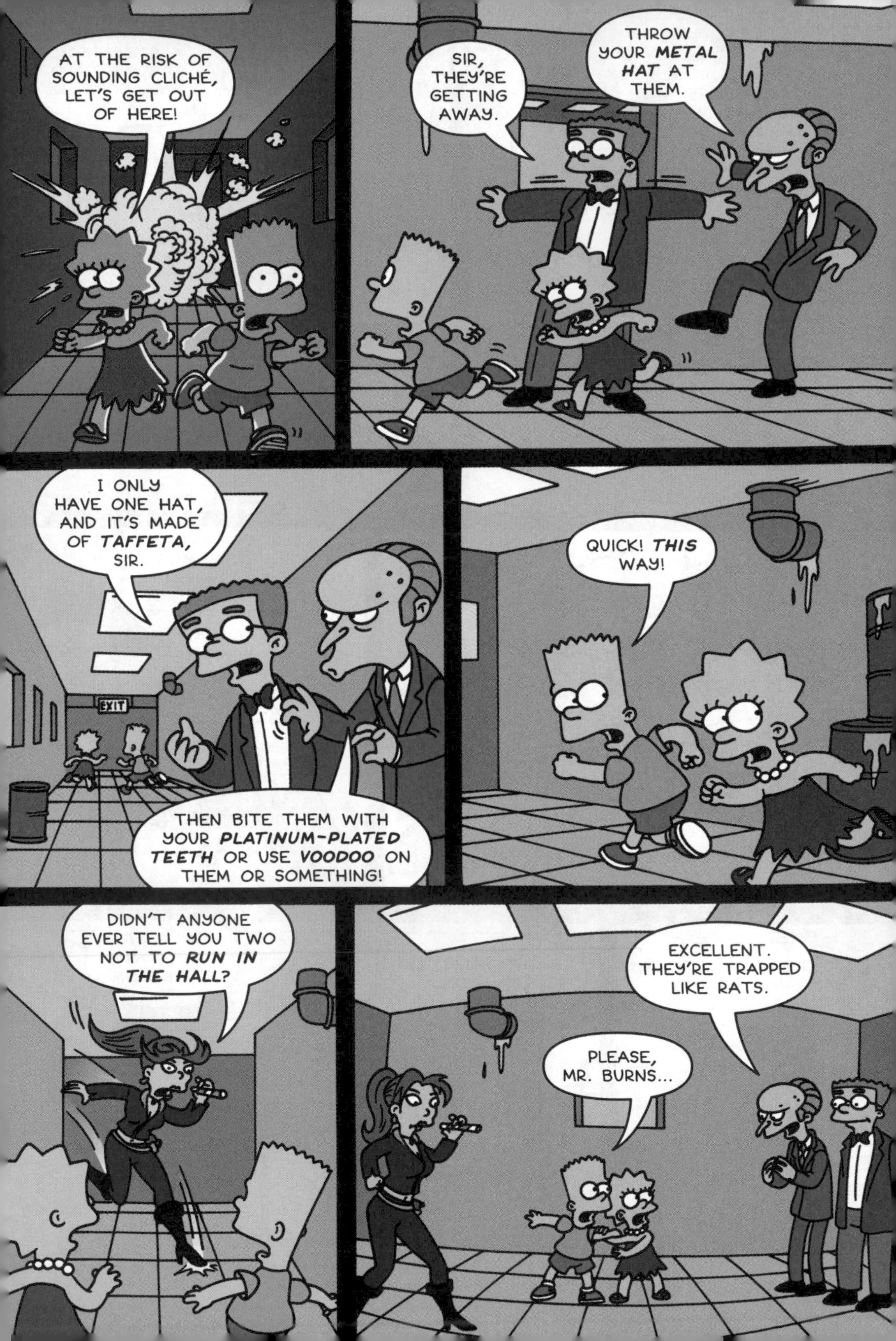
AT THE RISK OF SOUNDING CLICHÉ, LET'S GET OUT OF HERE!
SIR, THEY'RE GETTING AWAY.
THROW YOUR METAL HAT AT THEM.
I ONLY HAVE ONE HAT, AND IT'S MADE OF TAFFETA, SIR.
EXIT
THEN BITE THEM WITH YOUR PLATINUM-PLATED TEETH OR USE VOODOO ON THEM OR SOMETHING!
QUICK! THIS WAY!
DIDN'T ANYONE EVER TELL YOU TWO NOT TO RUN IN THE HALL?
EXCELLENT. THEY'RE TRAPPED LIKE RATS.
PLEASE, MR. BURNS...

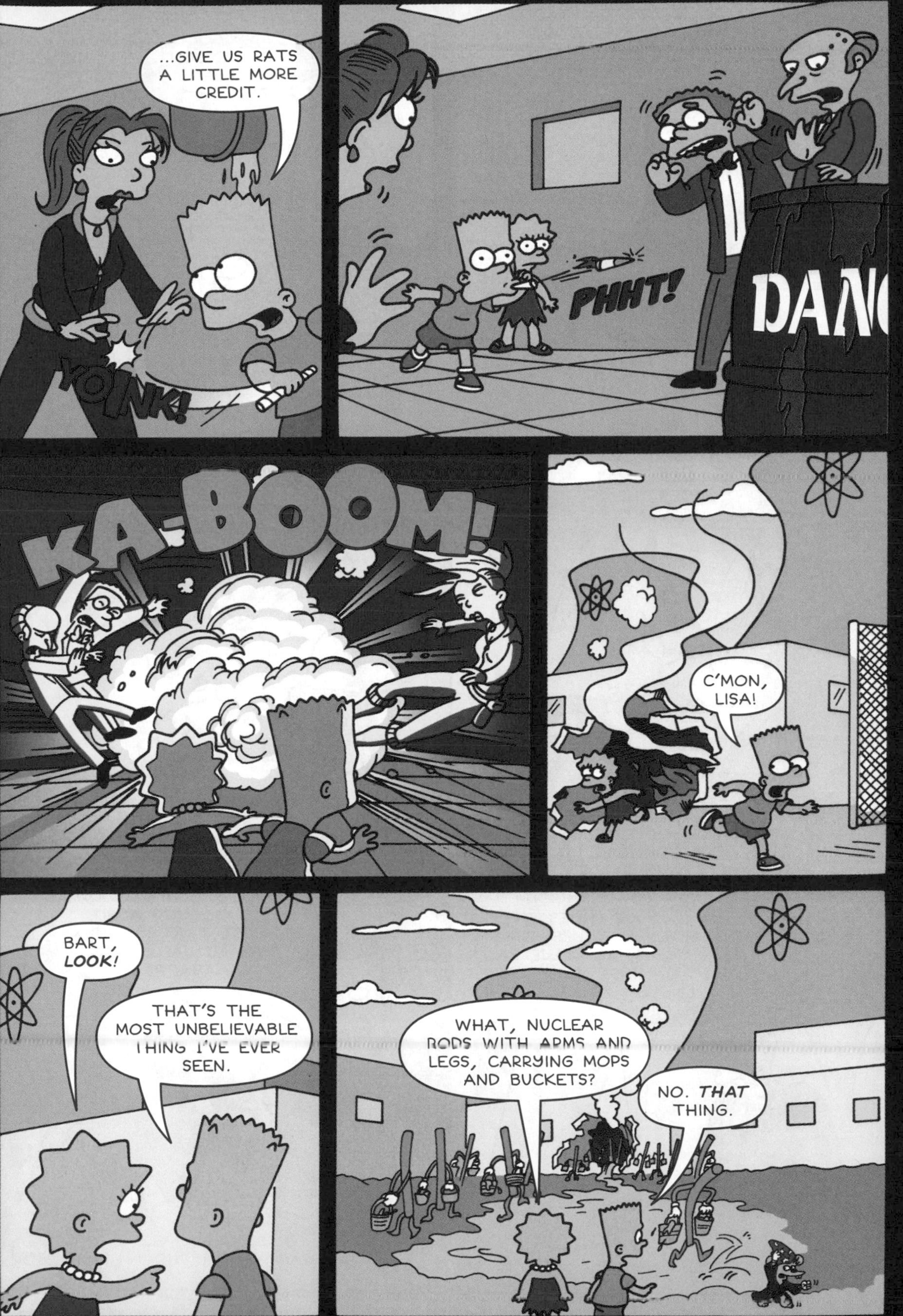
...GIVE US RATS A LITTLE MORE CREDIT.
YOINK!
PHHT!
DANG
KA-BOOM!
C'MON, LISA!
BART, LOOK!
THAT'S THE MOST UNBELIEVABLE THING I'VE EVER SEEN.
WHAT, NUCLEAR RODS WITH ARMS AND LEGS, CARRYING MOPS AND BUCKETS?
NO. THAT THING.

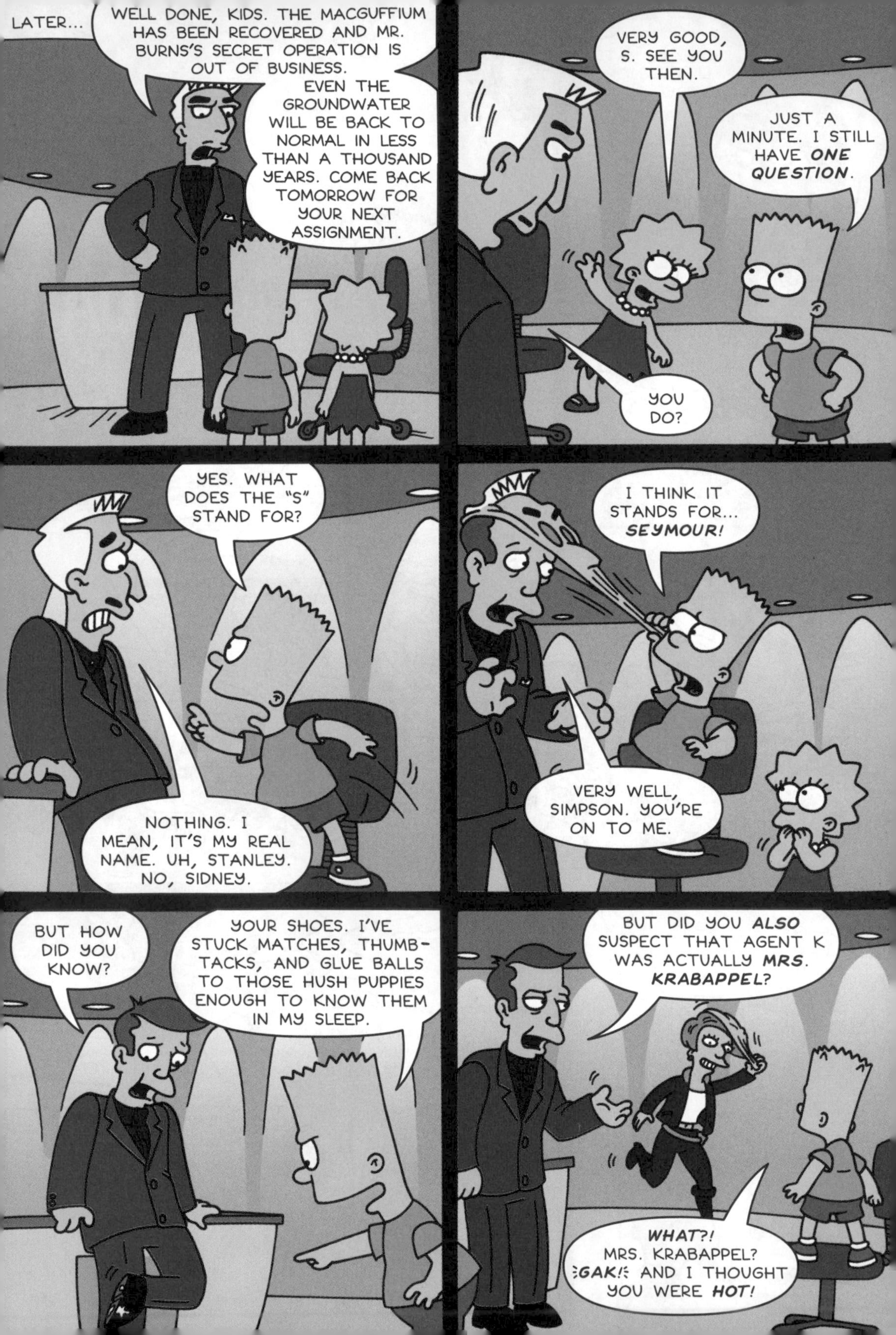
LATER...
WELL DONE, KIDS. THE MACGUFFIUM HAS BEEN RECOVERED AND MR. BURNS'S SECRET OPERATION IS OUT OF BUSINESS.
EVEN THE GROUNDWATER WILL BE BACK TO NORMAL IN LESS THAN A THOUSAND YEARS. COME BACK TOMORROW FOR YOUR NEXT ASSIGNMENT.
VERY GOOD, S. SEE YOU THEN.
JUST A MINUTE. I STILL HAVE **ONE QUESTION**.
YOU DO?
YES. WHAT DOES THE "S" STAND FOR?
NOTHING. I MEAN, IT'S MY REAL NAME. UH, STANLEY. NO, SIDNEY.
I THINK IT STANDS FOR... **SEYMOUR!**
VERY WELL, SIMPSON. YOU'RE ON TO ME.
BUT HOW DID YOU KNOW?
YOUR SHOES. I'VE STUCK MATCHES, THUMB-TACKS, AND GLUE BALLS TO THOSE HUSH PUPPIES ENOUGH TO KNOW THEM IN MY SLEEP.
BUT DID YOU **ALSO** SUSPECT THAT AGENT K WAS ACTUALLY **MRS. KRABAPPEL**?
WHAT?! MRS. KRABAPPEL? **GAK!** AND I THOUGHT YOU WERE **HOT**!

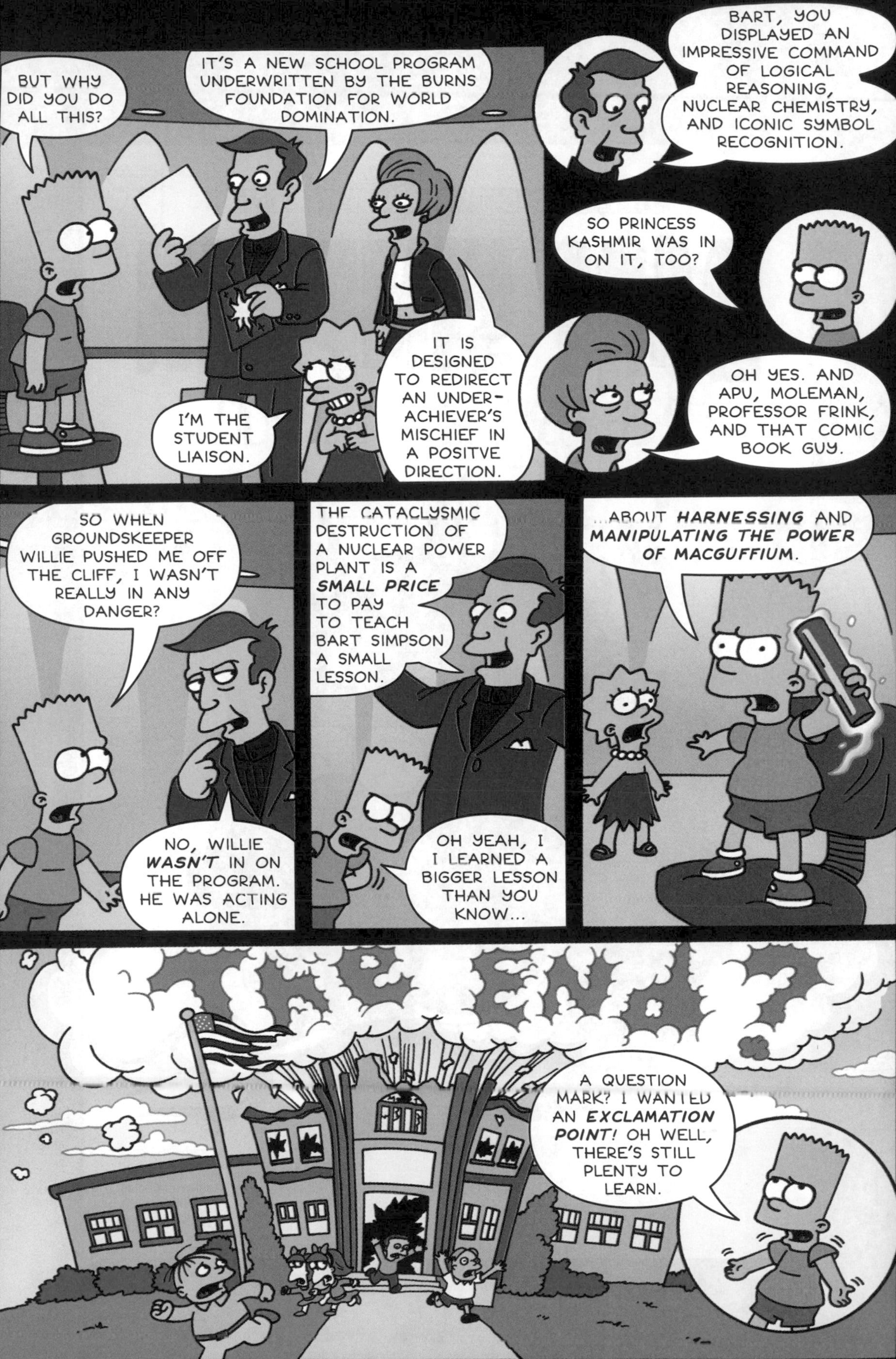
BUT WHY DID YOU DO ALL THIS?
IT'S A NEW SCHOOL PROGRAM UNDERWRITTEN BY THE BURNS FOUNDATION FOR WORLD DOMINATION.
I'M THE STUDENT LIAISON.
IT IS DESIGNED TO REDIRECT AN UNDER-ACHIEVER'S MISCHIEF IN A POSITVE DIRECTION.
BART, YOU DISPLAYED AN IMPRESSIVE COMMAND OF LOGICAL REASONING, NUCLEAR CHEMISTRY, AND ICONIC SYMBOL RECOGNITION.
SO PRINCESS KASHMIR WAS IN ON IT, TOO?
OH YES. AND APU, MOLEMAN, PROFESSOR FRINK, AND THAT COMIC BOOK GUY.
SO WHEN GROUNDSKEEPER WILLIE PUSHED ME OFF THE CLIFF, I WASN'T REALLY IN ANY DANGER?
NO, WILLIE WASN'T IN ON THE PROGRAM. HE WAS ACTING ALONE.
THE CATACLYSMIC DESTRUCTION OF A NUCLEAR POWER PLANT IS A SMALL PRICE TO PAY TO TEACH BART SIMPSON A SMALL LESSON.
OH YEAH, I I LEARNED A BIGGER LESSON THAN YOU KNOW...
...ABOUT HARNESSING AND MANIPULATING THE POWER OF MACGUFFIUM.
A QUESTION MARK? I WANTED AN EXCLAMATION POINT! OH WELL, THERE'S STILL PLENTY TO LEARN.

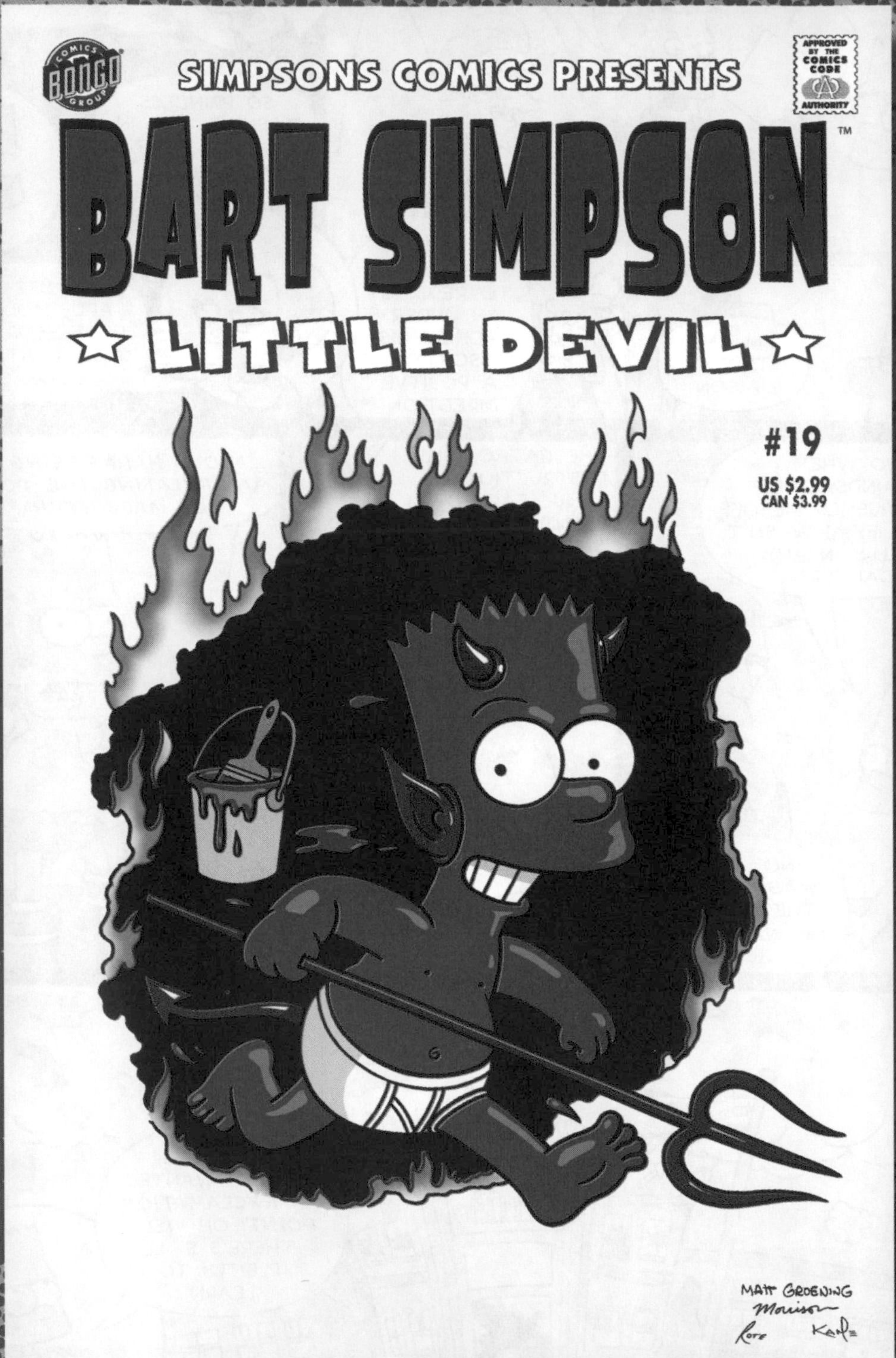
SIMPSONS COMICS PRESENTS
BART SIMPSON
LITTLE DEVIL
#19
US $2.99
CAN $3.99
APPROVED BY THE COMICS CODE AUTHORITY
MATT GROENING

MATT GROENING PRESENTS

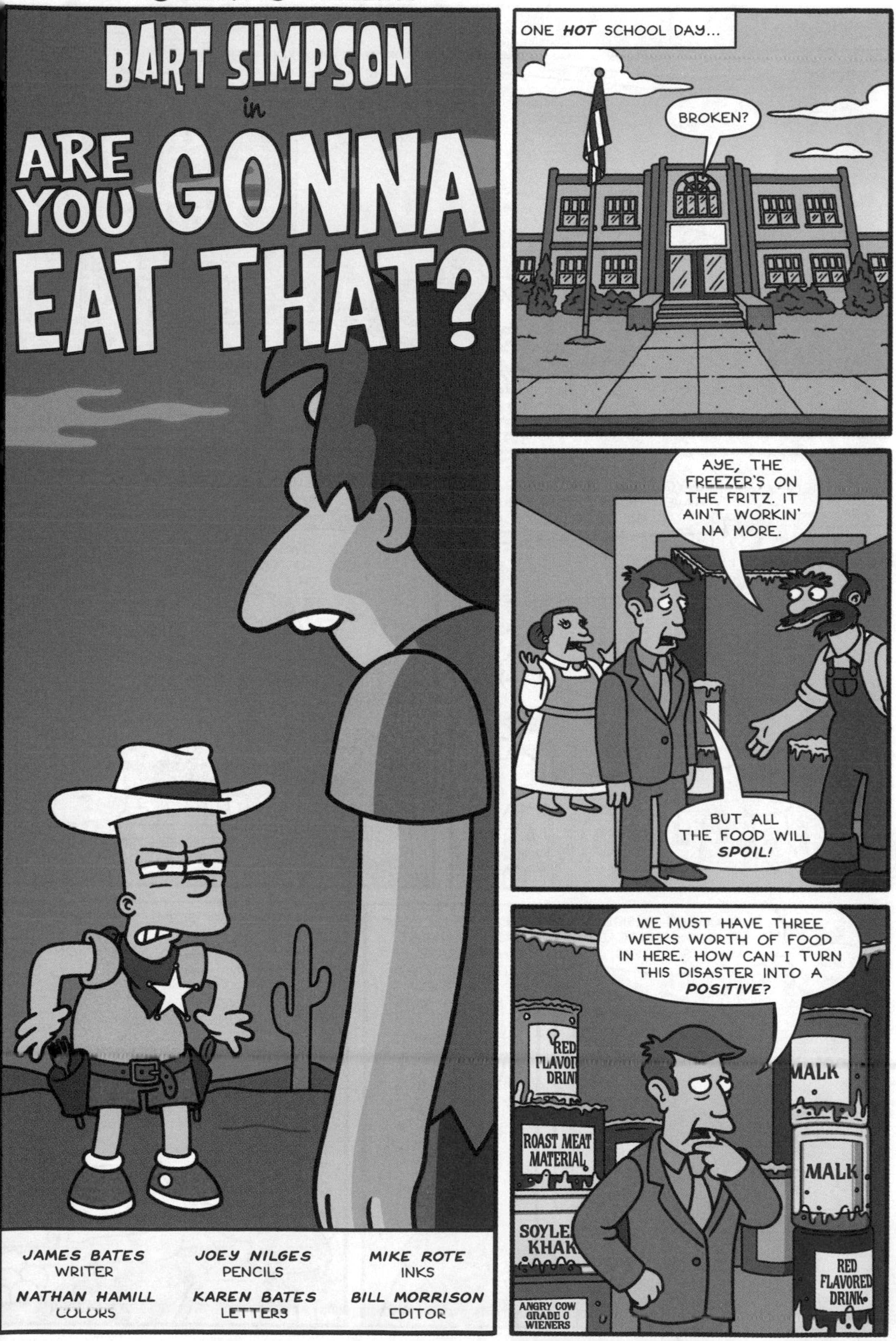
BART SIMPSON
in
ARE YOU GONNA EAT THAT?
JAMES BATES WRITER
JOEY NILGES PENCILS
MIKE ROTE INKS
NATHAN HAMILL COLORS
KAREN BATES LETTERS
BILL MORRISON EDITOR
ONE HOT SCHOOL DAY...
BROKEN?
AYE, THE FREEZER'S ON THE FRITZ. IT AIN'T WORKIN' NA MORE.
BUT ALL THE FOOD WILL SPOIL!
WE MUST HAVE THREE WEEKS WORTH OF FOOD IN HERE. HOW CAN I TURN THIS DISASTER INTO A POSITIVE?
ROAST MEAT MATERIAL
MALK
MALK
RED FLAVORED DRINK
ANGRY COW GRADE 0 WIENERS

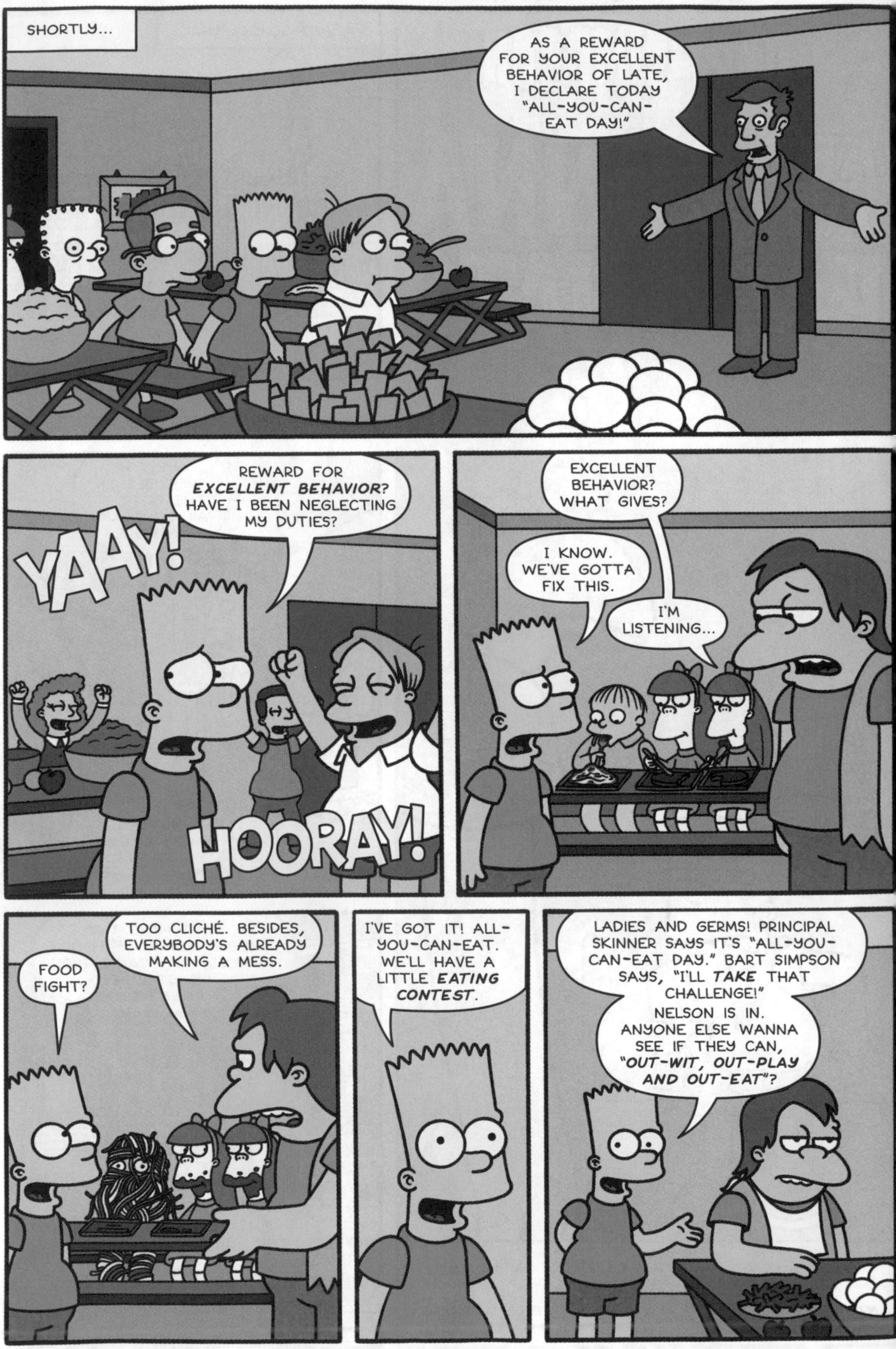
SHORTLY...
AS A REWARD FOR YOUR EXCELLENT BEHAVIOR OF LATE, I DECLARE TODAY "ALL-YOU-CAN-EAT DAY!"
YAAY!
REWARD FOR EXCELLENT BEHAVIOR? HAVE I BEEN NEGLECTING MY DUTIES?
HOORAY!
EXCELLENT BEHAVIOR? WHAT GIVES?
I KNOW. WE'VE GOTTA FIX THIS.
I'M LISTENING...
FOOD FIGHT?
TOO CLICHÉ. BESIDES, EVERYBODY'S ALREADY MAKING A MESS.
I'VE GOT IT! ALL-YOU-CAN-EAT. WE'LL HAVE A LITTLE EATING CONTEST.
LADIES AND GERMS! PRINCIPAL SKINNER SAYS IT'S "ALL-YOU-CAN-EAT DAY." BART SIMPSON SAYS, "I'LL TAKE THAT CHALLENGE!"
NELSON IS IN. ANYONE ELSE WANNA SEE IF THEY CAN, "OUT-WIT, OUT-PLAY AND OUT-EAT"?

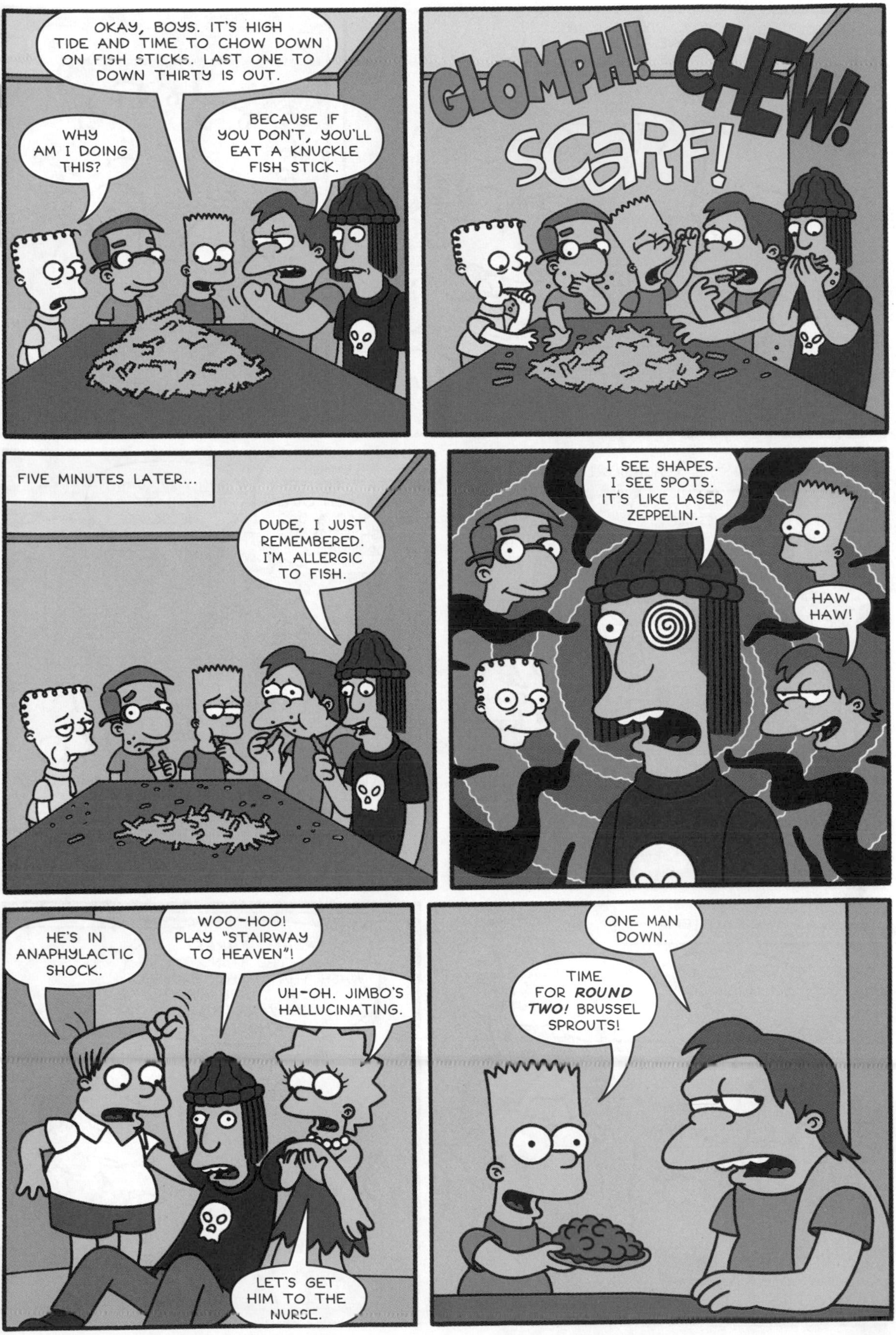
OKAY, BOYS. IT'S HIGH TIDE AND TIME TO CHOW DOWN ON FISH STICKS. LAST ONE TO DOWN THIRTY IS OUT.
WHY AM I DOING THIS?
BECAUSE IF YOU DON'T, YOU'LL EAT A KNUCKLE FISH STICK.
GLOMPH! CHEW! SCARF!
FIVE MINUTES LATER...
DUDE, I JUST REMEMBERED. I'M ALLERGIC TO FISH.
I SEE SHAPES. I SEE SPOTS. IT'S LIKE LASER ZEPPELIN.
HAW HAW!
HE'S IN ANAPHYLACTIC SHOCK.
WOO-HOO! PLAY "STAIRWAY TO HEAVEN"!
UH-OH. JIMBO'S HALLUCINATING.
LET'S GET HIM TO THE NURSE.
ONE MAN DOWN.
TIME FOR ROUND TWO! BRUSSEL SPROUTS!

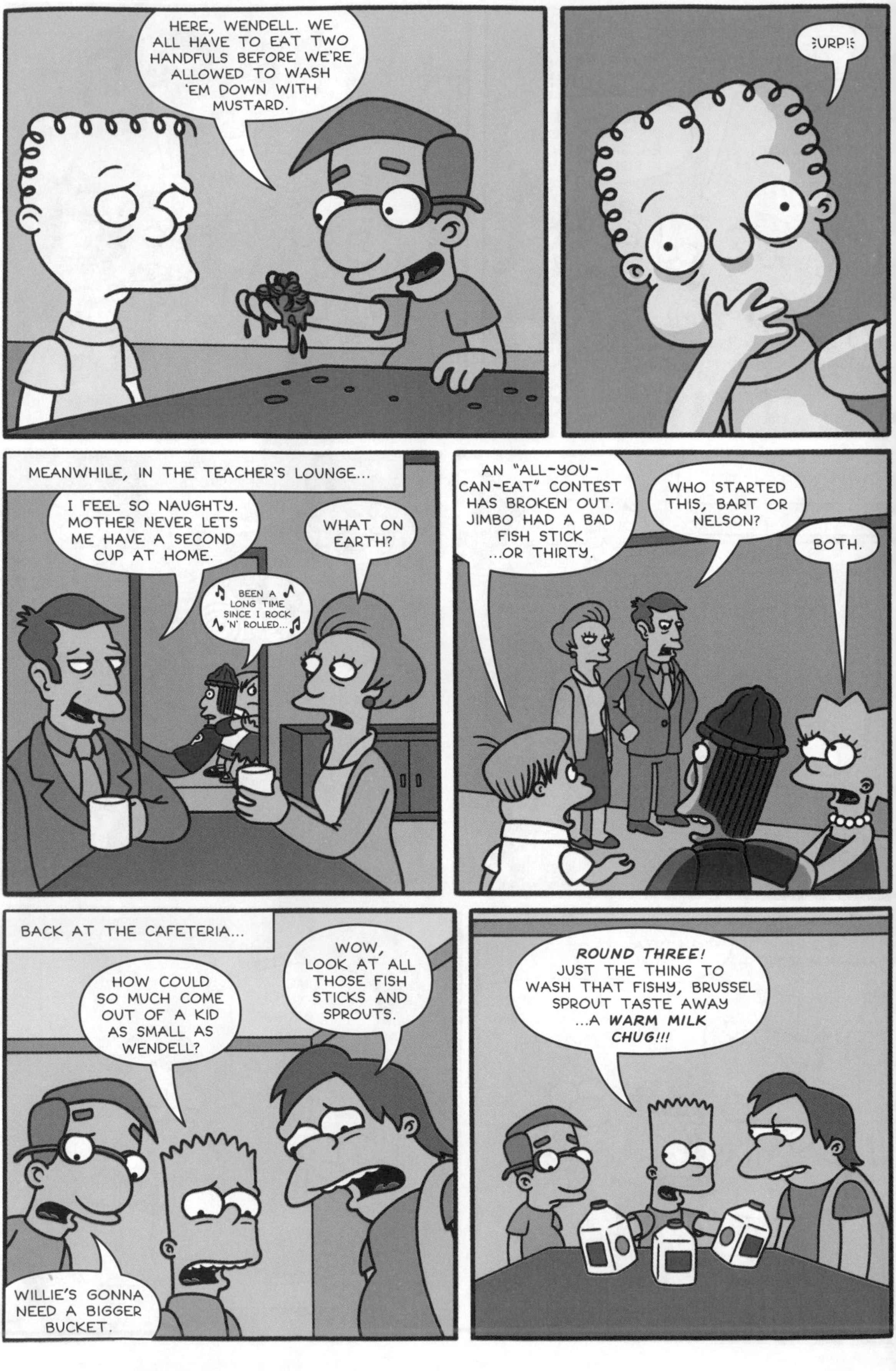
HERE, WENDELL. WE ALL HAVE TO EAT TWO HANDFULS BEFORE WE'RE ALLOWED TO WASH 'EM DOWN WITH MUSTARD.
URP!
MEANWHILE, IN THE TEACHER'S LOUNGE...
I FEEL SO NAUGHTY. MOTHER NEVER LETS ME HAVE A SECOND CUP AT HOME.
WHAT ON EARTH?
BEEN A LONG TIME SINCE I ROCK 'N' ROLLED...
AN "ALL-YOU-CAN-EAT" CONTEST HAS BROKEN OUT. JIMBO HAD A BAD FISH STICK ...OR THIRTY.
WHO STARTED THIS, BART OR NELSON?
BOTH.
BACK AT THE CAFETERIA...
HOW COULD SO MUCH COME OUT OF A KID AS SMALL AS WENDELL?
WOW, LOOK AT ALL THOSE FISH STICKS AND SPROUTS.
WILLIE'S GONNA NEED A BIGGER BUCKET.
ROUND THREE! JUST THE THING TO WASH THAT FISHY, BRUSSEL SPROUT TASTE AWAY ...A WARM MILK CHUG!!!

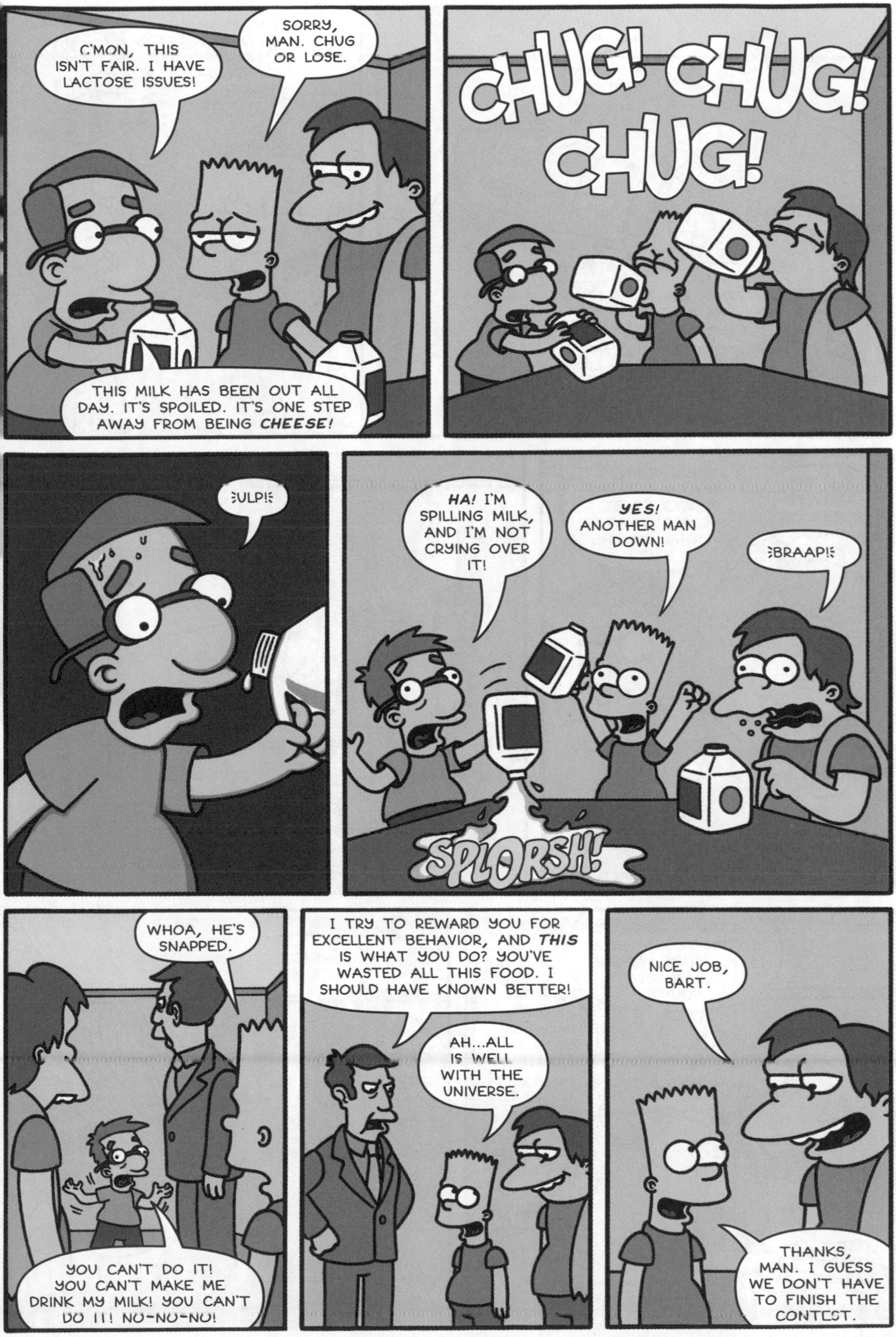
C'MON, THIS ISN'T FAIR. I HAVE LACTOSE ISSUES!
SORRY, MAN. CHUG OR LOSE.
THIS MILK HAS BEEN OUT ALL DAY. IT'S SPOILED. IT'S ONE STEP AWAY FROM BEING *CHEESE!*
CHUG! CHUG! CHUG!
ULP!
HA! I'M SPILLING MILK, AND I'M NOT CRYING OVER IT!
YES! ANOTHER MAN DOWN!
BRAAP!
SPLORSH!
WHOA, HE'S SNAPPED.
YOU CAN'T DO IT! YOU CAN'T MAKE ME DRINK MY MILK! YOU CAN'T DO IT! NO-NO-NO!
I TRY TO REWARD YOU FOR EXCELLENT BEHAVIOR, AND *THIS* IS WHAT YOU DO? YOU'VE WASTED ALL THIS FOOD. I SHOULD HAVE KNOWN BETTER!
AH...ALL IS WELL WITH THE UNIVERSE.
NICE JOB, BART.
THANKS, MAN. I GUESS WE DON'T HAVE TO FINISH THE CONTEST.

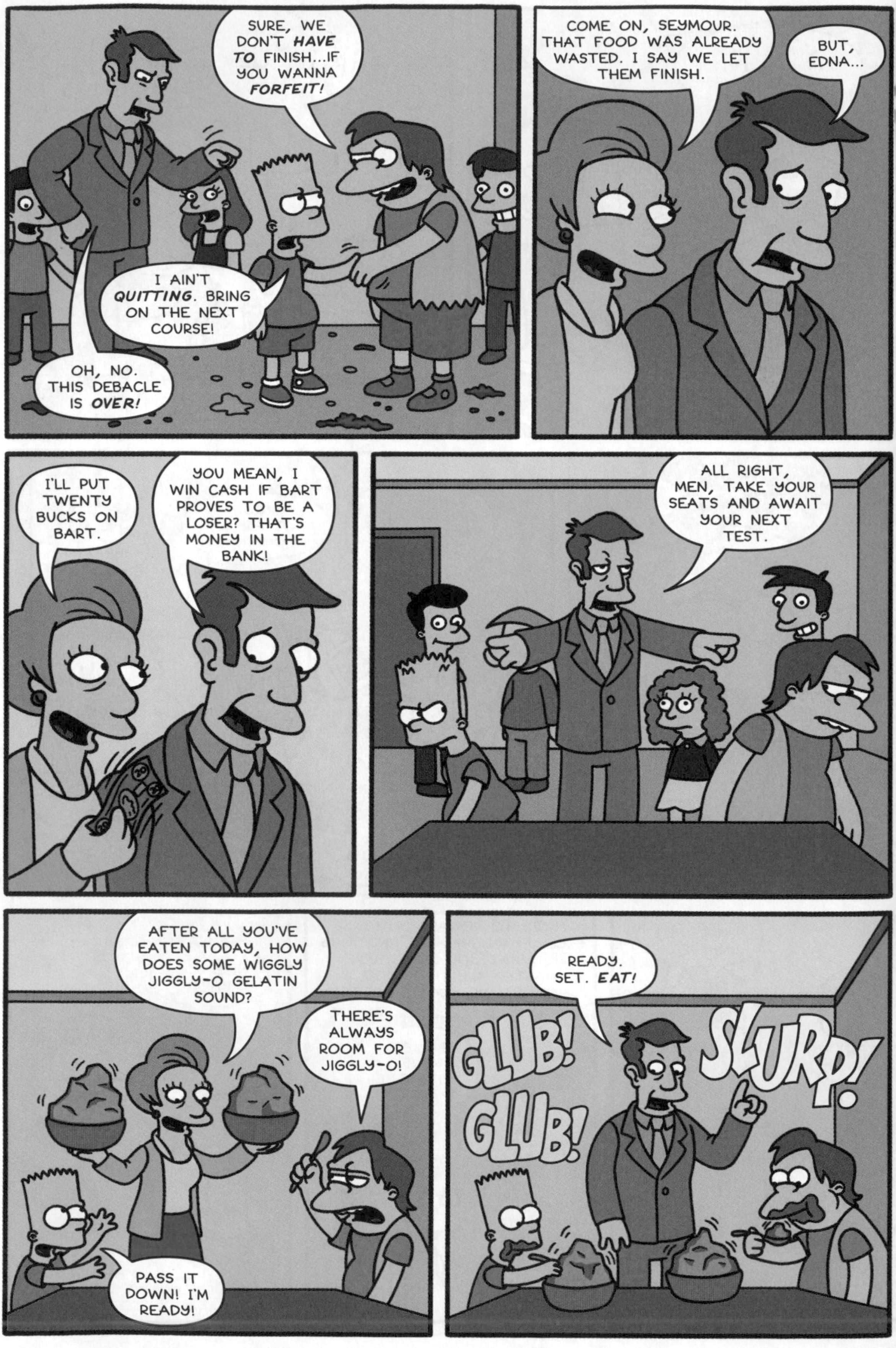

SURE, WE DON'T *HAVE TO* FINISH...IF YOU WANNA *FORFEIT!*
I AIN'T *QUITTING*. BRING ON THE NEXT COURSE!
OH, NO. THIS DEBACLE IS *OVER!*
COME ON, SEYMOUR. THAT FOOD WAS ALREADY WASTED. I SAY WE LET THEM FINISH.
BUT, EDNA...
I'LL PUT TWENTY BUCKS ON BART.
YOU MEAN, I WIN CASH IF BART PROVES TO BE A LOSER? THAT'S MONEY IN THE BANK!
ALL RIGHT, MEN, TAKE YOUR SEATS AND AWAIT YOUR NEXT TEST.
AFTER ALL YOU'VE EATEN TODAY, HOW DOES SOME WIGGLY JIGGLY-O GELATIN SOUND?
THERE'S ALWAYS ROOM FOR JIGGLY-O!
PASS IT DOWN! I'M READY!
READY. SET. *EAT!*
GLUB! GLUB!
SLURP!

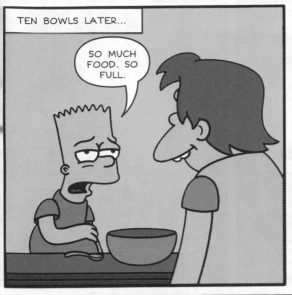

TEN BOWLS LATER...

SO MUCH FOOD. SO FULL.

HOW ABOUT SOME MINT ICE CREAM? TWO BOWLS EACH.

THIS SHOULD GIVE US A WINNER. BON APPETIT!

CAN'T EAT MORE...MUST EAT MORE... CAN'T...

MUST...

UH-OH. I KNOW THAT LOOK. *TAKE COVER!*

OH NO!

LOOKS LIKE BART IS GONNA BLOW. YOU MIGHT AS WELL FORK OVER THAT TWENTY, EDNA.

BART, STOP IT! NOTHING GOOD CAN COME OF EATING UNTIL YOU'RE SICK. HAVEN'T YOU LEARNED ANYTHING FROM WATCHING DAD?

ξGLUGξ

C'MON, SIMPSON. PLAY OR FORFEIT!

LISA'S RIGHT! I'VE BEEN WATCHING HOMER PACK IT AWAY FOR YEARS. I CAN *DO* THIS!

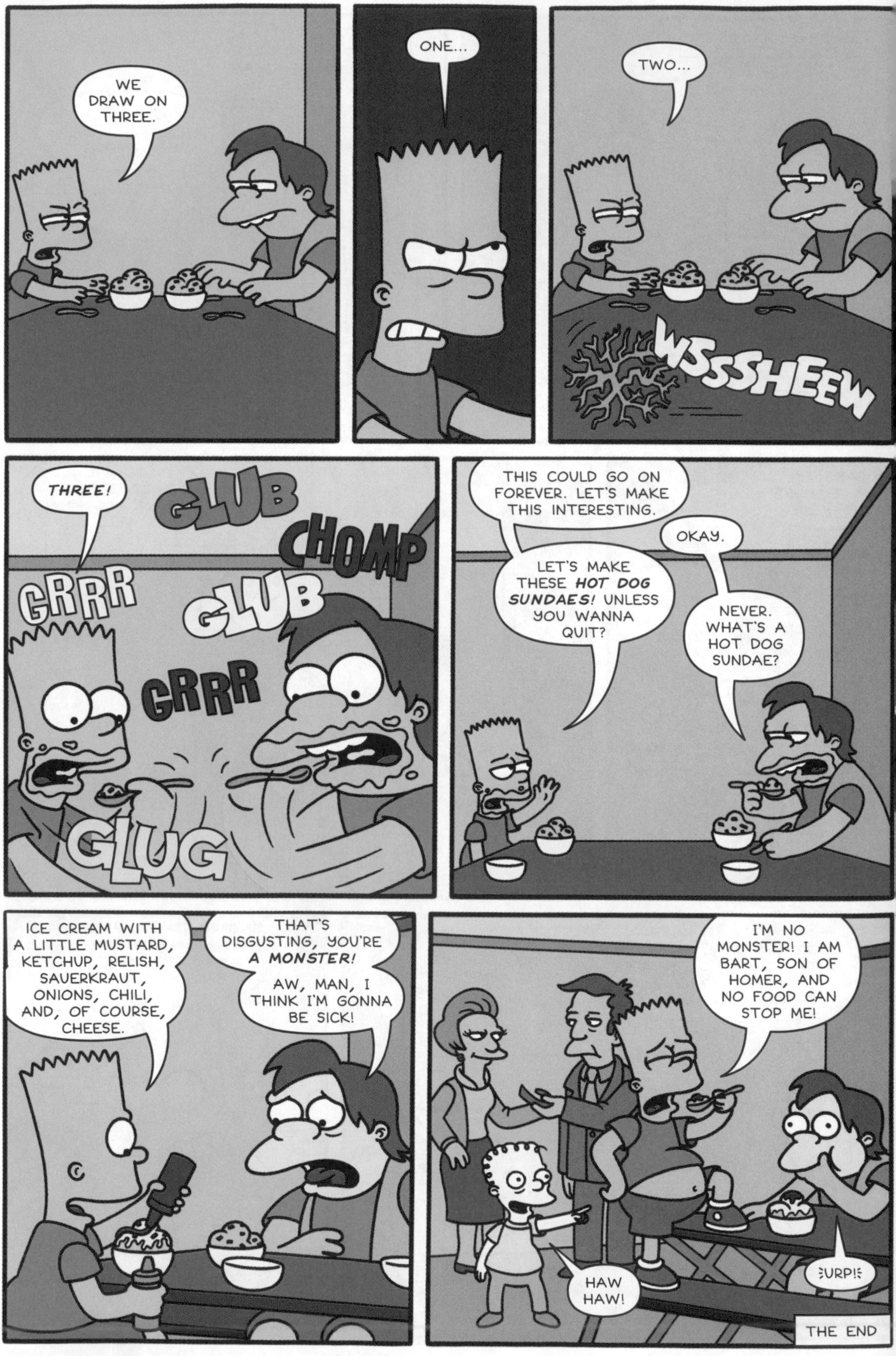

WE DRAW ON THREE.
ONE...
TWO...
WSSSHEEW
THREE!
GLUB
CHOMP
GRRR
GLUB
GRRR
GLUG
THIS COULD GO ON FOREVER. LET'S MAKE THIS INTERESTING.
OKAY.
LET'S MAKE THESE **HOT DOG SUNDAES!** UNLESS YOU WANNA QUIT?
NEVER. WHAT'S A HOT DOG SUNDAE?
ICE CREAM WITH A LITTLE MUSTARD, KETCHUP, RELISH, SAUERKRAUT, ONIONS, CHILI, AND, OF COURSE, CHEESE.
THAT'S DISGUSTING, YOU'RE **A MONSTER!**
AW, MAN, I THINK I'M GONNA BE SICK!
I'M NO MONSTER! I AM BART, SON OF HOMER, AND NO FOOD CAN STOP ME!
HAW HAW!
URP!
THE END

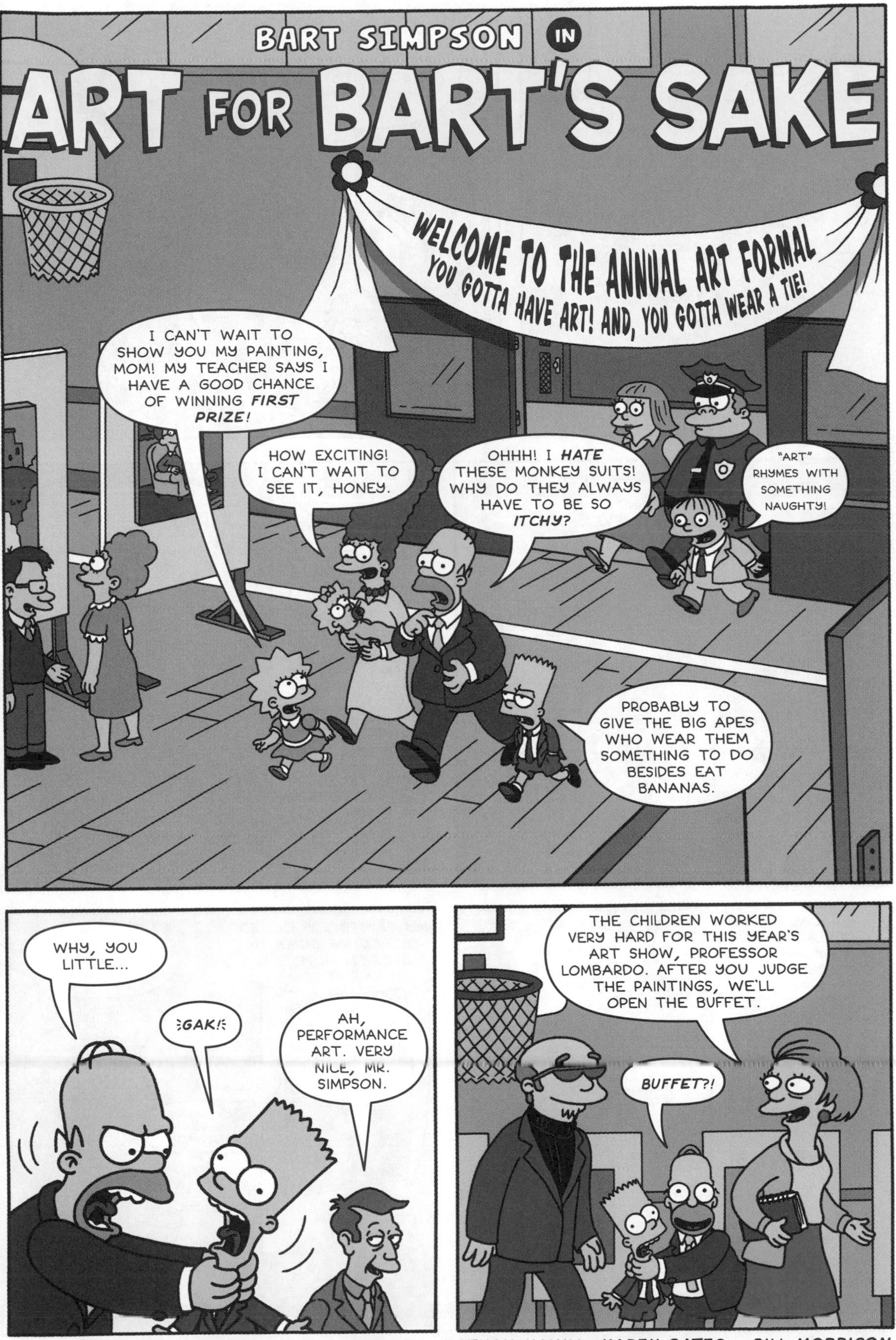
BART SIMPSON IN
ART FOR BART'S SAKE
WELCOME TO THE ANNUAL ART FORMAL
YOU GOTTA HAVE ART! AND, YOU GOTTA WEAR A TIE!
I CAN'T WAIT TO SHOW YOU MY PAINTING, MOM! MY TEACHER SAYS I HAVE A GOOD CHANCE OF WINNING *FIRST PRIZE*!
HOW EXCITING! I CAN'T WAIT TO SEE IT, HONEY.
OHHH! I *HATE* THESE MONKEY SUITS! WHY DO THEY ALWAYS HAVE TO BE SO *ITCHY*?
"ART" RHYMES WITH SOMETHING NAUGHTY!
PROBABLY TO GIVE THE BIG APES WHO WEAR THEM SOMETHING TO DO BESIDES EAT BANANAS.
WHY, YOU LITTLE...
GAK!
AH, PERFORMANCE ART. VERY NICE, MR. SIMPSON.
THE CHILDREN WORKED VERY HARD FOR THIS YEAR'S ART SHOW, PROFESSOR LOMBARDO. AFTER YOU JUDGE THE PAINTINGS, WE'LL OPEN THE BUFFET.
BUFFET?!

CHRIS YAMBAR WRITER | **MIKE KAZALEH** PENCILS | **JASON HO** INKS | **NATHAN HAMILL** COLORS | **KAREN BATES** LETTERS | **BILL MORRISON** EDITOR

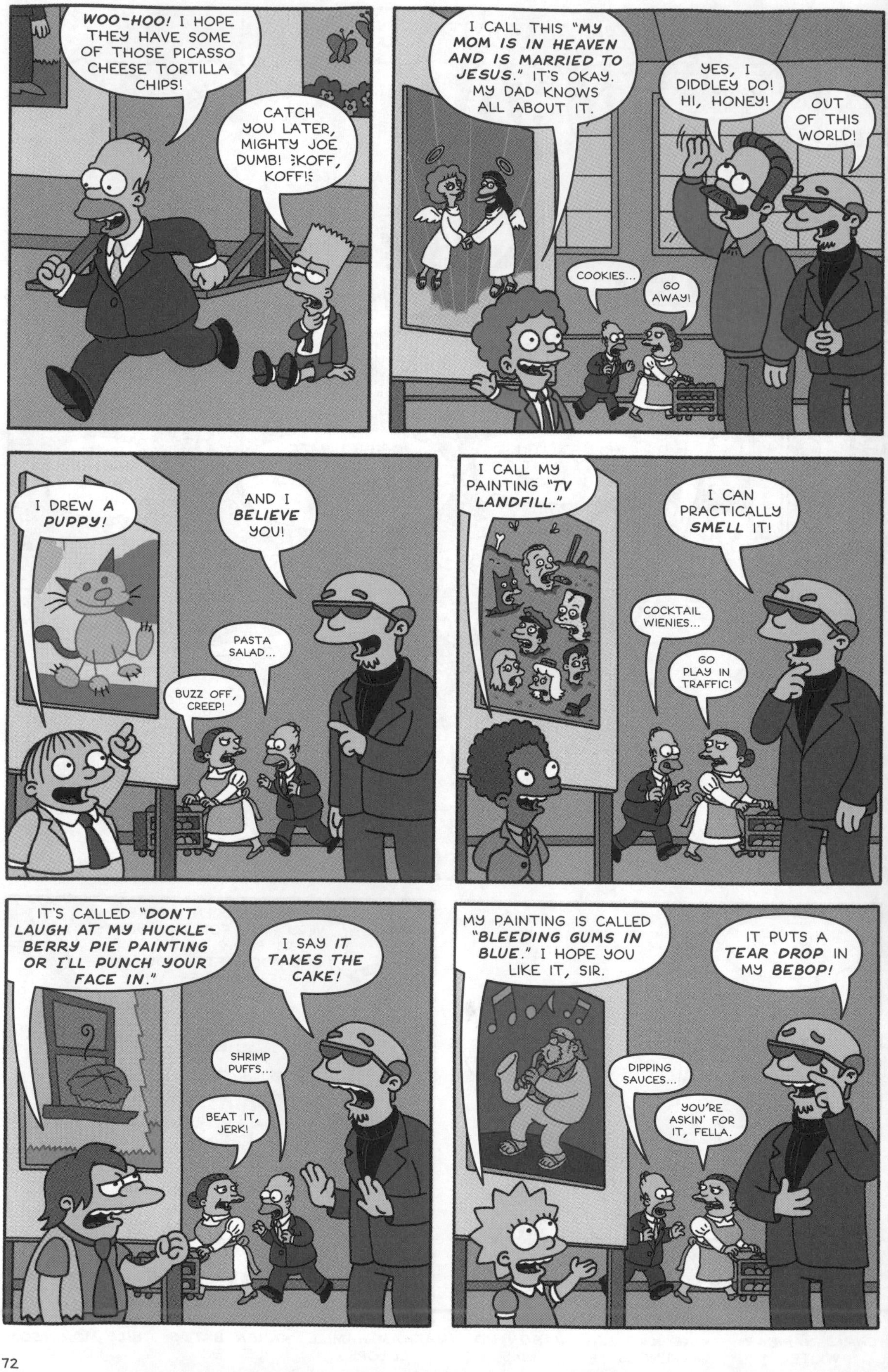
WOO-HOO! I HOPE THEY HAVE SOME OF THOSE PICASSO CHEESE TORTILLA CHIPS!
CATCH YOU LATER, MIGHTY JOE DUMB! KOFF, KOFF!
I CALL THIS "MY MOM IS IN HEAVEN AND IS MARRIED TO JESUS." IT'S OKAY. MY DAD KNOWS ALL ABOUT IT.
YES, I DIDDLEY DO! HI, HONEY!
OUT OF THIS WORLD!
COOKIES...
GO AWAY!
I DREW A PUPPY!
AND I BELIEVE YOU!
PASTA SALAD...
BUZZ OFF, CREEP!
I CALL MY PAINTING "TV LANDFILL."
I CAN PRACTICALLY SMELL IT!
COCKTAIL WIENIES...
GO PLAY IN TRAFFIC!
IT'S CALLED "DON'T LAUGH AT MY HUCKLEBERRY PIE PAINTING OR I'LL PUNCH YOUR FACE IN."
I SAY IT TAKES THE CAKE!
SHRIMP PUFFS...
BEAT IT, JERK!
MY PAINTING IS CALLED "BLEEDING GUMS IN BLUE." I HOPE YOU LIKE IT, SIR.
IT PUTS A TEAR DROP IN MY BEBOP!
DIPPING SAUCES...
YOU'RE ASKIN' FOR IT, FELLA.

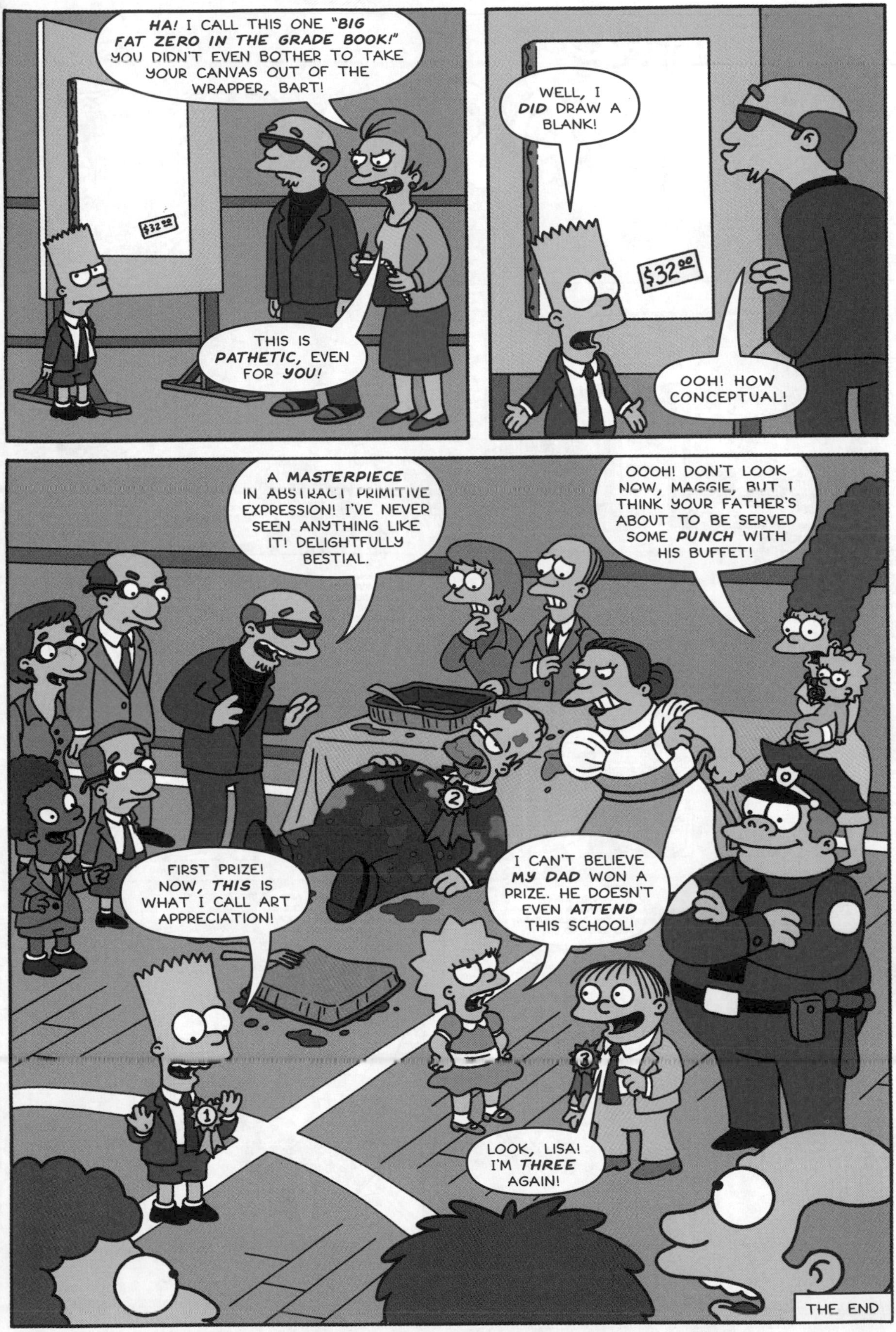
HA! I CALL THIS ONE "BIG FAT ZERO IN THE GRADE BOOK!" YOU DIDN'T EVEN BOTHER TO TAKE YOUR CANVAS OUT OF THE WRAPPER, BART!
THIS IS PATHETIC, EVEN FOR YOU!
$32.00
WELL, I DID DRAW A BLANK!
OOH! HOW CONCEPTUAL!
$32.00
A MASTERPIECE IN ABSTRACT PRIMITIVE EXPRESSION! I'VE NEVER SEEN ANYTHING LIKE IT! DELIGHTFULLY BESTIAL.
OOOH! DON'T LOOK NOW, MAGGIE, BUT I THINK YOUR FATHER'S ABOUT TO BE SERVED SOME PUNCH WITH HIS BUFFET!
FIRST PRIZE! NOW, THIS IS WHAT I CALL ART APPRECIATION!
I CAN'T BELIEVE MY DAD WON A PRIZE. HE DOESN'T EVEN ATTEND THIS SCHOOL!
LOOK, LISA! I'M THREE AGAIN!
THE END

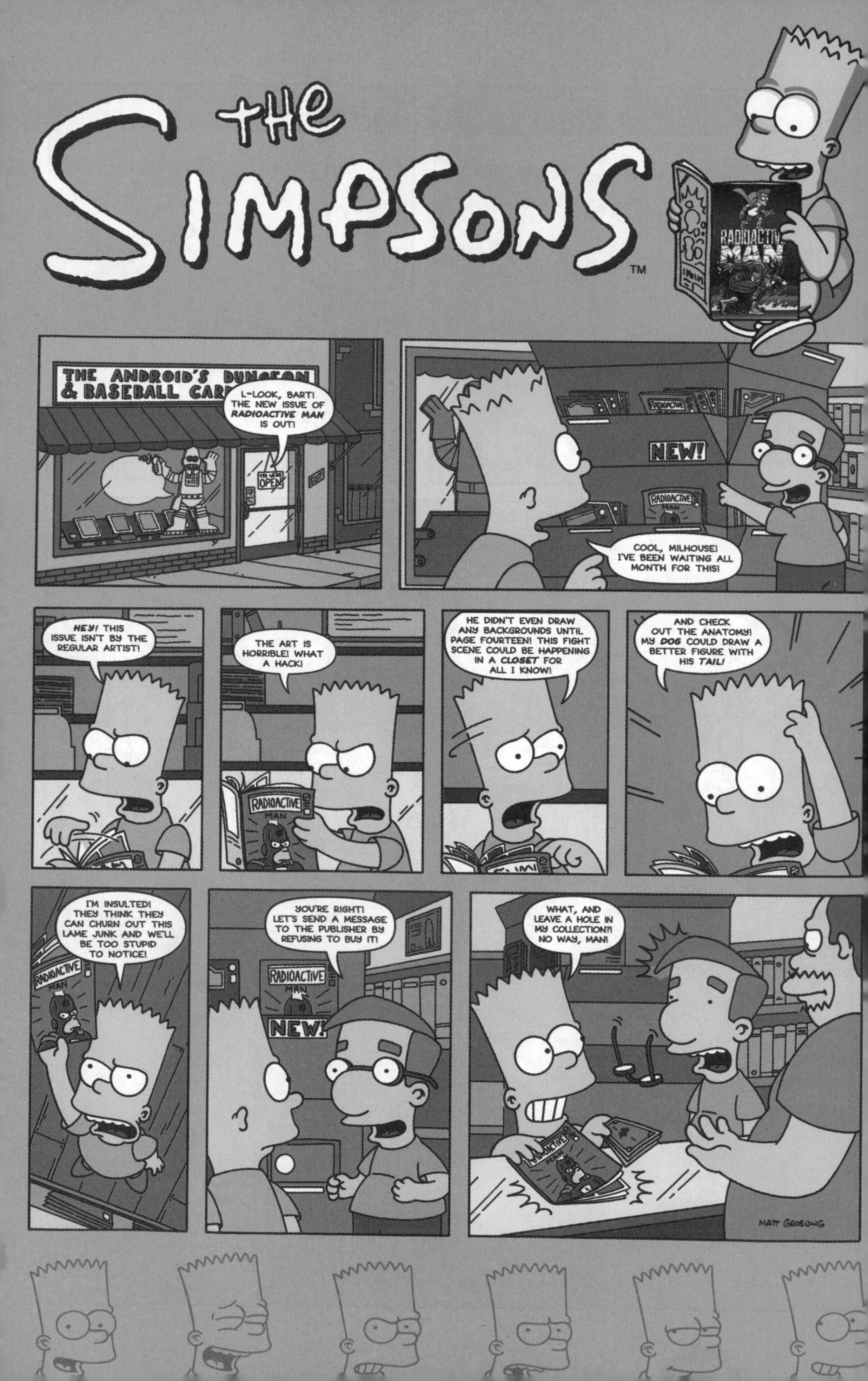
THE SIMPSONS™
RADIOACTIVE MAN
THE ANDROID'S
L-LOOK, BART! THE NEW ISSUE OF *RADIOACTIVE MAN* IS OUT!
OPEN
NEW!
RADIOACTIVE MAN
COOL, MILHOUSE! I'VE BEEN WAITING ALL MONTH FOR THIS!
HEY! THIS ISSUE ISN'T BY THE REGULAR ARTIST!
THE ART IS HORRIBLE! WHAT A HACK!
RADIOACTIVE MAN
HE DIDN'T EVEN DRAW ANY BACKGROUNDS UNTIL PAGE FOURTEEN! THIS FIGHT SCENE COULD BE HAPPENING IN A *CLOSET* FOR ALL I KNOW!
AND CHECK OUT THE ANATOMY! MY *DOG* COULD DRAW A BETTER FIGURE WITH HIS *TAIL!*
I'M INSULTED! THEY THINK THEY CAN CHURN OUT THIS LAME JUNK AND WE'LL BE TOO STUPID TO NOTICE!
RADIOACTIVE MAN
YOU'RE RIGHT! LET'S SEND A MESSAGE TO THE PUBLISHER BY REFUSING TO BUY IT!
RADIOACTIVE MAN
NEW!
WHAT, AND LEAVE A HOLE IN MY COLLECTION?! NO WAY, MAN!
RADIOACTIVE MAN
MATT GROENING

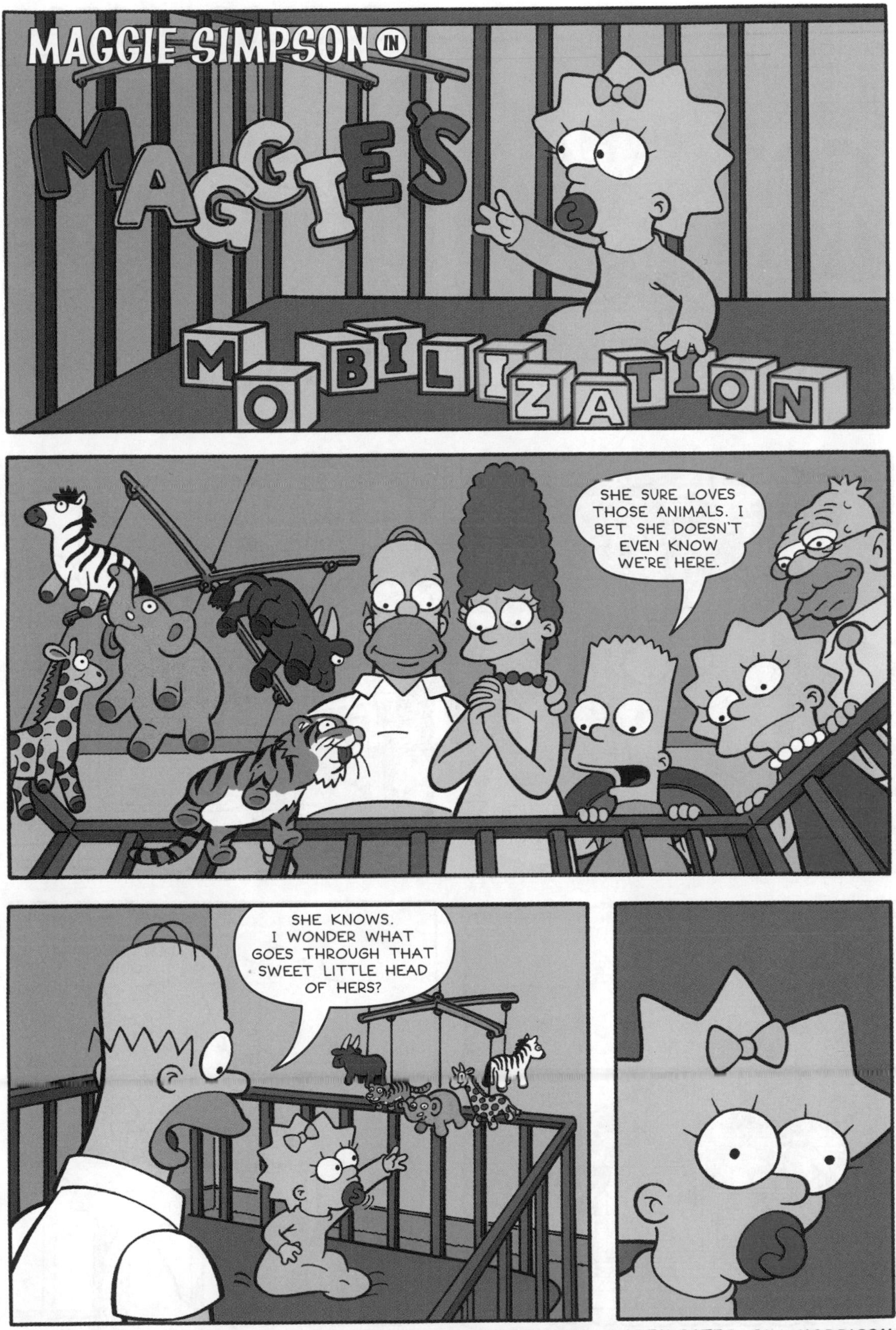
MAGGIE SIMPSON IN
MAGGIE'S
MOBILIZATION
SHE SURE LOVES THOSE ANIMALS. I BET SHE DOESN'T EVEN KNOW WE'RE HERE.
SHE KNOWS. I WONDER WHAT GOES THROUGH THAT SWEET LITTLE HEAD OF HERS?

JAMES BATES WRITER | *MARK ERVIN* PENCILS | *MIKE DECARLO* INKS | *NATHAN HAMILL* COLORS | *KAREN BATES* LETTERS | *BILL MORRISON* EDITOR

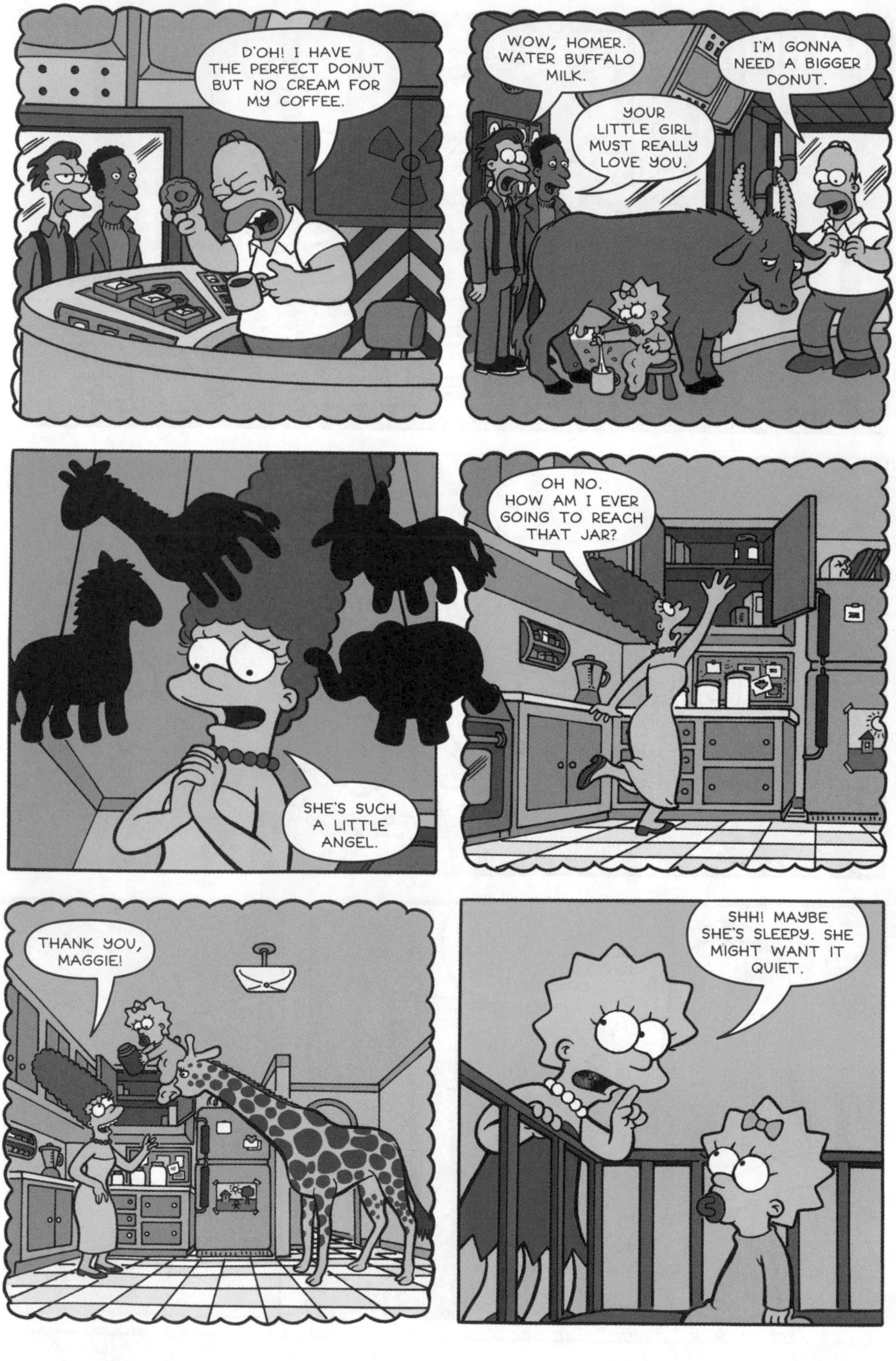
D'OH! I HAVE THE PERFECT DONUT BUT NO CREAM FOR MY COFFEE.
WOW, HOMER. WATER BUFFALO MILK.
YOUR LITTLE GIRL MUST REALLY LOVE YOU.
I'M GONNA NEED A BIGGER DONUT.
SHE'S SUCH A LITTLE ANGEL.
OH NO. HOW AM I EVER GOING TO REACH THAT JAR?
THANK YOU, MAGGIE!
SHH! MAYBE SHE'S SLEEPY. SHE MIGHT WANT IT QUIET.

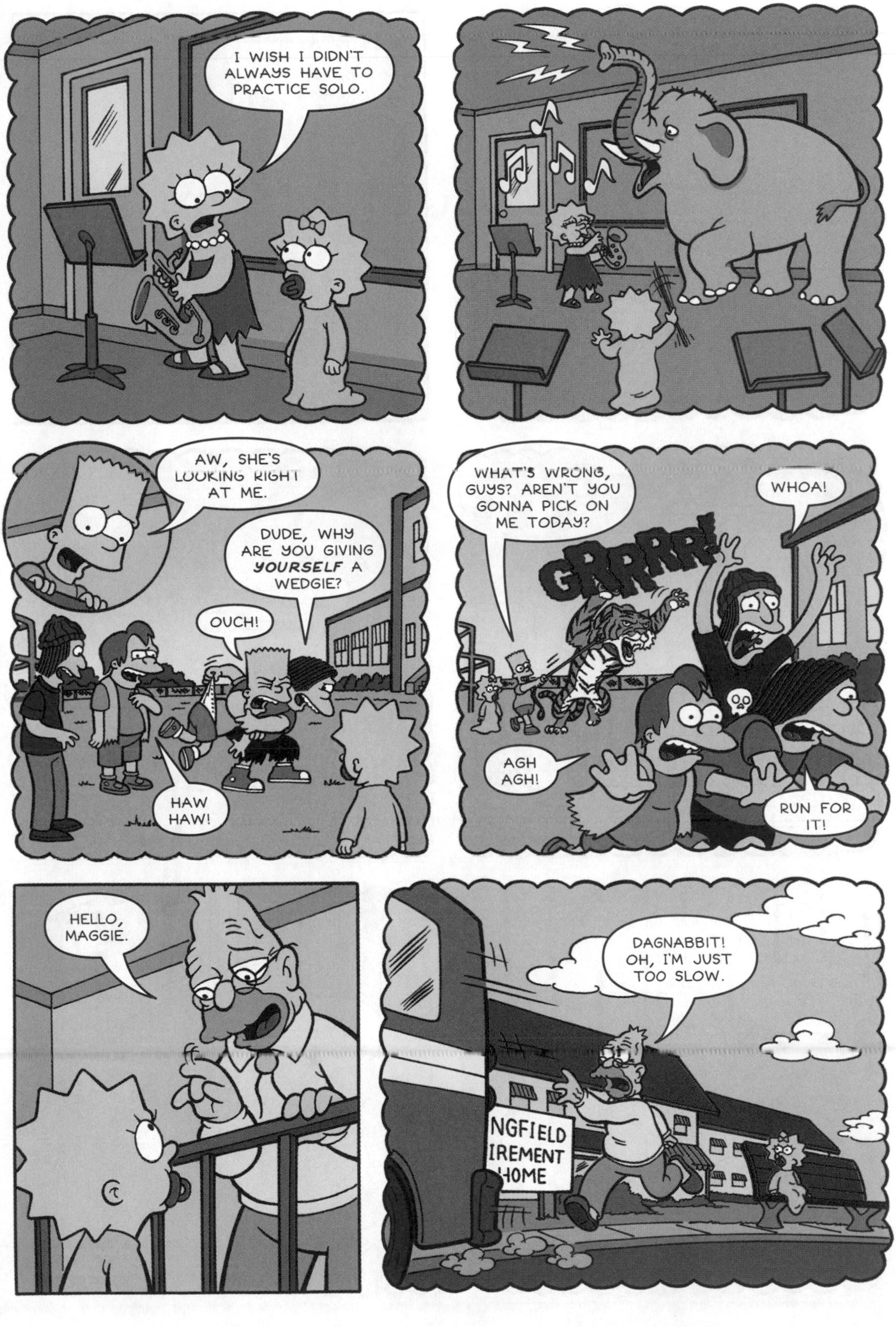
I WISH I DIDN'T ALWAYS HAVE TO PRACTICE SOLO.
AW, SHE'S LOOKING RIGHT AT ME.
DUDE, WHY ARE YOU GIVING **YOURSELF** A WEDGIE?
OUCH!
HAW HAW!
WHAT'S WRONG, GUYS? AREN'T YOU GONNA PICK ON ME TODAY?
WHOA!
GRRRR!
AGH AGH!
RUN FOR IT!
HELLO, MAGGIE.
DAGNABBIT! OH, I'M JUST TOO SLOW.
NGFIELD
IREMENT
HOME

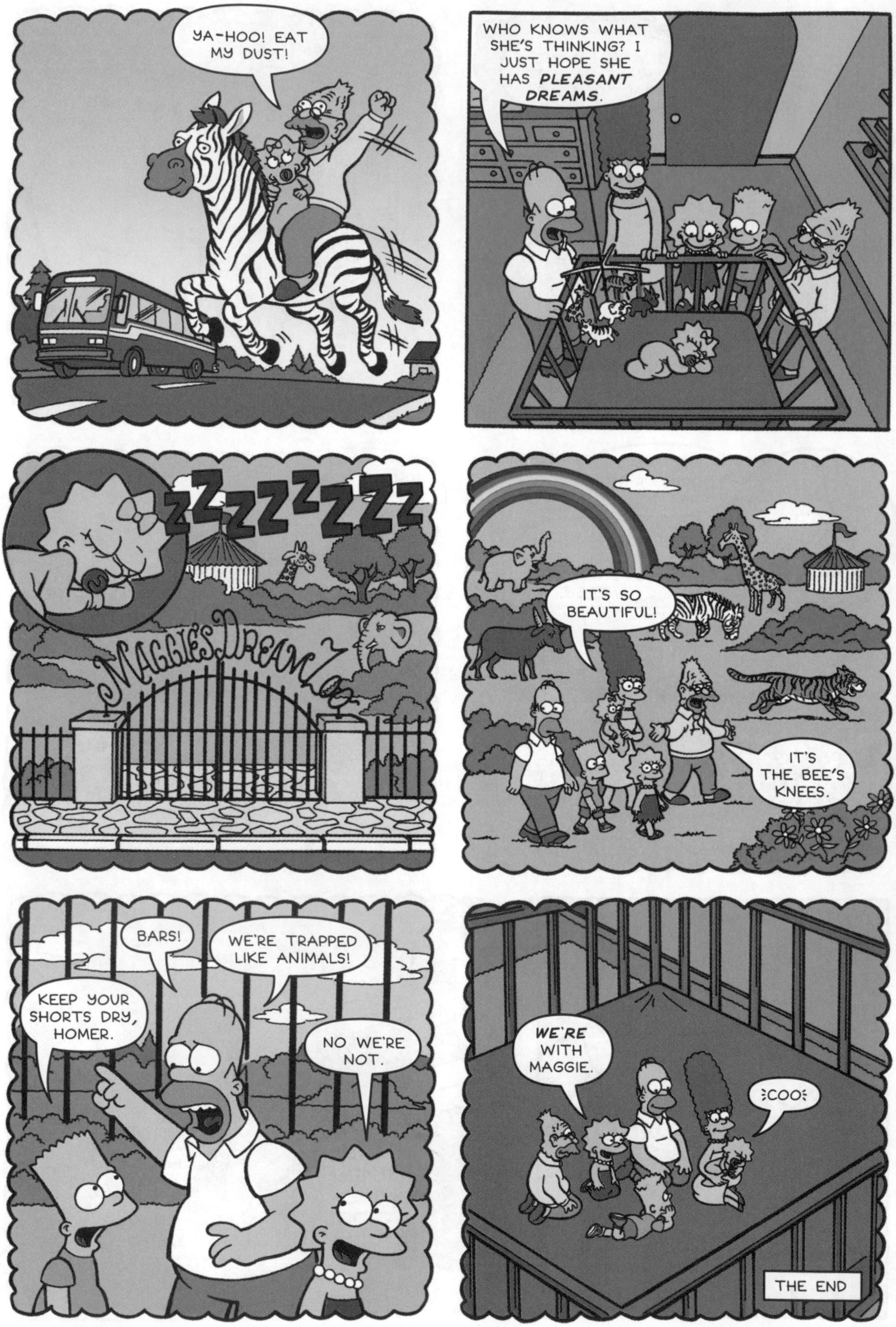
YA-HOO! EAT MY DUST!
WHO KNOWS WHAT SHE'S THINKING? I JUST HOPE SHE HAS **PLEASANT DREAMS**.
ZZZZZZZZZ
MAGGIE'S DREAM ZOO
IT'S SO BEAUTIFUL!
IT'S THE BEE'S KNEES.
BARS!
WE'RE TRAPPED LIKE ANIMALS!
KEEP YOUR SHORTS DRY, HOMER.
NO WE'RE NOT.
WE'RE WITH MAGGIE.
COO
THE END

THE MEDIOCRE MISADVENTURES OF MARTIN & MILHOUSE!
BARTLESS ON A TUESDAY

HEY, MARTIN. COOL ROBOT!

THIS IS MY GREATEST CREATION, *THE PRINCE 5000!* IT'S A ROBOT DESIGNED TO TAKE A BULLY'S BEATING!

REALLY? *WOW!*

CAN YOU BUILD ME ONE? DOES IT REALLY WORK?

OH MY YES! IT WORKS SO WELL, I'M SORELY TEMPTED TO BEAT THE LITTLE CIRCUIT MONKEY MYSELF!

NYAH!

BUT THAT WILL HAVE TO WAIT. BART IS FINALLY TAKING US TO SEE PROFESSOR FRINK'S LABORATORY SO THAT HE CAN CRITIQUE MY WORK! ISN'T IT EXCITING?

UH, ACTUALLY, I'D BE UP FOR ANYTHING THAT WOULD GET ME OUT OF THE HOUSE AND AWAY FROM MY MOM AND NEW "WEEK-END DAD."

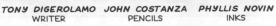

TONY DIGEROLAMO
WRITER

JOHN COSTANZA
PENCILS

PHYLLIS NOVIN
INKS

ART VILLANUEVA
COLORS

KAREN BATES
LETTERS

BILL MORRISON
EDITOR

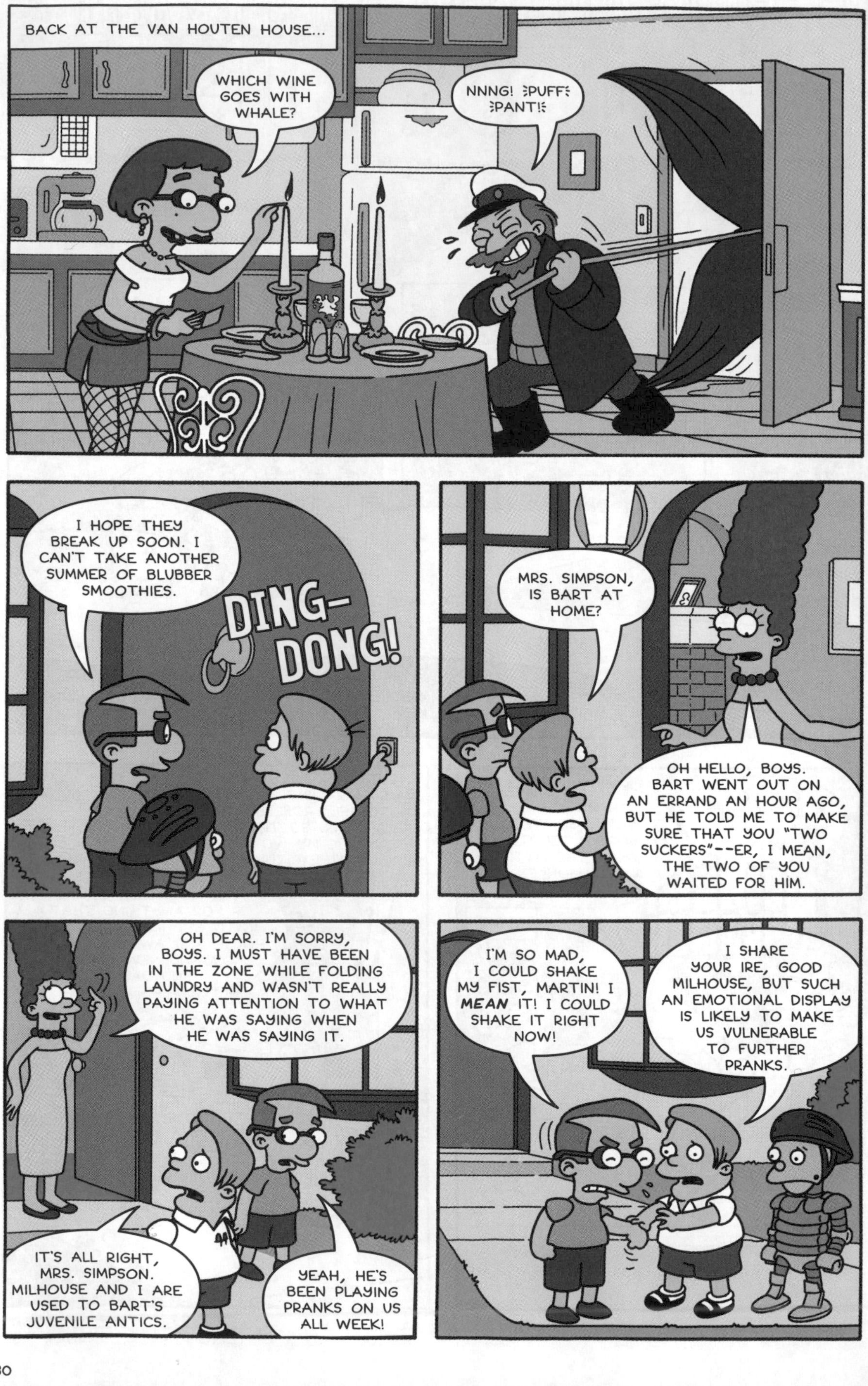
BACK AT THE VAN HOUTEN HOUSE...
WHICH WINE GOES WITH WHALE?
NNNG! PUFF PANT!
I HOPE THEY BREAK UP SOON. I CAN'T TAKE ANOTHER SUMMER OF BLUBBER SMOOTHIES.
DING-DONG!
MRS. SIMPSON, IS BART AT HOME?
OH HELLO, BOYS. BART WENT OUT ON AN ERRAND AN HOUR AGO, BUT HE TOLD ME TO MAKE SURE THAT YOU "TWO SUCKERS"--ER, I MEAN, THE TWO OF YOU WAITED FOR HIM.
OH DEAR. I'M SORRY, BOYS. I MUST HAVE BEEN IN THE ZONE WHILE FOLDING LAUNDRY AND WASN'T REALLY PAYING ATTENTION TO WHAT HE WAS SAYING WHEN HE WAS SAYING IT.
IT'S ALL RIGHT, MRS. SIMPSON. MILHOUSE AND I ARE USED TO BART'S JUVENILE ANTICS.
YEAH, HE'S BEEN PLAYING PRANKS ON US ALL WEEK!
I'M SO MAD, I COULD SHAKE MY FIST, MARTIN! I MEAN IT! I COULD SHAKE IT RIGHT NOW!
I SHARE YOUR IRE, GOOD MILHOUSE, BUT SUCH AN EMOTIONAL DISPLAY IS LIKELY TO MAKE US VULNERABLE TO FURTHER PRANKS.

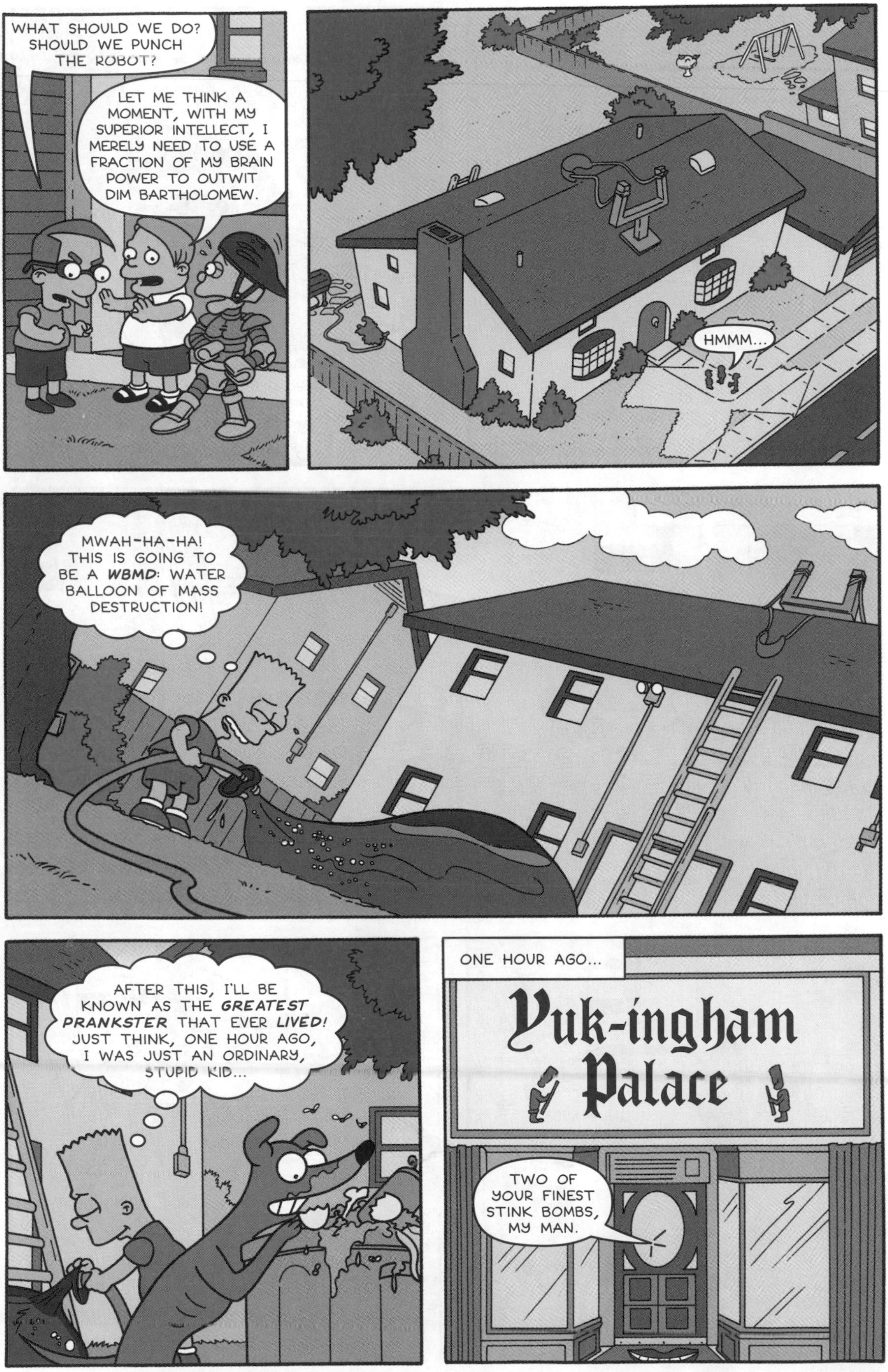
WHAT SHOULD WE DO? SHOULD WE PUNCH THE ROBOT?
LET ME THINK A MOMENT, WITH MY SUPERIOR INTELLECT, I MERELY NEED TO USE A FRACTION OF MY BRAIN POWER TO OUTWIT DIM BARTHOLOMEW.
HMMM...
MWAH-HA-HA! THIS IS GOING TO BE A WBMD: WATER BALLOON OF MASS DESTRUCTION!
AFTER THIS, I'LL BE KNOWN AS THE GREATEST PRANKSTER THAT EVER LIVED! JUST THINK, ONE HOUR AGO, I WAS JUST AN ORDINARY, STUPID KID...
ONE HOUR AGO...
Yuk-ingham Palace
TWO OF YOUR FINEST STINK BOMBS, MY MAN.

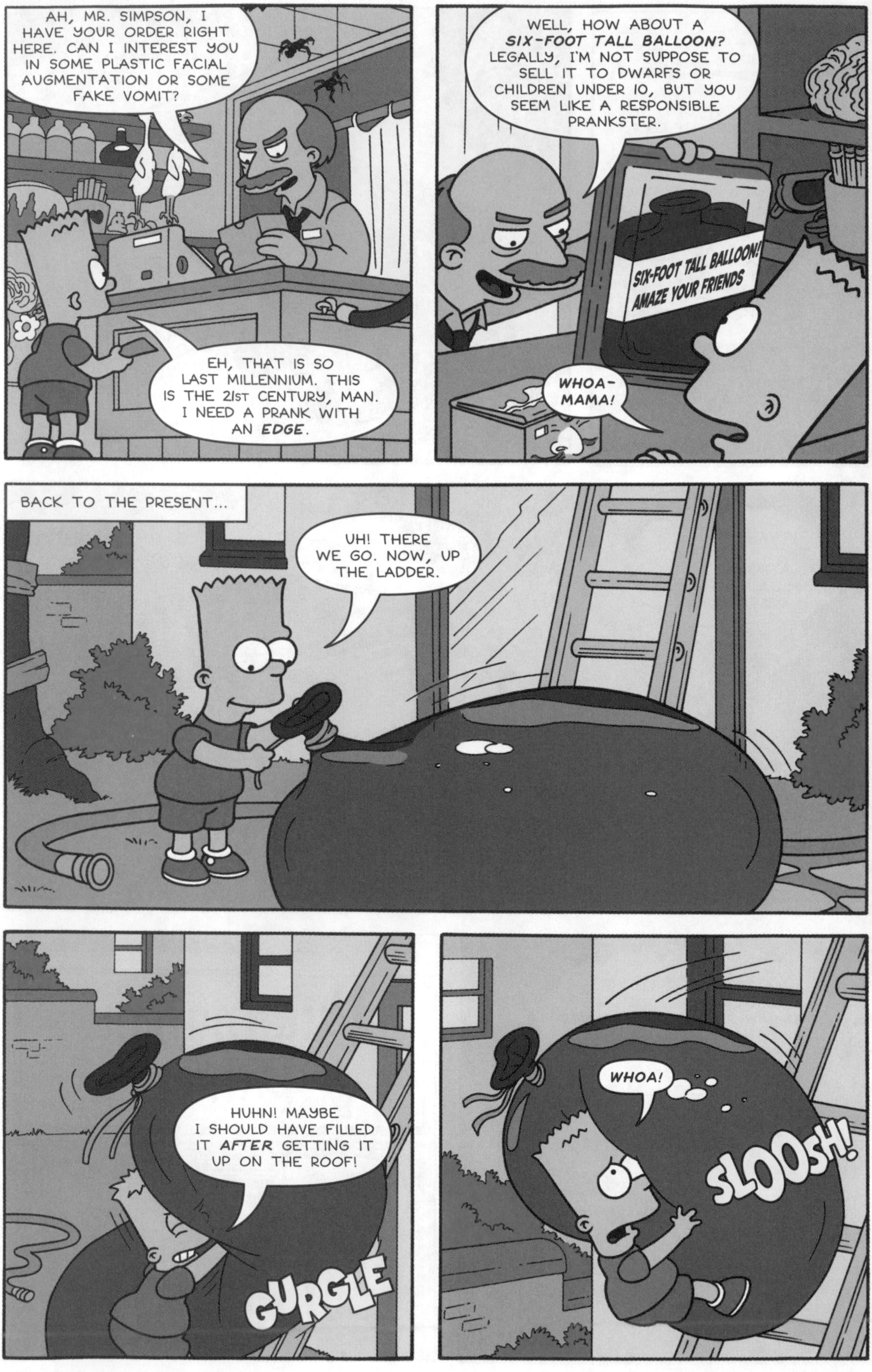
AH, MR. SIMPSON, I HAVE YOUR ORDER RIGHT HERE. CAN I INTEREST YOU IN SOME PLASTIC FACIAL AUGMENTATION OR SOME FAKE VOMIT?
EH, THAT IS SO LAST MILLENNIUM. THIS IS THE 21ST CENTURY, MAN. I NEED A PRANK WITH AN EDGE.
WELL, HOW ABOUT A SIX-FOOT TALL BALLOON? LEGALLY, I'M NOT SUPPOSE TO SELL IT TO DWARFS OR CHILDREN UNDER 10, BUT YOU SEEM LIKE A RESPONSIBLE PRANKSTER.
SIX-FOOT TALL BALLOON! AMAZE YOUR FRIENDS
WHOA-MAMA!
BACK TO THE PRESENT...
UH! THERE WE GO. NOW, UP THE LADDER.
HUHN! MAYBE I SHOULD HAVE FILLED IT AFTER GETTING IT UP ON THE ROOF!
GURGLE
WHOA!
SLOOSH!

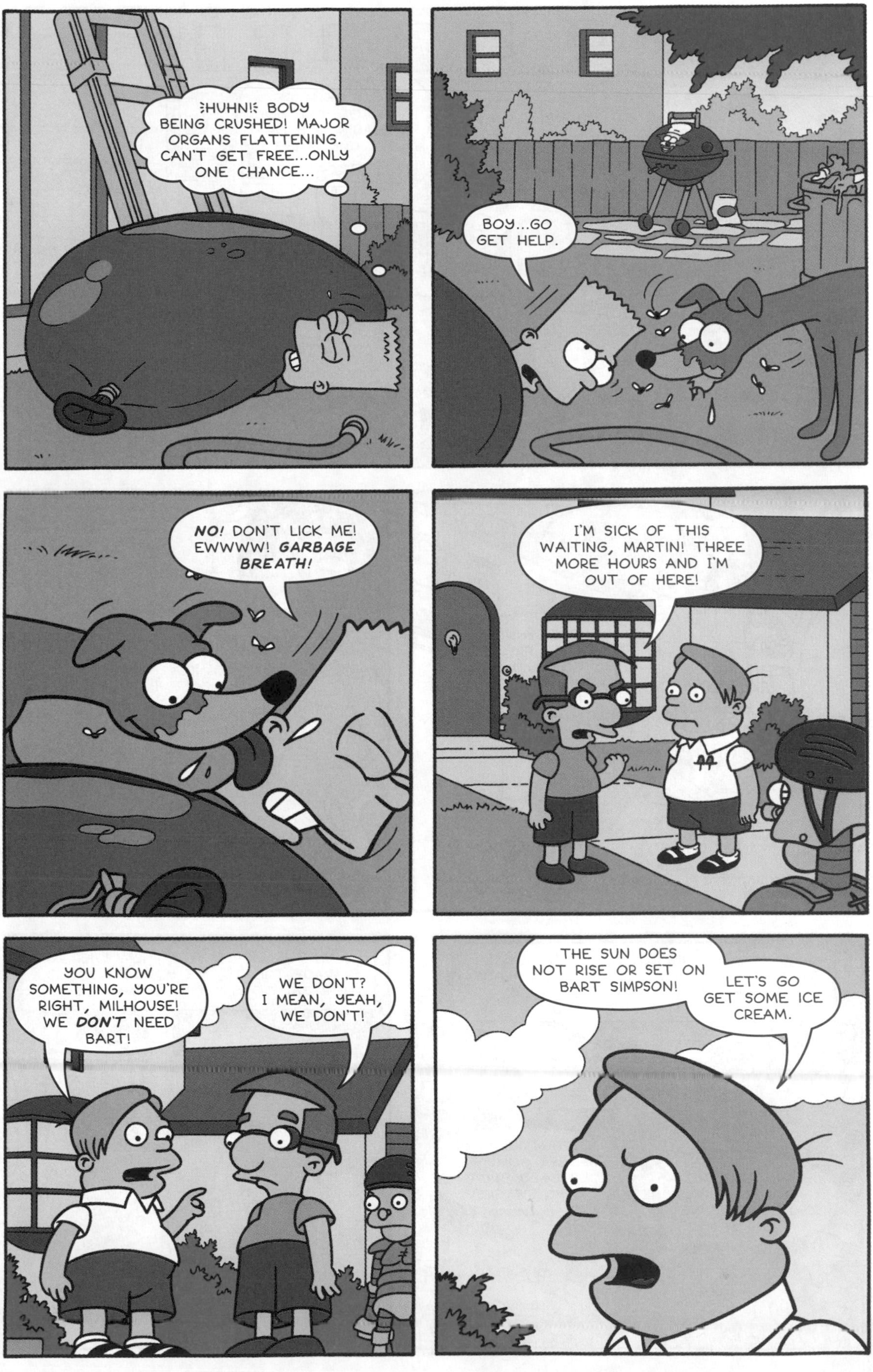

HUHN! BODY BEING CRUSHED! MAJOR ORGANS FLATTENING. CAN'T GET FREE...ONLY ONE CHANCE...
BOY...GO GET HELP.
NO! DON'T LICK ME! EWWWW! GARBAGE BREATH!
I'M SICK OF THIS WAITING, MARTIN! THREE MORE HOURS AND I'M OUT OF HERE!
YOU KNOW SOMETHING, YOU'RE RIGHT, MILHOUSE! WE DON'T NEED BART!
WE DON'T? I MEAN, YEAH, WE DON'T!
THE SUN DOES NOT RISE OR SET ON BART SIMPSON!
LET'S GO GET SOME ICE CREAM.

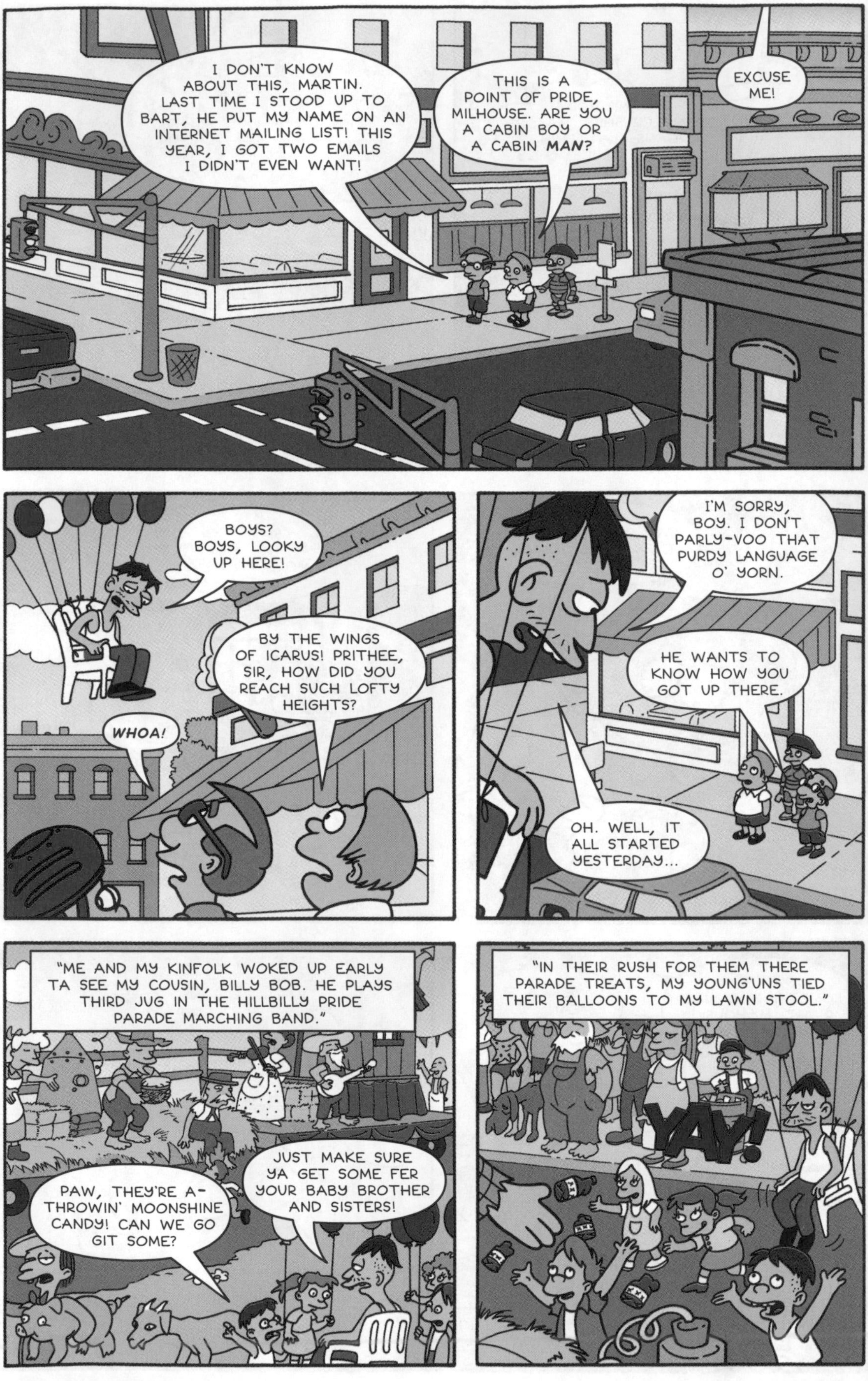
I DON'T KNOW ABOUT THIS, MARTIN. LAST TIME I STOOD UP TO BART, HE PUT MY NAME ON AN INTERNET MAILING LIST! THIS YEAR, I GOT TWO EMAILS I DIDN'T EVEN WANT!
THIS IS A POINT OF PRIDE, MILHOUSE. ARE YOU A CABIN BOY OR A CABIN ***MAN***?
EXCUSE ME!
BOYS? BOYS, LOOKY UP HERE!
WHOA!
BY THE WINGS OF ICARUS! PRITHEE, SIR, HOW DID YOU REACH SUCH LOFTY HEIGHTS?
I'M SORRY, BOY. I DON'T PARLY-VOO THAT PURDY LANGUAGE O' YORN.
HE WANTS TO KNOW HOW YOU GOT UP THERE.
OH. WELL, IT ALL STARTED YESTERDAY...
"ME AND MY KINFOLK WOKED UP EARLY TA SEE MY COUSIN, BILLY BOB. HE PLAYS THIRD JUG IN THE HILLBILLY PRIDE PARADE MARCHING BAND."
PAW, THEY'RE A-THROWIN' MOONSHINE CANDY! CAN WE GO GIT SOME?
JUST MAKE SURE YA GET SOME FER YOUR BABY BROTHER AND SISTERS!
"IN THEIR RUSH FOR THEM THERE PARADE TREATS, MY YOUNG'UNS TIED THEIR BALLOONS TO MY LAWN STOOL."
YAY!

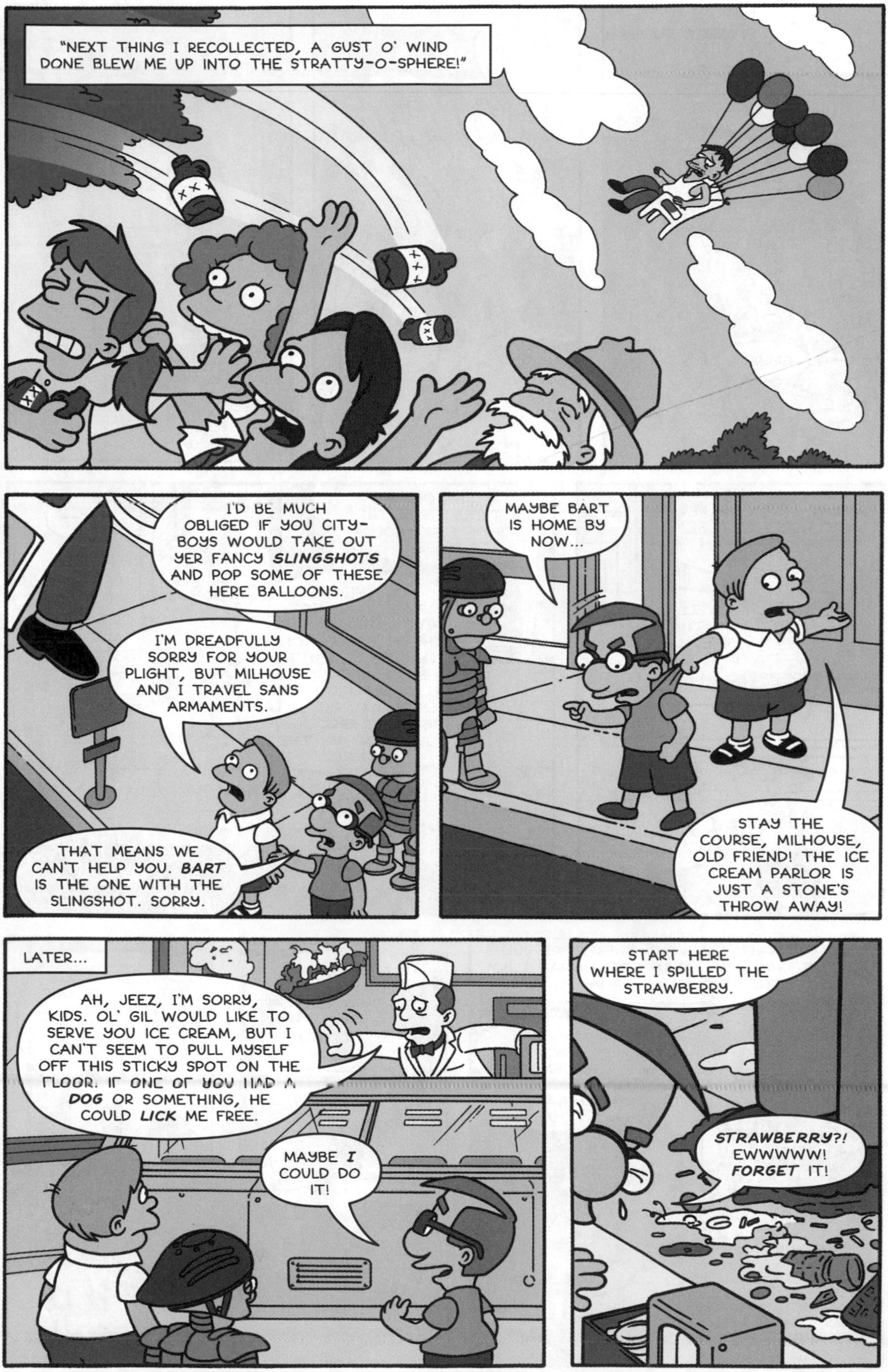
"NEXT THING I RECOLLECTED, A GUST O' WIND DONE BLEW ME UP INTO THE STRATTY-O-SPHERE!"
I'D BE MUCH OBLIGED IF YOU CITY-BOYS WOULD TAKE OUT YER FANCY *SLINGSHOTS* AND POP SOME OF THESE HERE BALLOONS.
I'M DREADFULLY SORRY FOR YOUR PLIGHT, BUT MILHOUSE AND I TRAVEL SANS ARMAMENTS.
THAT MEANS WE CAN'T HELP YOU. *BART* IS THE ONE WITH THE SLINGSHOT. SORRY.
MAYBE BART IS HOME BY NOW...
STAY THE COURSE, MILHOUSE, OLD FRIEND! THE ICE CREAM PARLOR IS JUST A STONE'S THROW AWAY!
LATER...
AH, JEEZ, I'M SORRY, KIDS. OL' GIL WOULD LIKE TO SERVE YOU ICE CREAM, BUT I CAN'T SEEM TO PULL MYSELF OFF THIS STICKY SPOT ON THE FLOOR. IF ONE OF YOU HAD A *DOG* OR SOMETHING, HE COULD *LICK* ME FREE.
MAYBE *I* COULD DO IT!
START HERE WHERE I SPILLED THE STRAWBERRY.
STRAWBERRY?! EWWWWW! *FORGET* IT!

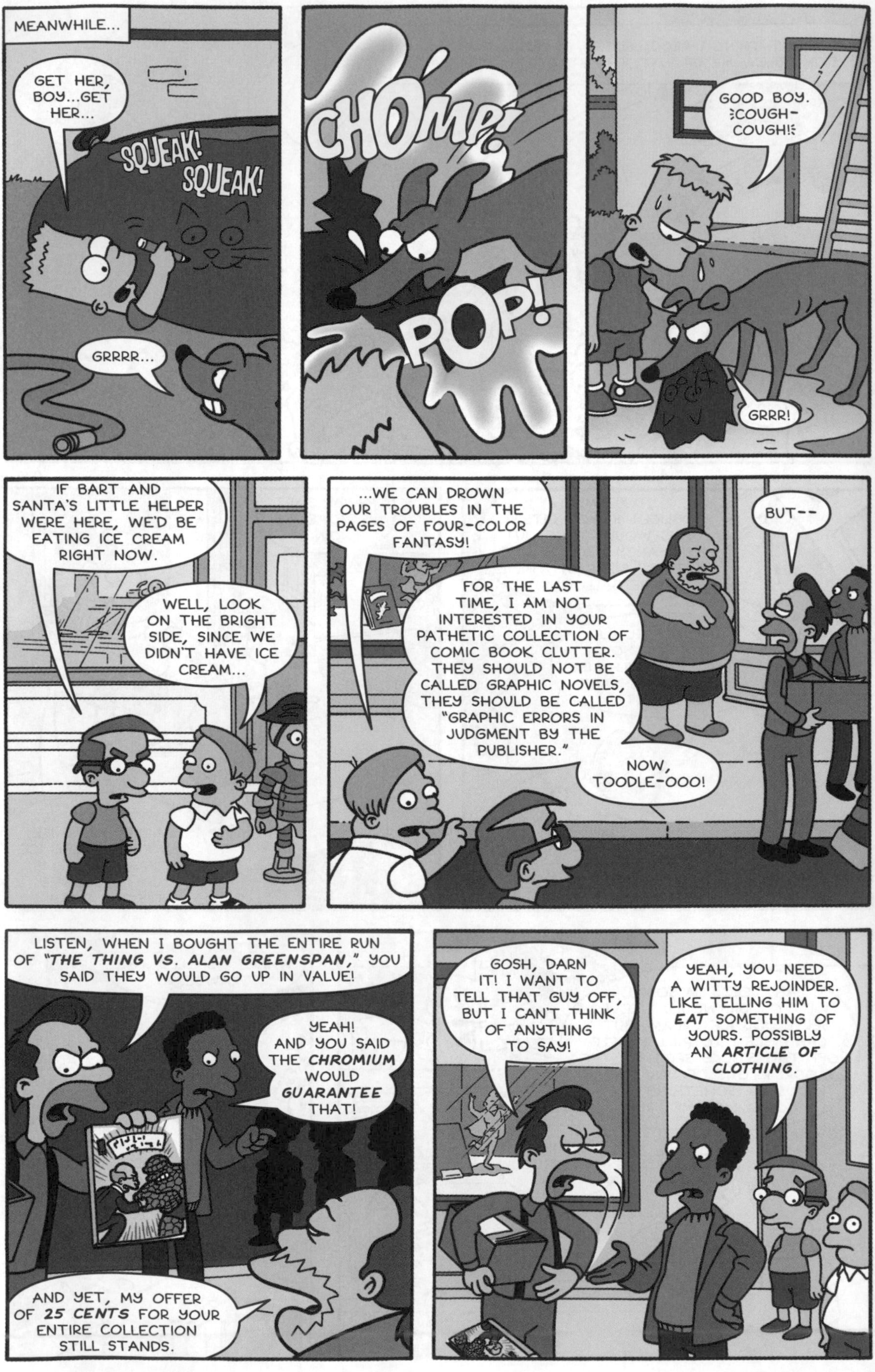
MEANWHILE...
GET HER, BOY...GET HER...
SQUEAK! SQUEAK!
GRRRR...
CHOMP!
POP!
GOOD BOY. COUGH-COUGH!
GRRR!
IF BART AND SANTA'S LITTLE HELPER WERE HERE, WE'D BE EATING ICE CREAM RIGHT NOW.
WELL, LOOK ON THE BRIGHT SIDE, SINCE WE DIDN'T HAVE ICE CREAM...
...WE CAN DROWN OUR TROUBLES IN THE PAGES OF FOUR-COLOR FANTASY!
FOR THE LAST TIME, I AM NOT INTERESTED IN YOUR PATHETIC COLLECTION OF COMIC BOOK CLUTTER. THEY SHOULD NOT BE CALLED GRAPHIC NOVELS, THEY SHOULD BE CALLED "GRAPHIC ERRORS IN JUDGMENT BY THE PUBLISHER."
NOW, TOODLE-OOO!
BUT--
LISTEN, WHEN I BOUGHT THE ENTIRE RUN OF *"THE THING VS. ALAN GREENSPAN,"* YOU SAID THEY WOULD GO UP IN VALUE!
YEAH! AND YOU SAID THE *CHROMIUM* WOULD *GUARANTEE* THAT!
AND YET, MY OFFER OF **25 CENTS** FOR YOUR ENTIRE COLLECTION STILL STANDS.
GOSH, DARN IT! I WANT TO TELL THAT GUY OFF, BUT I CAN'T THINK OF ANYTHING TO SAY!
YEAH, YOU NEED A WITTY REJOINDER. LIKE TELLING HIM TO *EAT* SOMETHING OF YOURS. POSSIBLY AN *ARTICLE OF CLOTHING*.

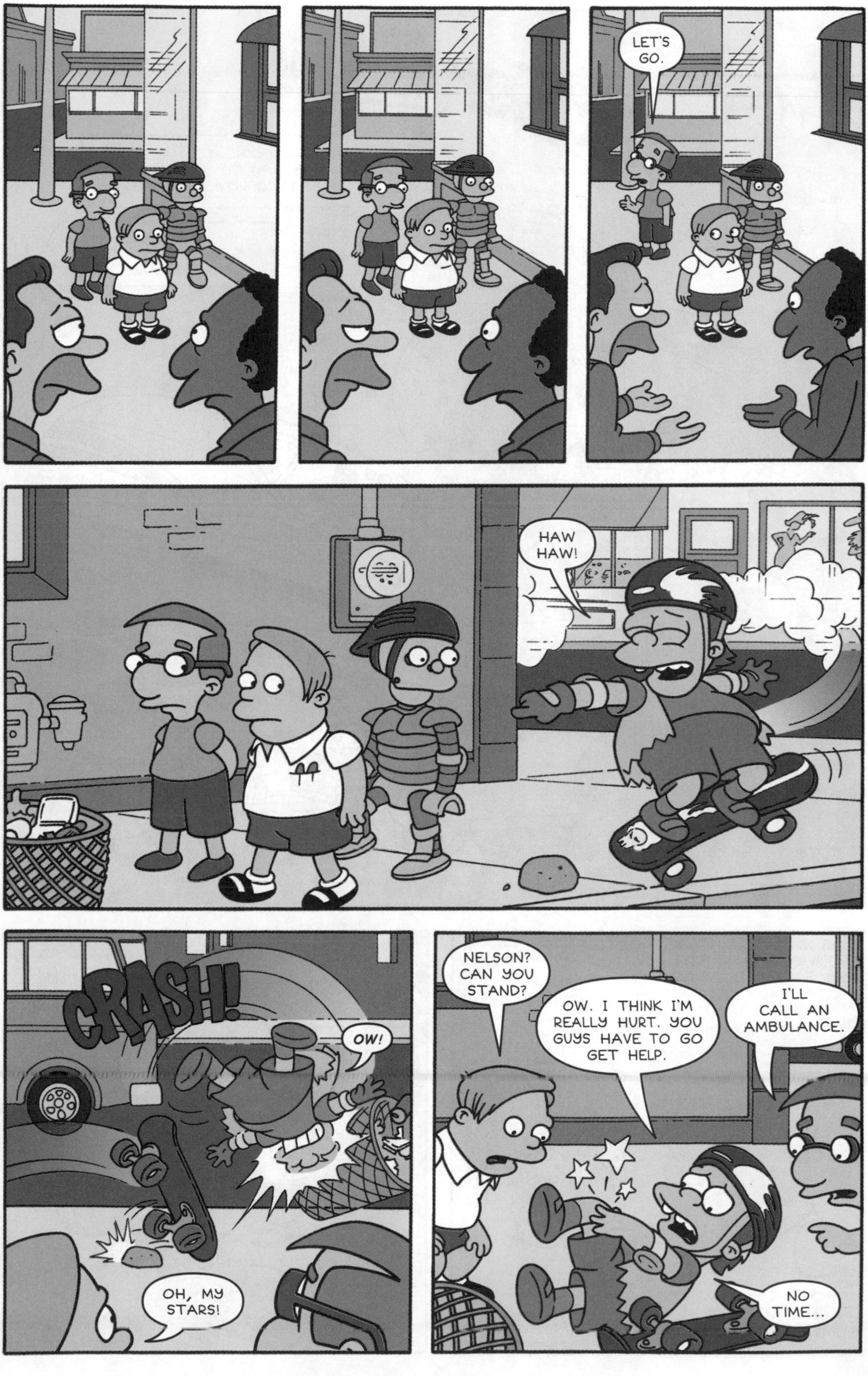
LET'S GO.
HAW HAW!
CRASH!
OW!
OH, MY STARS!
NELSON? CAN YOU STAND?
OW. I THINK I'M REALLY HURT. YOU GUYS HAVE TO GO GET HELP.
I'LL CALL AN AMBULANCE.
NO TIME...

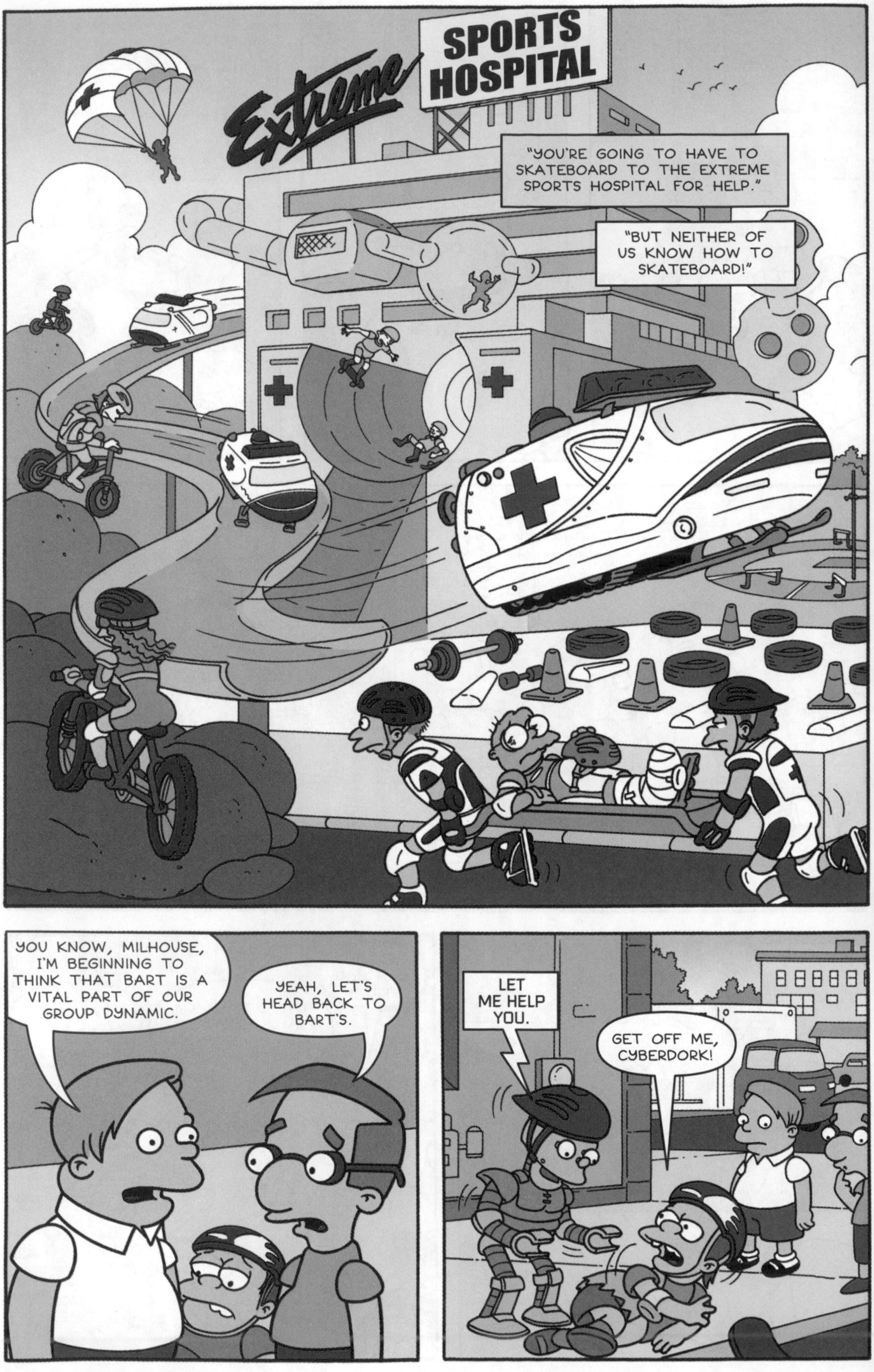
Extreme
SPORTS HOSPITAL
"YOU'RE GOING TO HAVE TO SKATEBOARD TO THE EXTREME SPORTS HOSPITAL FOR HELP."
"BUT NEITHER OF US KNOW HOW TO SKATEBOARD!"
YOU KNOW, MILHOUSE, I'M BEGINNING TO THINK THAT BART IS A VITAL PART OF OUR GROUP DYNAMIC.
YEAH, LET'S HEAD BACK TO BART'S.
LET ME HELP YOU.
GET OFF ME, CYBERDORK!

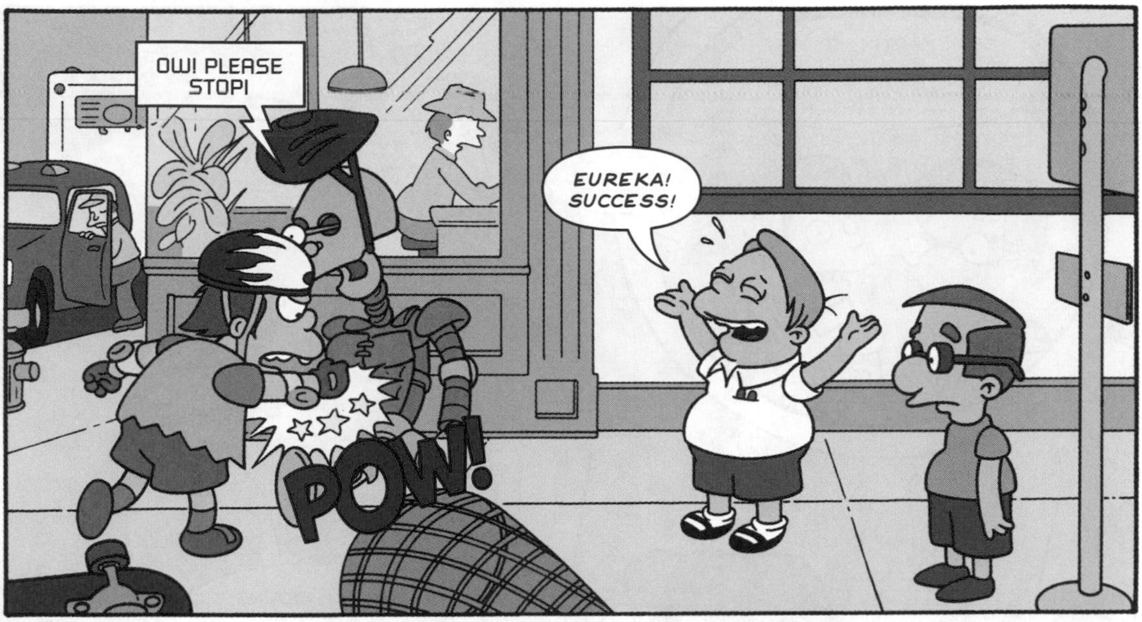
OW! PLEASE STOP!
EUREKA! SUCCESS!
POW!

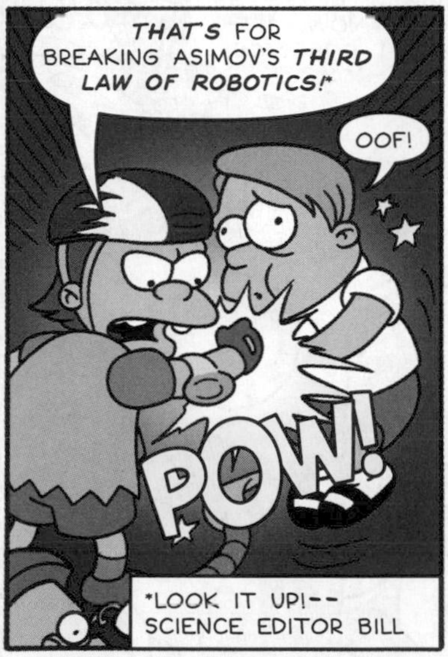
THAT'S FOR BREAKING ASIMOV'S THIRD LAW OF ROBOTICS!*
OOF!
POW!
*LOOK IT UP!-- SCIENCE EDITOR BILL

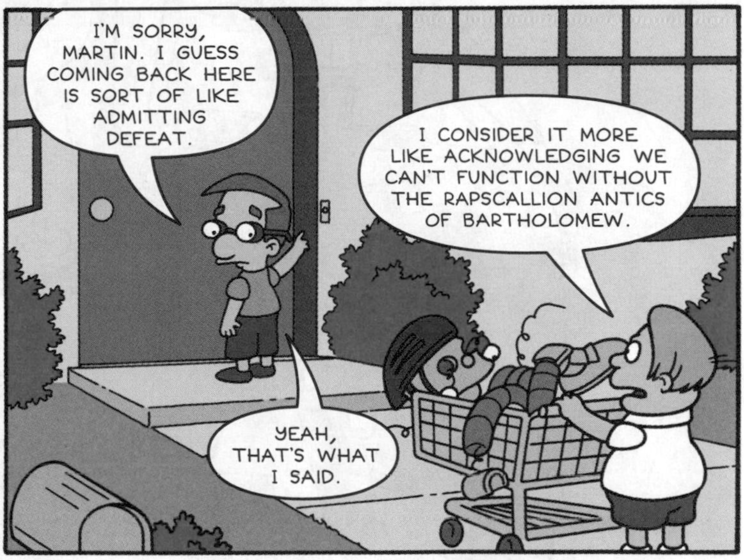
I'M SORRY, MARTIN. I GUESS COMING BACK HERE IS SORT OF LIKE ADMITTING DEFEAT.
I CONSIDER IT MORE LIKE ACKNOWLEDGING WE CAN'T FUNCTION WITHOUT THE RAPSCALLION ANTICS OF BARTHOLOMEW.
YEAH, THAT'S WHAT I SAID.

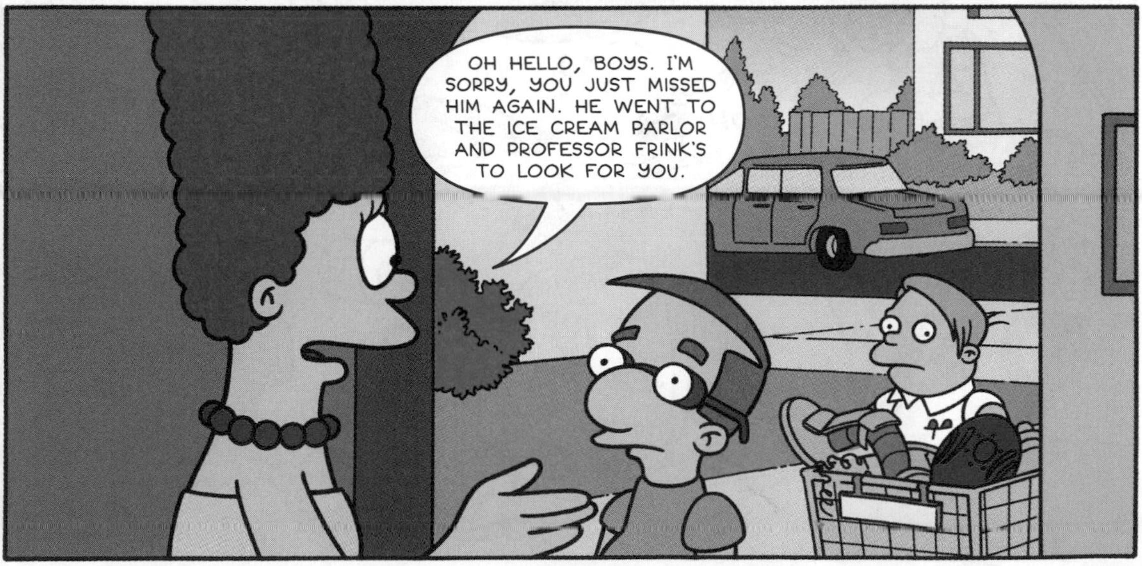
OH HELLO, BOYS. I'M SORRY, YOU JUST MISSED HIM AGAIN. HE WENT TO THE ICE CREAM PARLOR AND PROFESSOR FRINK'S TO LOOK FOR YOU.

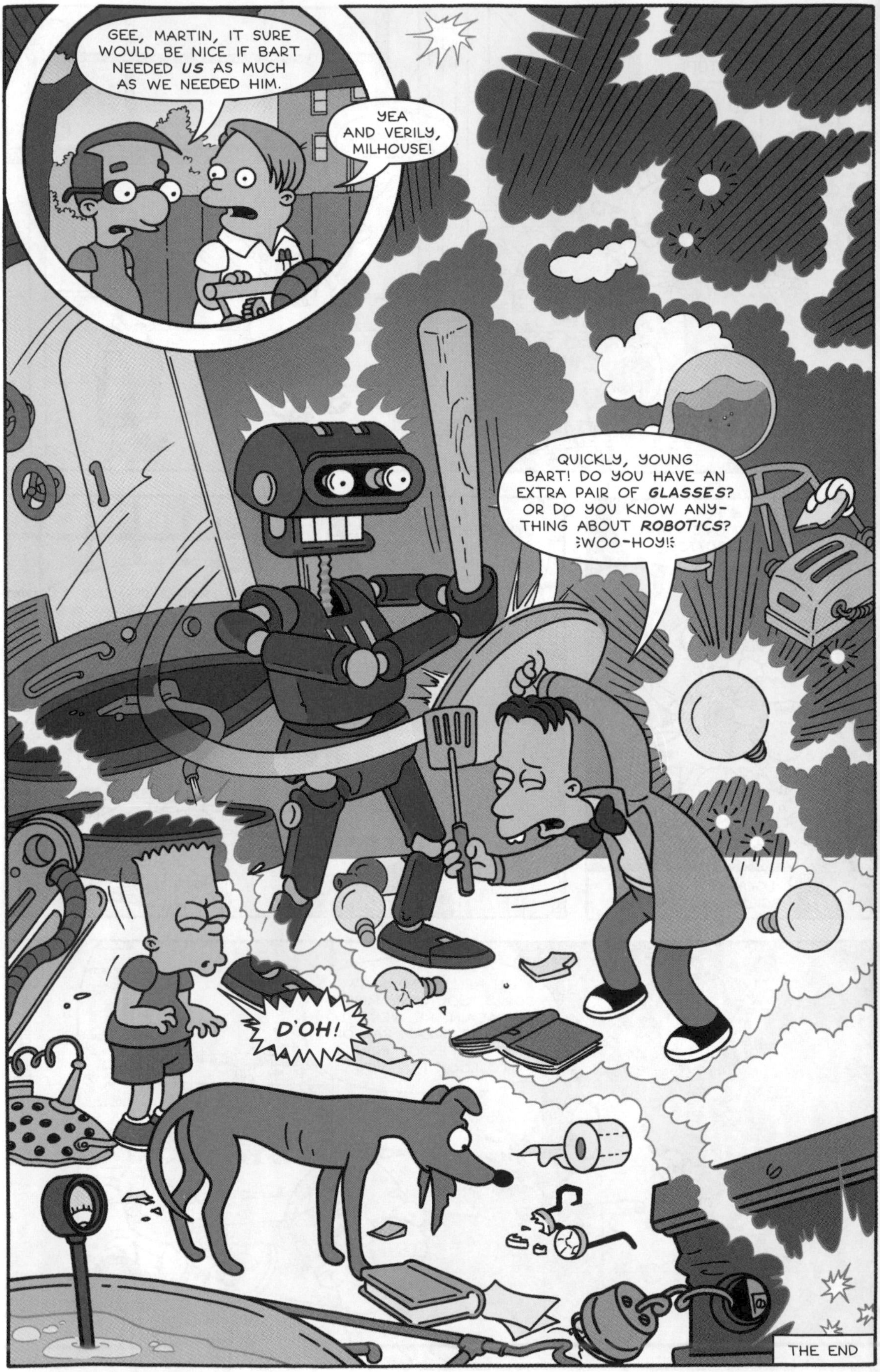
GEE, MARTIN, IT SURE WOULD BE NICE IF BART NEEDED US AS MUCH AS WE NEEDED HIM.
YEA AND VERILY, MILHOUSE!
QUICKLY, YOUNG BART! DO YOU HAVE AN EXTRA PAIR OF GLASSES? OR DO YOU KNOW ANYTHING ABOUT ROBOTICS? WOO-HOY!
D'OH!
THE END

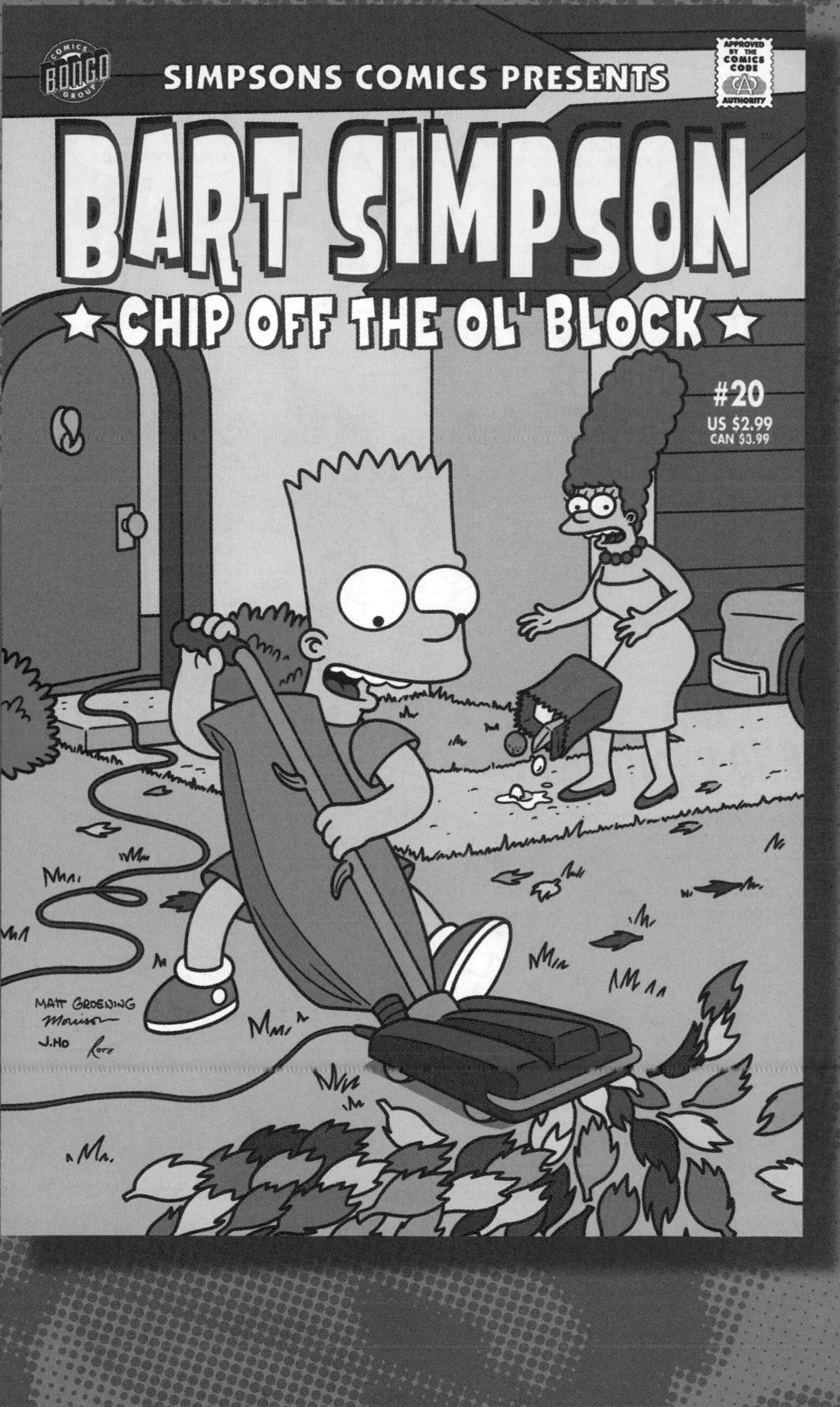

SIMPSONS COMICS PRESENTS
BART SIMPSON
CHIP OFF THE OL' BLOCK
#20
US $2.99
CAN $3.99
APPROVED BY THE COMICS CODE AUTHORITY
MATT GROENING
J.HO

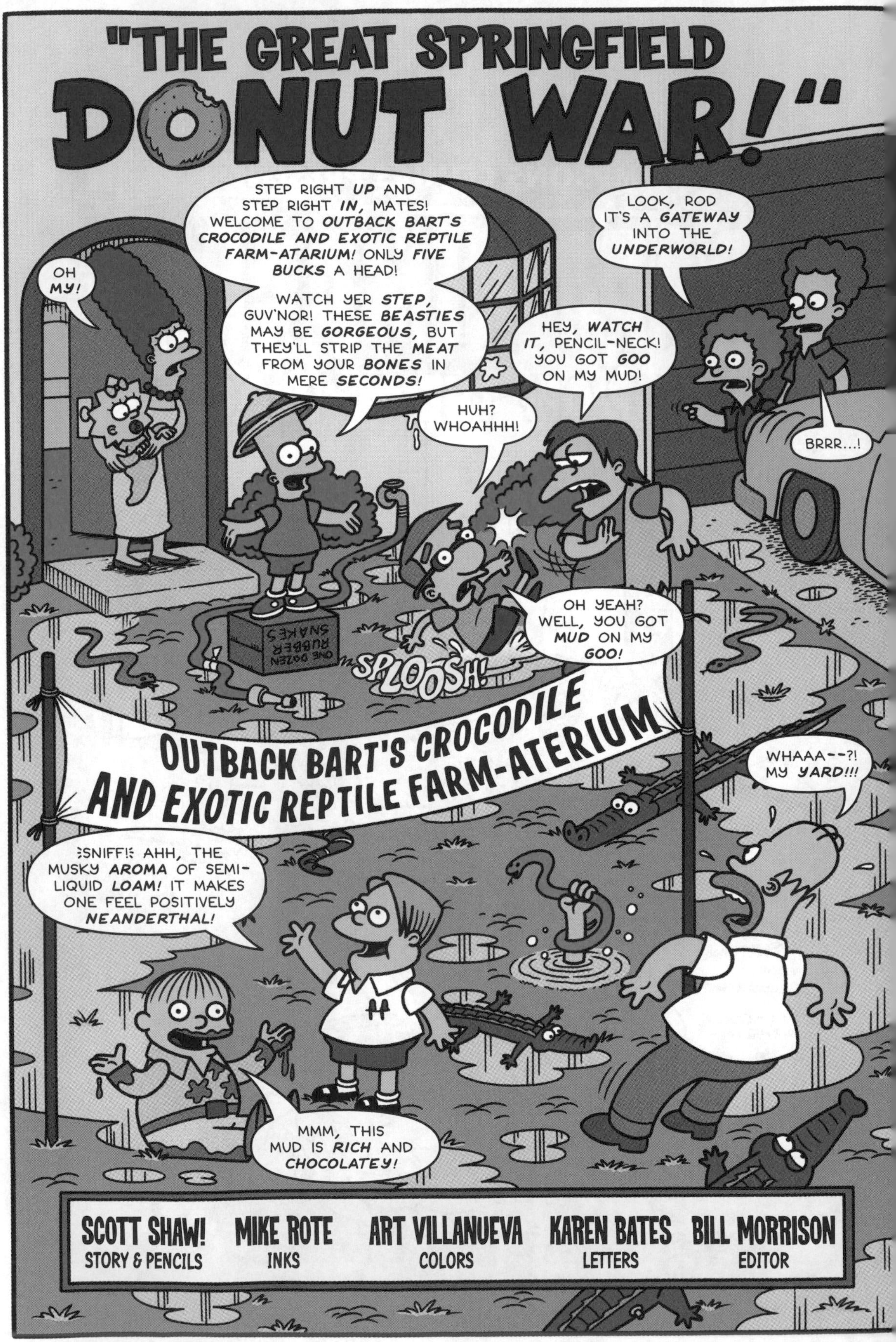
"THE GREAT SPRINGFIELD DONUT WAR!"
STEP RIGHT UP AND STEP RIGHT IN, MATES! WELCOME TO OUTBACK BART'S CROCODILE AND EXOTIC REPTILE FARM-ATARIUM! ONLY FIVE BUCKS A HEAD!
WATCH YER STEP, GUV'NOR! THESE BEASTIES MAY BE GORGEOUS, BUT THEY'LL STRIP THE MEAT FROM YOUR BONES IN MERE SECONDS!
OH MY!
LOOK, ROD IT'S A GATEWAY INTO THE UNDERWORLD!
HEY, WATCH IT, PENCIL-NECK! YOU GOT GOO ON MY MUD!
HUH? WHOAHHH!
BRRR...!
ONE DOZEN RUBBER SNAKES
OH YEAH? WELL, YOU GOT MUD ON MY GOO!
SPLOOSH!
OUTBACK BART'S CROCODILE AND EXOTIC REPTILE FARM-ATERIUM
WHAAA--?! MY YARD!!!
:SNIFF!: AHH, THE MUSKY AROMA OF SEMI-LIQUID LOAM! IT MAKES ONE FEEL POSITIVELY NEANDERTHAL!
MMM, THIS MUD IS RICH AND CHOCOLATEY!
SCOTT SHAW! STORY & PENCILS
MIKE ROTE INKS
ART VILLANUEVA COLORS
KAREN BATES LETTERS
BILL MORRISON EDITOR

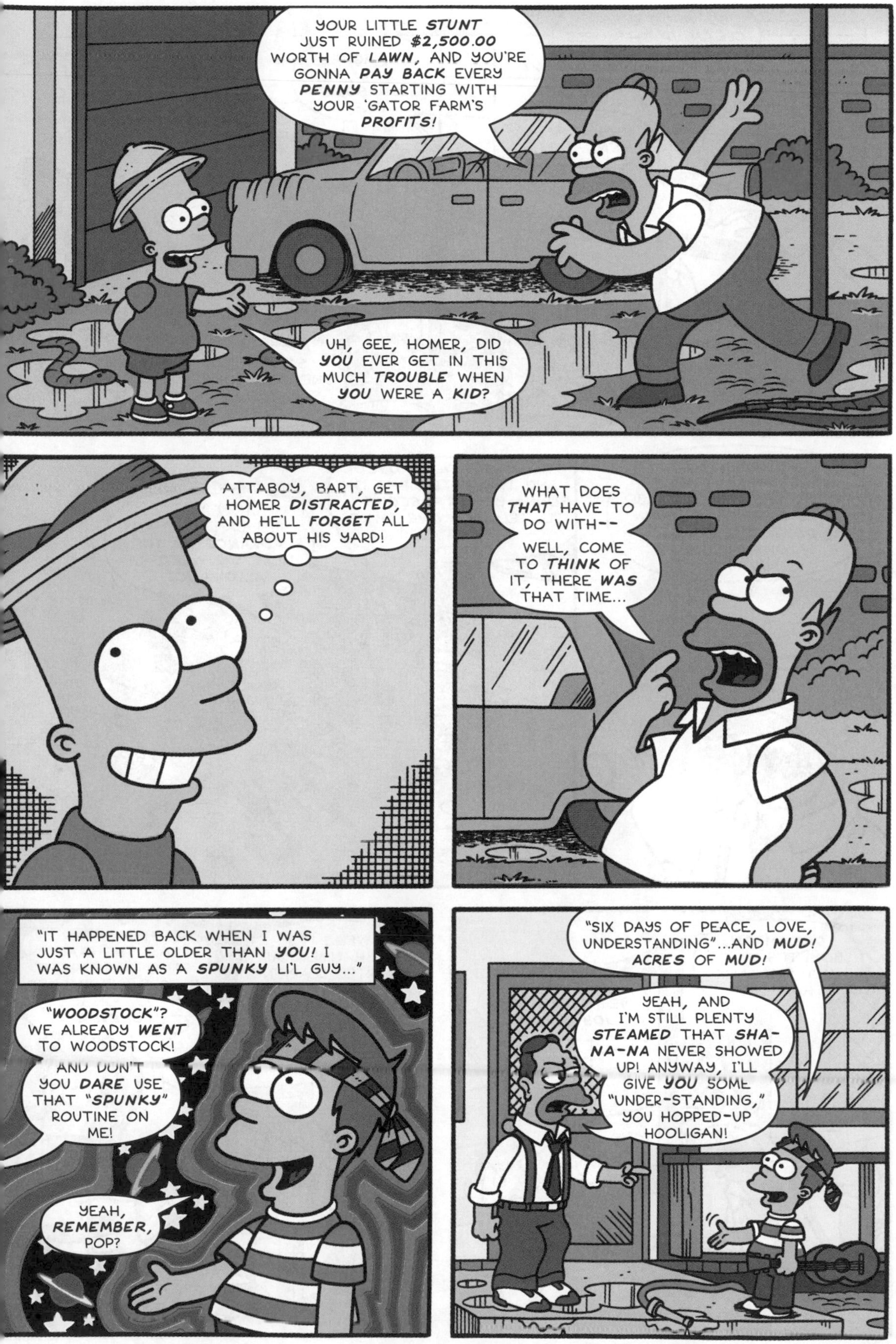

YOUR LITTLE STUNT JUST RUINED $2,500.00 WORTH OF LAWN, AND YOU'RE GONNA PAY BACK EVERY PENNY STARTING WITH YOUR 'GATOR FARM'S PROFITS!
UH, GEE, HOMER, DID YOU EVER GET IN THIS MUCH TROUBLE WHEN YOU WERE A KID?
ATTABOY, BART, GET HOMER DISTRACTED, AND HE'LL FORGET ALL ABOUT HIS YARD!
WHAT DOES THAT HAVE TO DO WITH--
WELL, COME TO THINK OF IT, THERE WAS THAT TIME...
"IT HAPPENED BACK WHEN I WAS JUST A LITTLE OLDER THAN YOU! I WAS KNOWN AS A SPUNKY LI'L GUY..."
"WOODSTOCK"? WE ALREADY WENT TO WOODSTOCK!
AND DON'T YOU DARE USE THAT "SPUNKY" ROUTINE ON ME!
YEAH, REMEMBER, POP?
"SIX DAYS OF PEACE, LOVE, UNDERSTANDING"...AND MUD! ACRES OF MUD!
YEAH, AND I'M STILL PLENTY STEAMED THAT SHA-NA-NA NEVER SHOWED UP! ANYWAY, I'LL GIVE YOU SOME "UNDER-STANDING," YOU HOPPED-UP HOOLIGAN!

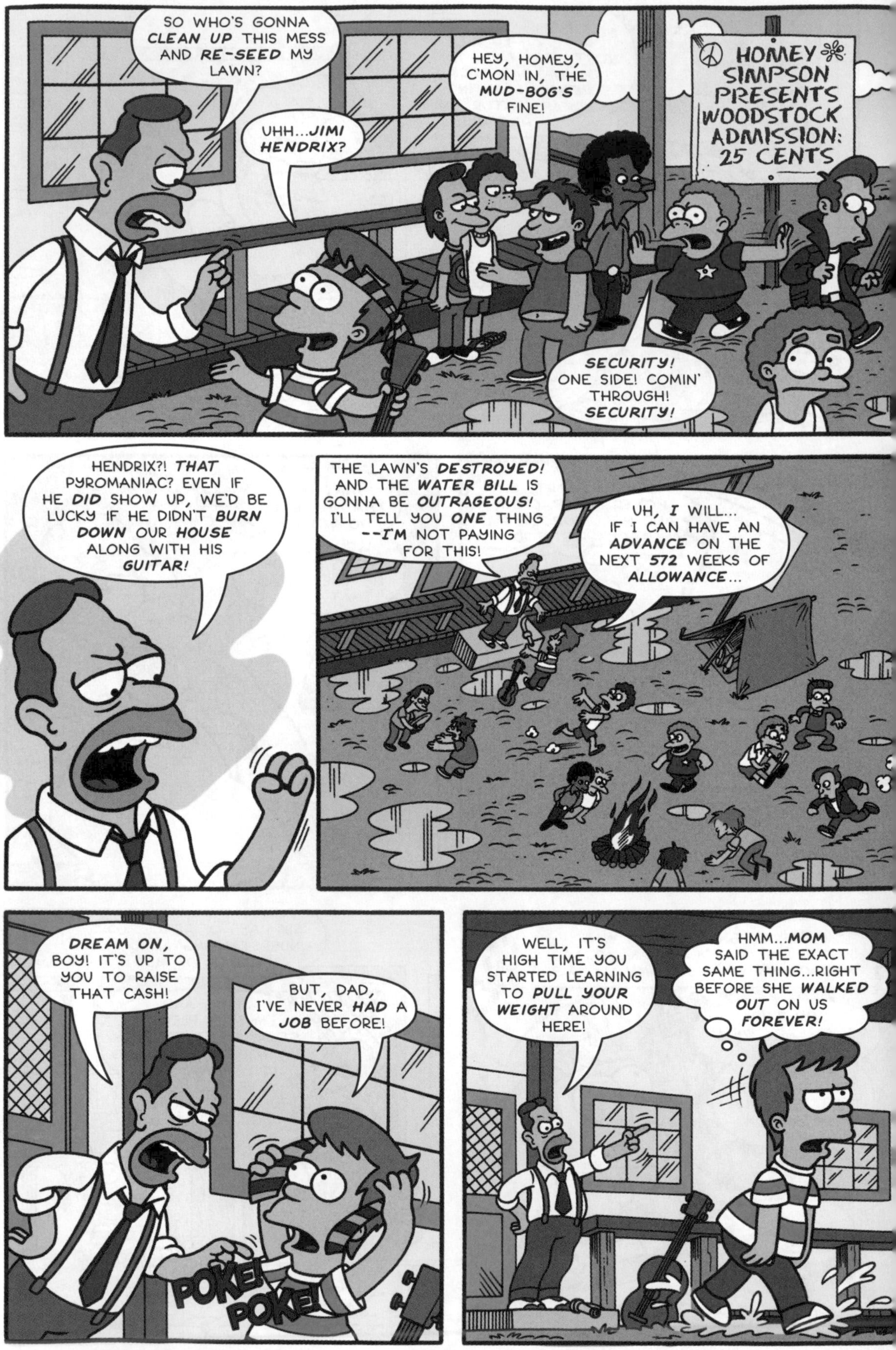

SO WHO'S GONNA CLEAN UP THIS MESS AND RE-SEED MY LAWN?
UHH...JIMI HENDRIX?
HEY, HOMEY, C'MON IN, THE MUD-BOG'S FINE!
HOMEY SIMPSON PRESENTS WOODSTOCK ADMISSION: 25 CENTS
SECURITY! ONE SIDE! COMIN' THROUGH! SECURITY!
HENDRIX?! THAT PYROMANIAC? EVEN IF HE DID SHOW UP, WE'D BE LUCKY IF HE DIDN'T BURN DOWN OUR HOUSE ALONG WITH HIS GUITAR!
THE LAWN'S DESTROYED! AND THE WATER BILL IS GONNA BE OUTRAGEOUS! I'LL TELL YOU ONE THING --I'M NOT PAYING FOR THIS!
UH, I WILL... IF I CAN HAVE AN ADVANCE ON THE NEXT 572 WEEKS OF ALLOWANCE...
DREAM ON, BOY! IT'S UP TO YOU TO RAISE THAT CASH!
BUT, DAD, I'VE NEVER HAD A JOB BEFORE!
POKE! POKE!
WELL, IT'S HIGH TIME YOU STARTED LEARNING TO PULL YOUR WEIGHT AROUND HERE!
HMM...MOM SAID THE EXACT SAME THING...RIGHT BEFORE SHE WALKED OUT ON US FOREVER!

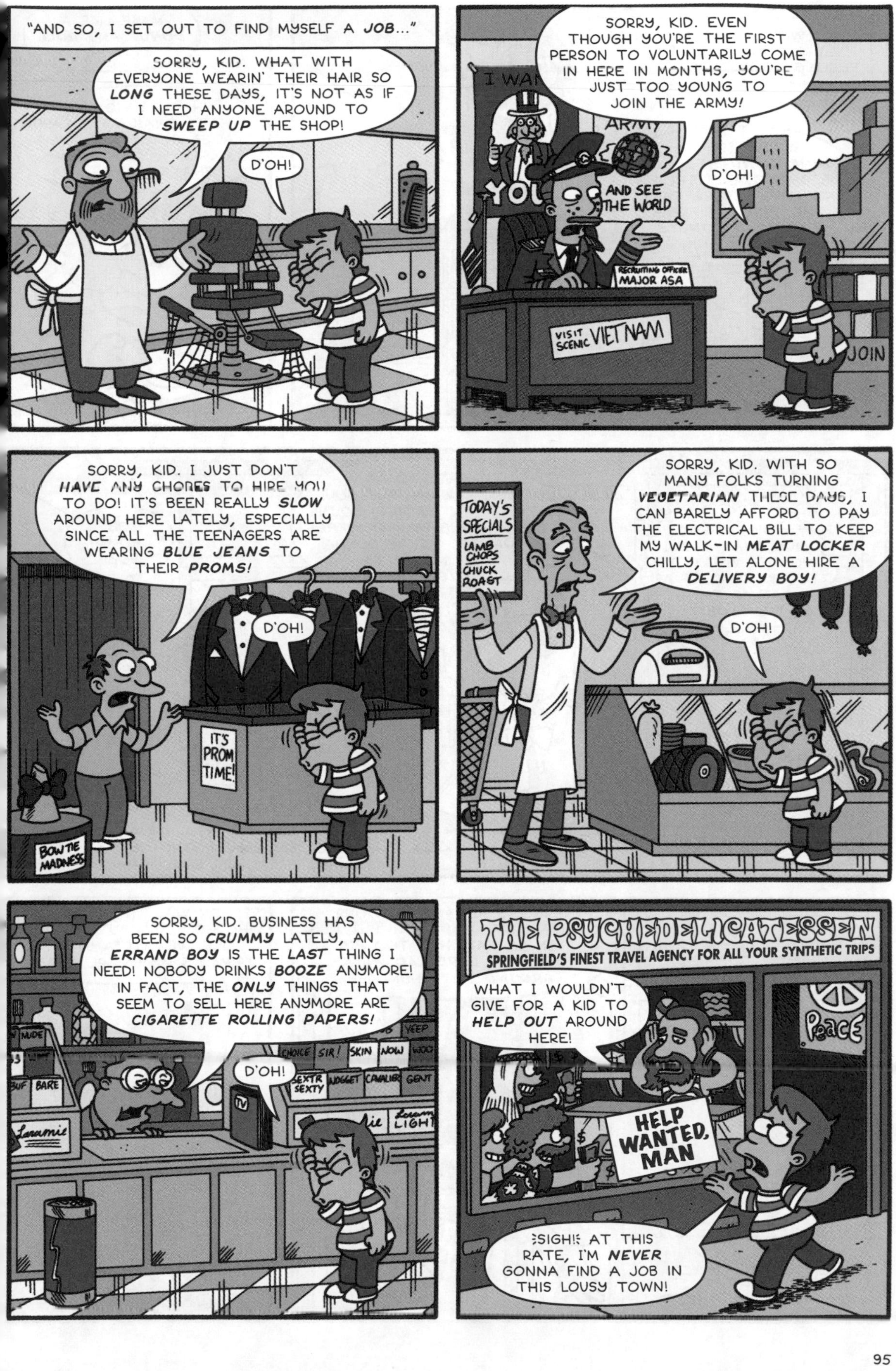
"AND SO, I SET OUT TO FIND MYSELF A JOB..."
SORRY, KID. WHAT WITH EVERYONE WEARIN' THEIR HAIR SO LONG THESE DAYS, IT'S NOT AS IF I NEED ANYONE AROUND TO SWEEP UP THE SHOP!
D'OH!
SORRY, KID. EVEN THOUGH YOU'RE THE FIRST PERSON TO VOLUNTARILY COME IN HERE IN MONTHS, YOU'RE JUST TOO YOUNG TO JOIN THE ARMY!
AND SEE THE WORLD
RECRUITING OFFICER MAJOR ASA
VISIT SCENIC VIETNAM
JOIN
D'OH!
SORRY, KID. I JUST DON'T HAVE ANY CHORES TO HIRE YOU TO DO! IT'S BEEN REALLY SLOW AROUND HERE LATELY, ESPECIALLY SINCE ALL THE TEENAGERS ARE WEARING BLUE JEANS TO THEIR PROMS!
D'OH!
IT'S PROM TIME!
BOW TIE MADNESS
TODAY'S SPECIALS
LAMB CHOPS
CHUCK ROAST
SORRY, KID. WITH SO MANY FOLKS TURNING VEGETARIAN THESE DAYS, I CAN BARELY AFFORD TO PAY THE ELECTRICAL BILL TO KEEP MY WALK-IN MEAT LOCKER CHILLY, LET ALONE HIRE A DELIVERY BOY!
D'OH!
SORRY, KID. BUSINESS HAS BEEN SO CRUMMY LATELY, AN ERRAND BOY IS THE LAST THING I NEED! NOBODY DRINKS BOOZE ANYMORE! IN FACT, THE ONLY THINGS THAT SEEM TO SELL HERE ANYMORE ARE CIGARETTE ROLLING PAPERS!
D'OH!
THE PSYCHEDELICATESSEN
SPRINGFIELD'S FINEST TRAVEL AGENCY FOR ALL YOUR SYNTHETIC TRIPS
WHAT I WOULDN'T GIVE FOR A KID TO HELP OUT AROUND HERE!
Peace
HELP WANTED, MAN
SIGH! AT THIS RATE, I'M NEVER GONNA FIND A JOB IN THIS LOUSY TOWN!

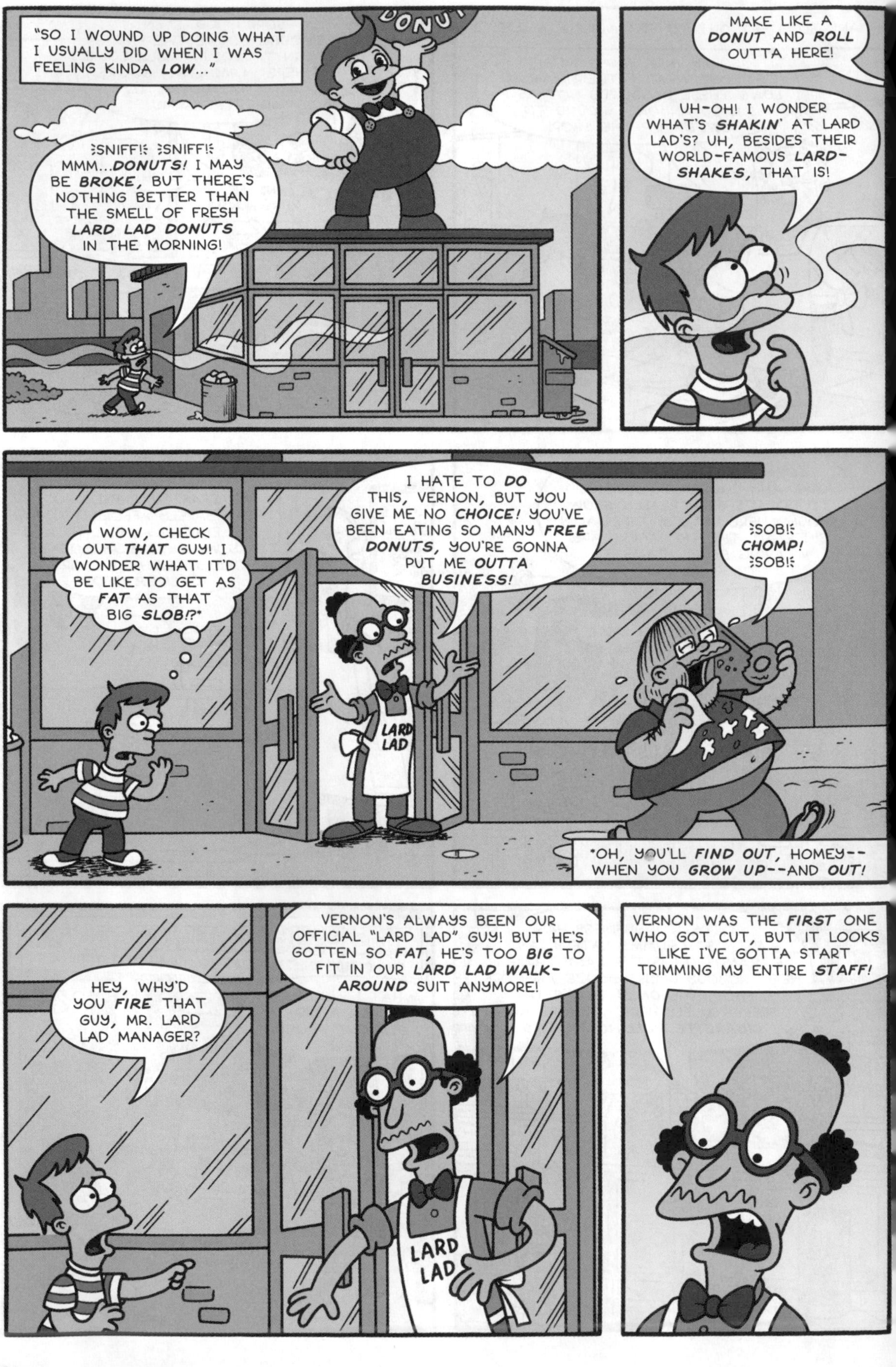
"SO I WOUND UP DOING WHAT I USUALLY DID WHEN I WAS FEELING KINDA LOW..."
DONUT
⁝SNIFF!⁝ ⁝SNIFF!⁝ MMM...DONUTS! I MAY BE BROKE, BUT THERE'S NOTHING BETTER THAN THE SMELL OF FRESH LARD LAD DONUTS IN THE MORNING!
MAKE LIKE A DONUT AND ROLL OUTTA HERE!
UH-OH! I WONDER WHAT'S SHAKIN' AT LARD LAD'S? UH, BESIDES THEIR WORLD-FAMOUS LARD-SHAKES, THAT IS!
WOW, CHECK OUT THAT GUY! I WONDER WHAT IT'D BE LIKE TO GET AS FAT AS THAT BIG SLOB!?*
I HATE TO DO THIS, VERNON, BUT YOU GIVE ME NO CHOICE! YOU'VE BEEN EATING SO MANY FREE DONUTS, YOU'RE GONNA PUT ME OUTTA BUSINESS!
LARD LAD
⁝SOB!⁝ CHOMP! ⁝SOB!⁝
*OH, YOU'LL FIND OUT, HOMEY--WHEN YOU GROW UP--AND OUT!
HEY, WHY'D YOU FIRE THAT GUY, MR. LARD LAD MANAGER?
VERNON'S ALWAYS BEEN OUR OFFICIAL "LARD LAD" GUY! BUT HE'S GOTTEN SO FAT, HE'S TOO BIG TO FIT IN OUR LARD LAD WALK-AROUND SUIT ANYMORE!
LARD LAD
VERNON WAS THE FIRST ONE WHO GOT CUT, BUT IT LOOKS LIKE I'VE GOTTA START TRIMMING MY ENTIRE STAFF!

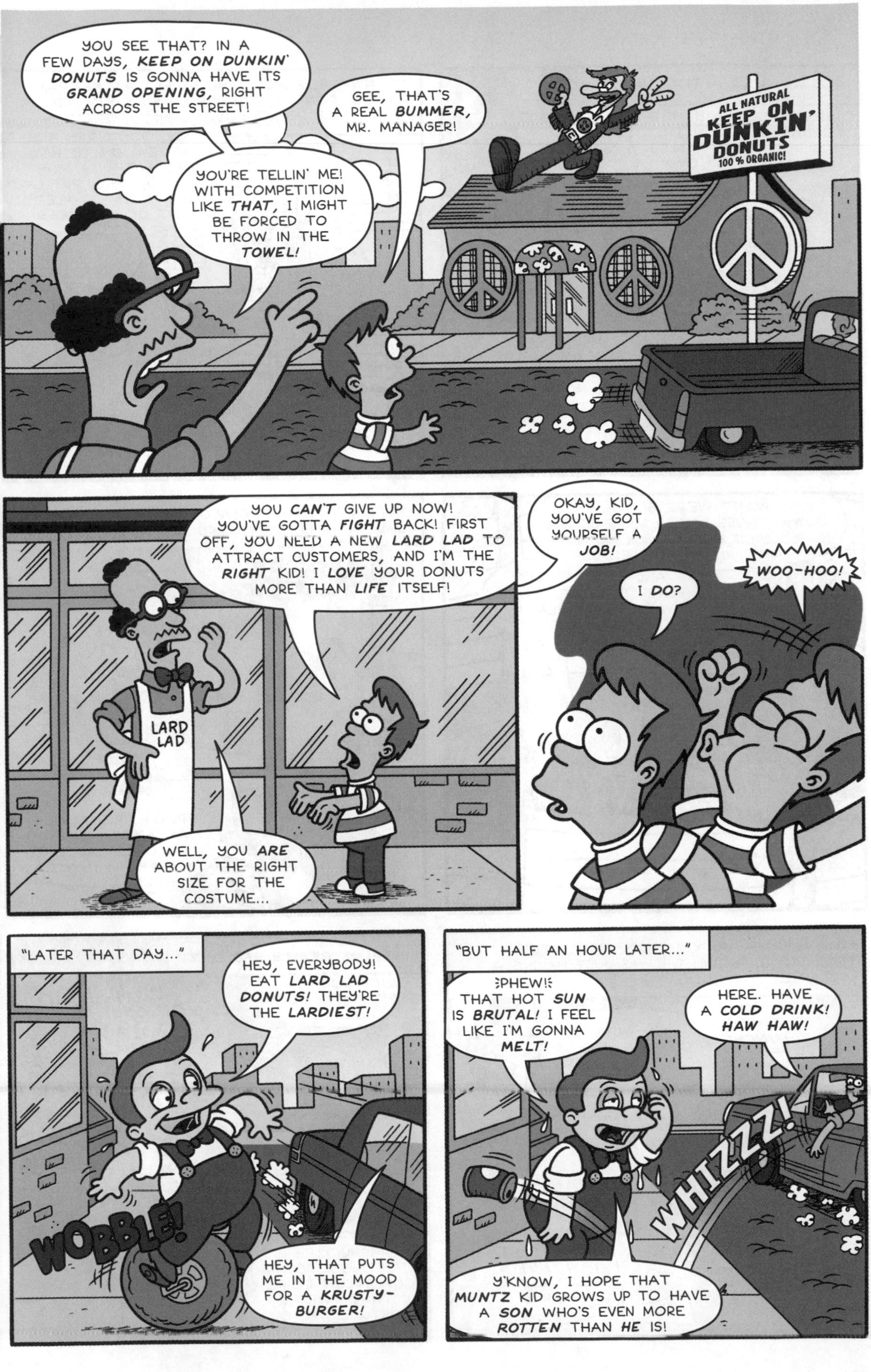
YOU SEE THAT? IN A FEW DAYS, KEEP ON DUNKIN' DONUTS IS GONNA HAVE ITS GRAND OPENING, RIGHT ACROSS THE STREET!
GEE, THAT'S A REAL BUMMER, MR. MANAGER!
ALL NATURAL KEEP ON DUNKIN' DONUTS 100 % ORGANIC!
YOU'RE TELLIN' ME! WITH COMPETITION LIKE THAT, I MIGHT BE FORCED TO THROW IN THE TOWEL!
YOU CAN'T GIVE UP NOW! YOU'VE GOTTA FIGHT BACK! FIRST OFF, YOU NEED A NEW LARD LAD TO ATTRACT CUSTOMERS, AND I'M THE RIGHT KID! I LOVE YOUR DONUTS MORE THAN LIFE ITSELF!
LARD LAD
WELL, YOU ARE ABOUT THE RIGHT SIZE FOR THE COSTUME...
OKAY, KID, YOU'VE GOT YOURSELF A JOB!
I DO?
WOO-HOO!
"LATER THAT DAY..."
HEY, EVERYBODY! EAT LARD LAD DONUTS! THEY'RE THE LARDIEST!
WOBBLE!
HEY, THAT PUTS ME IN THE MOOD FOR A KRUSTY-BURGER!
"BUT HALF AN HOUR LATER..."
PHEW! THAT HOT SUN IS BRUTAL! I FEEL LIKE I'M GONNA MELT!
HERE. HAVE A COLD DRINK! HAW HAW!
WHIZZZ!
Y'KNOW, I HOPE THAT MUNTZ KID GROWS UP TO HAVE A SON WHO'S EVEN MORE ROTTEN THAN HE IS!

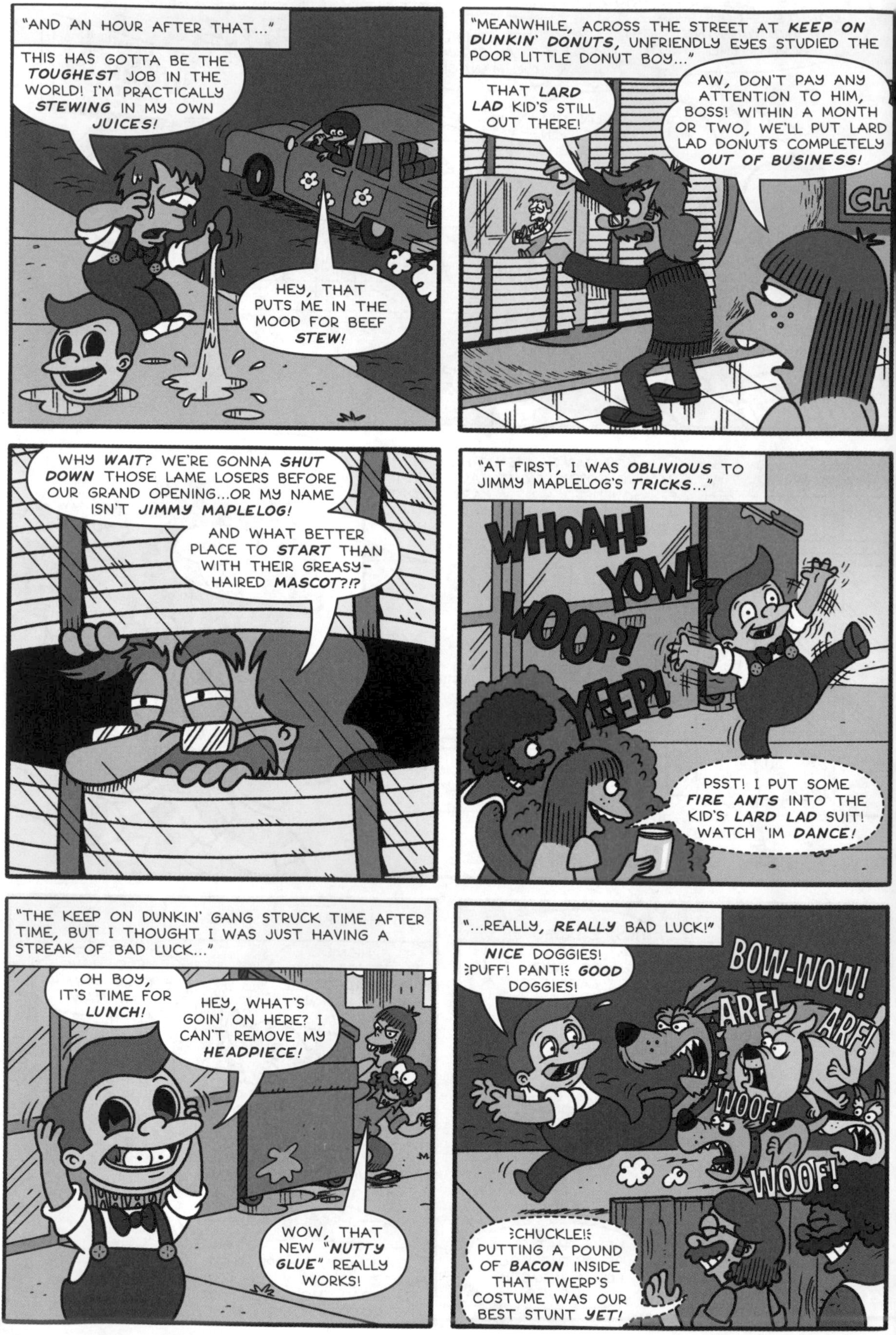
"AND AN HOUR AFTER THAT..."
THIS HAS GOTTA BE THE TOUGHEST JOB IN THE WORLD! I'M PRACTICALLY STEWING IN MY OWN JUICES!
HEY, THAT PUTS ME IN THE MOOD FOR BEEF STEW!
"MEANWHILE, ACROSS THE STREET AT KEEP ON DUNKIN' DONUTS, UNFRIENDLY EYES STUDIED THE POOR LITTLE DONUT BOY..."
THAT LARD LAD KID'S STILL OUT THERE!
AW, DON'T PAY ANY ATTENTION TO HIM, BOSS! WITHIN A MONTH OR TWO, WE'LL PUT LARD LAD DONUTS COMPLETELY OUT OF BUSINESS!
WHY WAIT? WE'RE GONNA SHUT DOWN THOSE LAME LOSERS BEFORE OUR GRAND OPENING...OR MY NAME ISN'T JIMMY MAPLELOG!
AND WHAT BETTER PLACE TO START THAN WITH THEIR GREASY-HAIRED MASCOT?!?
"AT FIRST, I WAS OBLIVIOUS TO JIMMY MAPLELOG'S TRICKS..."
WHOAH!
YOW!
WOOP!
YEEP!
PSST! I PUT SOME FIRE ANTS INTO THE KID'S LARD LAD SUIT! WATCH 'IM DANCE!
"THE KEEP ON DUNKIN' GANG STRUCK TIME AFTER TIME, BUT I THOUGHT I WAS JUST HAVING A STREAK OF BAD LUCK..."
OH BOY, IT'S TIME FOR LUNCH!
HEY, WHAT'S GOIN' ON HERE? I CAN'T REMOVE MY HEADPIECE!
WOW, THAT NEW "NUTTY GLUE" REALLY WORKS!
"...REALLY, REALLY BAD LUCK!"
NICE DOGGIES! ⁝PUFF! PANT!⁝ GOOD DOGGIES!
BOW-WOW!
ARF!
ARF!
WOOF!
WOOF!
⁝CHUCKLE!⁝ PUTTING A POUND OF BACON INSIDE THAT TWERP'S COSTUME WAS OUR BEST STUNT YET!

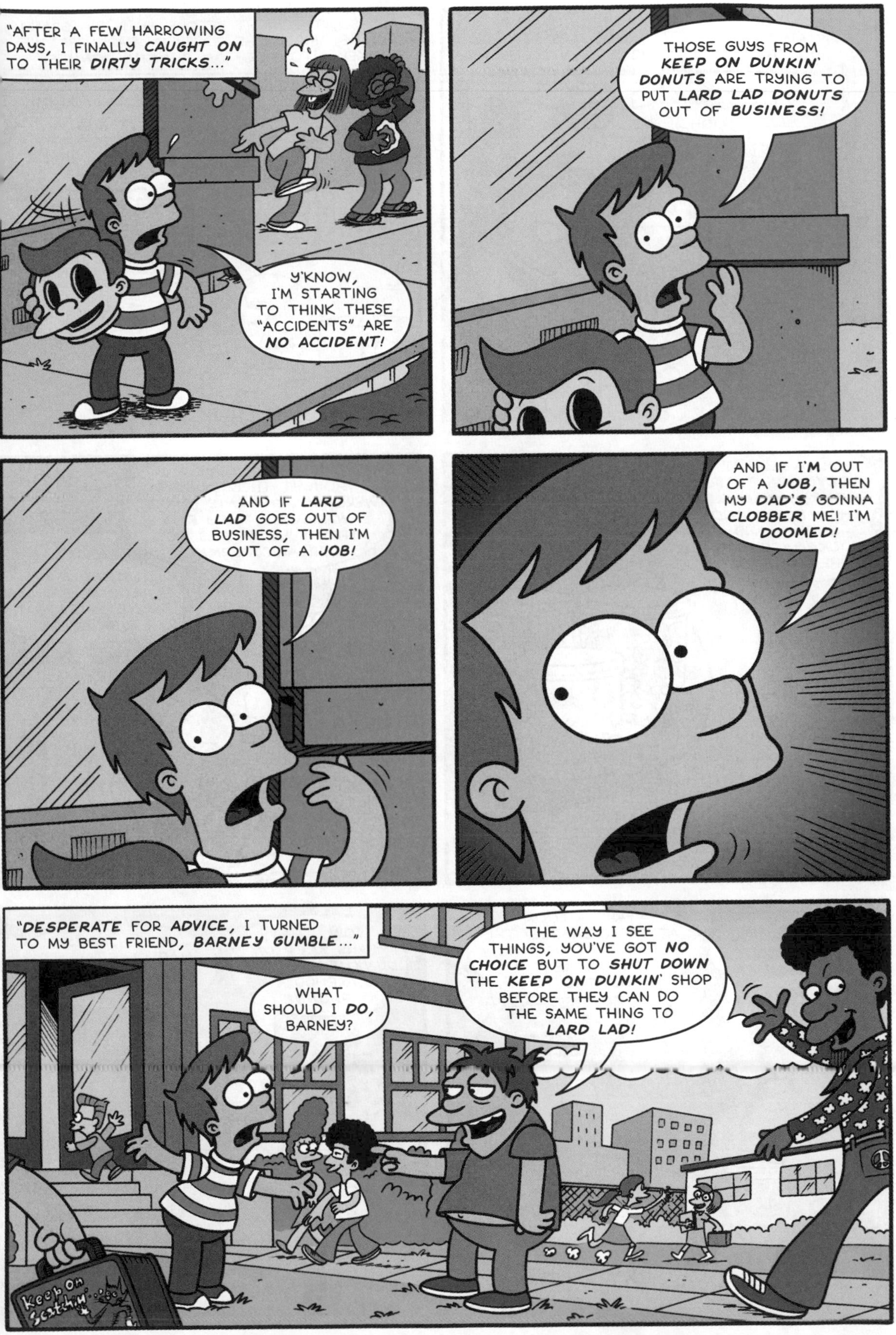
"AFTER A FEW HARROWING DAYS, I FINALLY CAUGHT ON TO THEIR DIRTY TRICKS..."
Y'KNOW, I'M STARTING TO THINK THESE "ACCIDENTS" ARE NO ACCIDENT!
THOSE GUYS FROM KEEP ON DUNKIN' DONUTS ARE TRYING TO PUT LARD LAD DONUTS OUT OF BUSINESS!
AND IF LARD LAD GOES OUT OF BUSINESS, THEN I'M OUT OF A JOB!
AND IF I'M OUT OF A JOB, THEN MY DAD'S GONNA CLOBBER ME! I'M DOOMED!
"DESPERATE FOR ADVICE, I TURNED TO MY BEST FRIEND, BARNEY GUMBLE..."
WHAT SHOULD I DO, BARNEY?
THE WAY I SEE THINGS, YOU'VE GOT NO CHOICE BUT TO SHUT DOWN THE KEEP ON DUNKIN' SHOP BEFORE THEY CAN DO THE SAME THING TO LARD LAD!
Keep On Scratchin'

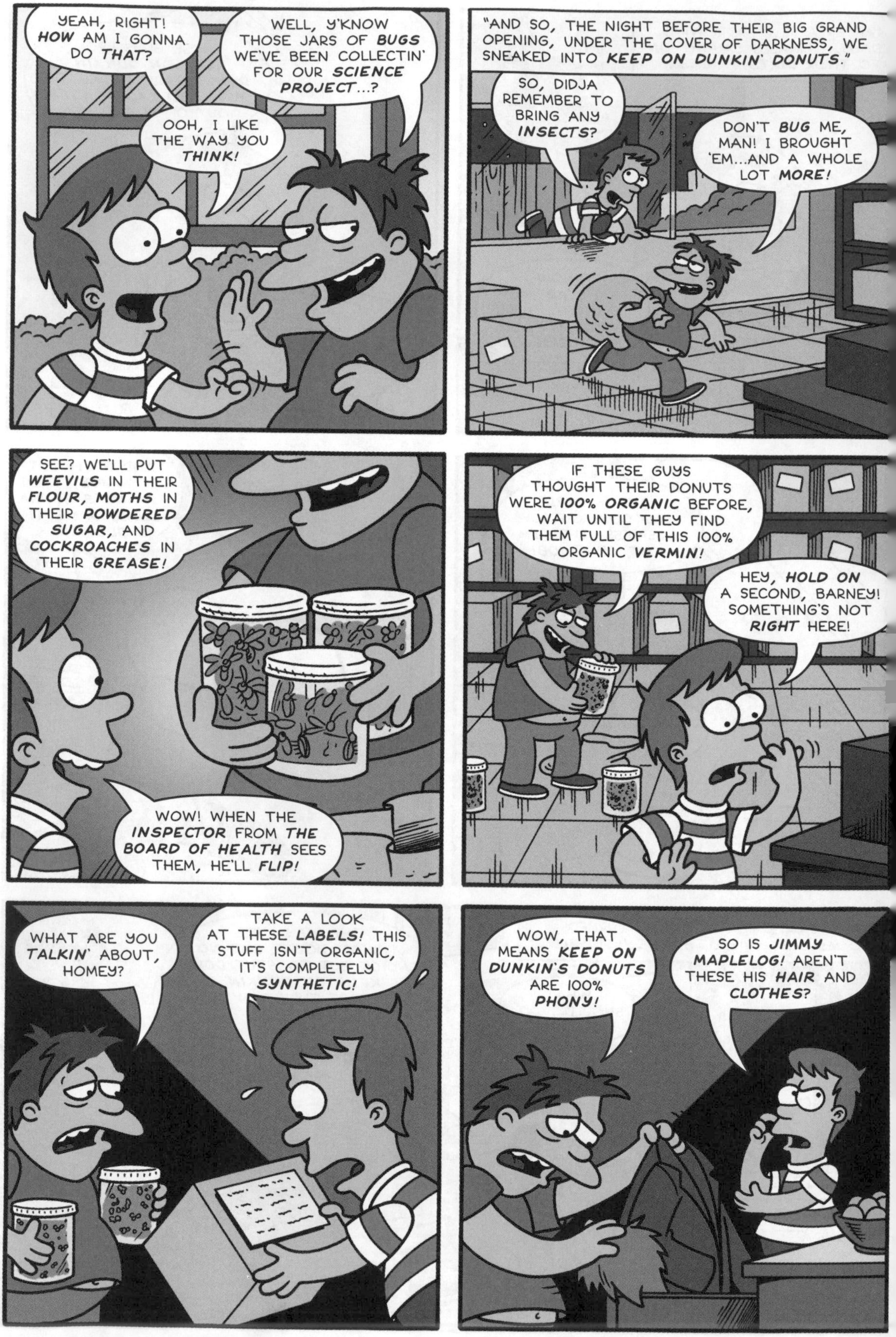
YEAH, RIGHT! HOW AM I GONNA DO THAT?
WELL, Y'KNOW THOSE JARS OF BUGS WE'VE BEEN COLLECTIN' FOR OUR SCIENCE PROJECT...?
OOH, I LIKE THE WAY YOU THINK!
"AND SO, THE NIGHT BEFORE THEIR BIG GRAND OPENING, UNDER THE COVER OF DARKNESS, WE SNEAKED INTO KEEP ON DUNKIN' DONUTS."
SO, DIDJA REMEMBER TO BRING ANY INSECTS?
DON'T BUG ME, MAN! I BROUGHT 'EM...AND A WHOLE LOT MORE!
SEE? WE'LL PUT WEEVILS IN THEIR FLOUR, MOTHS IN THEIR POWDERED SUGAR, AND COCKROACHES IN THEIR GREASE!
WOW! WHEN THE INSPECTOR FROM THE BOARD OF HEALTH SEES THEM, HE'LL FLIP!
IF THESE GUYS THOUGHT THEIR DONUTS WERE 100% ORGANIC BEFORE, WAIT UNTIL THEY FIND THEM FULL OF THIS 100% ORGANIC VERMIN!
HEY, HOLD ON A SECOND, BARNEY! SOMETHING'S NOT RIGHT HERE!
WHAT ARE YOU TALKIN' ABOUT, HOMEY?
TAKE A LOOK AT THESE LABELS! THIS STUFF ISN'T ORGANIC, IT'S COMPLETELY SYNTHETIC!
WOW, THAT MEANS KEEP ON DUNKIN'S DONUTS ARE 100% PHONY!
SO IS JIMMY MAPLELOG! AREN'T THESE HIS HAIR AND CLOTHES?

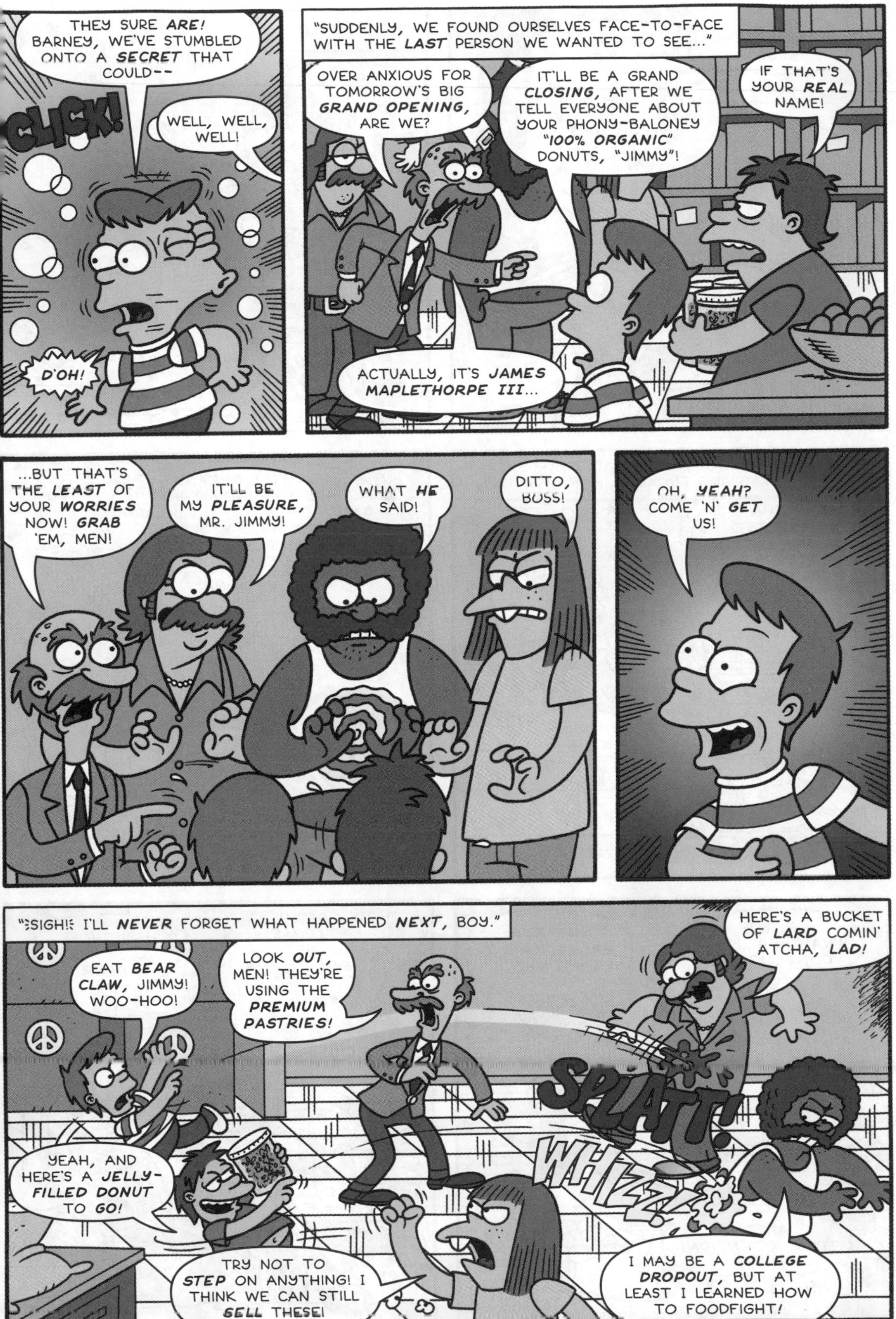
THEY SURE ARE! BARNEY, WE'VE STUMBLED ONTO A SECRET THAT COULD--
CLICK!
WELL, WELL, WELL!
D'OH!
"SUDDENLY, WE FOUND OURSELVES FACE-TO-FACE WITH THE LAST PERSON WE WANTED TO SEE..."
OVER ANXIOUS FOR TOMORROW'S BIG GRAND OPENING, ARE WE?
IT'LL BE A GRAND CLOSING, AFTER WE TELL EVERYONE ABOUT YOUR PHONY-BALONEY "100% ORGANIC" DONUTS, "JIMMY"!
IF THAT'S YOUR REAL NAME!
ACTUALLY, IT'S JAMES MAPLETHORPE III...
...BUT THAT'S THE LEAST OF YOUR WORRIES NOW! GRAB 'EM, MEN!
IT'LL BE MY PLEASURE, MR. JIMMY!
WHAT HE SAID!
DITTO, BOSS!
OH, YEAH? COME 'N' GET US!
"SIGH! I'LL NEVER FORGET WHAT HAPPENED NEXT, BOY."
EAT BEAR CLAW, JIMMY! WOO-HOO!
LOOK OUT, MEN! THEY'RE USING THE PREMIUM PASTRIES!
HERE'S A BUCKET OF LARD COMIN' ATCHA, LAD!
SPLATT!
WHIZZ!
YEAH, AND HERE'S A JELLY-FILLED DONUT TO GO!
TRY NOT TO STEP ON ANYTHING! I THINK WE CAN STILL SELL THESE!
I MAY BE A COLLEGE DROPOUT, BUT AT LEAST I LEARNED HOW TO FOODFIGHT!

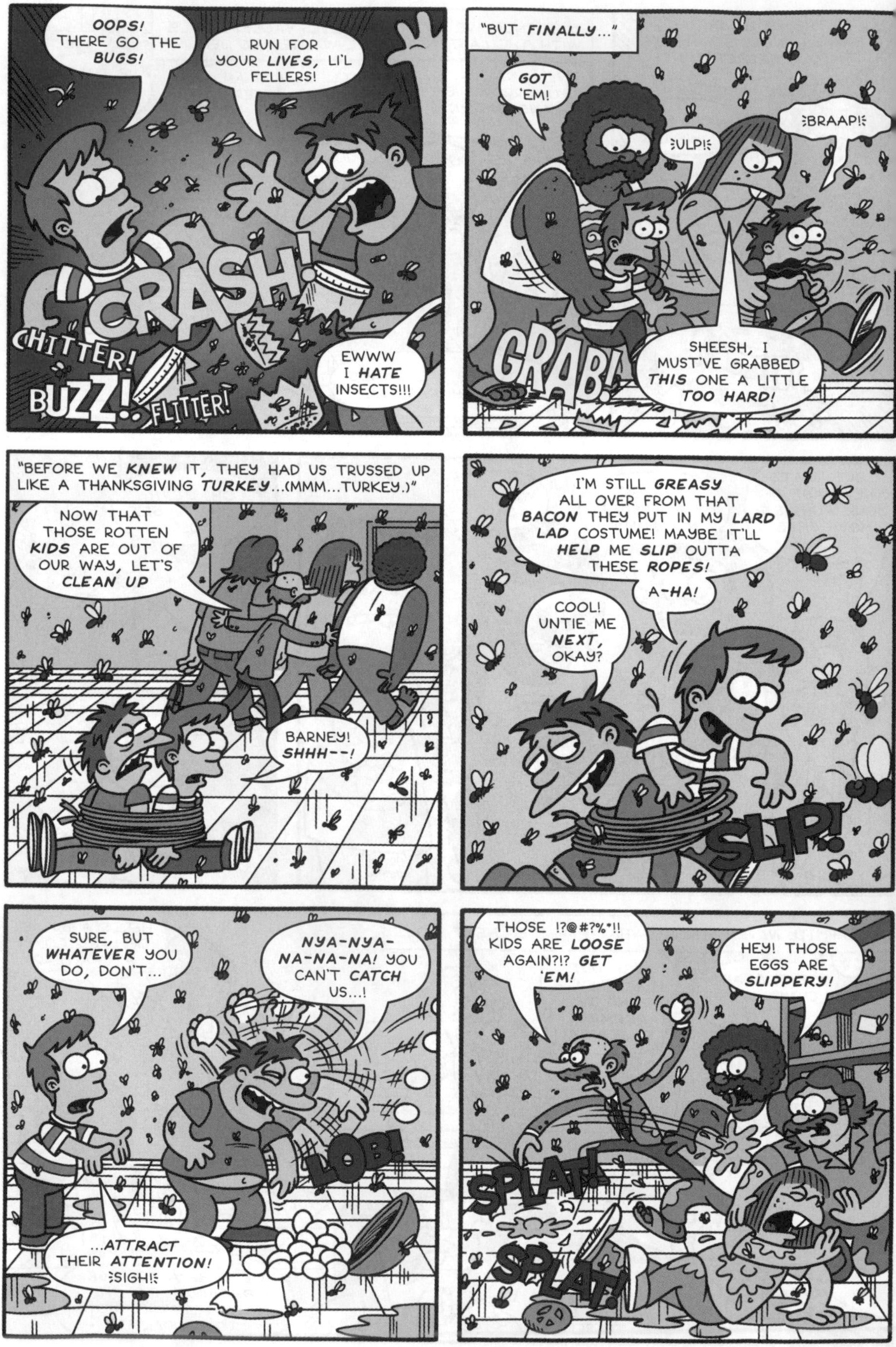
OOPS! THERE GO THE BUGS!
RUN FOR YOUR LIVES, LI'L FELLERS!
CRASH!
CHITTER!
BUZZ!
FLITTER!
EWWW I HATE INSECTS!!!
"BUT FINALLY..."
GOT 'EM!
ULP!
BRAAP!
GRAB!
SHEESH, I MUST'VE GRABBED THIS ONE A LITTLE TOO HARD!
"BEFORE WE KNEW IT, THEY HAD US TRUSSED UP LIKE A THANKSGIVING TURKEY...(MMM...TURKEY.)"
NOW THAT THOSE ROTTEN KIDS ARE OUT OF OUR WAY, LET'S CLEAN UP
BARNEY! SHHH--!
I'M STILL GREASY ALL OVER FROM THAT BACON THEY PUT IN MY LARD LAD COSTUME! MAYBE IT'LL HELP ME SLIP OUTTA THESE ROPES!
A-HA!
COOL! UNTIE ME NEXT, OKAY?
SLIP!
SURE, BUT WHATEVER YOU DO, DON'T...
NYA-NYA-NA-NA-NA! YOU CAN'T CATCH US...!
LOB!
...ATTRACT THEIR ATTENTION! SIGH!
THOSE !?@#?%*!! KIDS ARE LOOSE AGAIN?!? GET 'EM!
HEY! THOSE EGGS ARE SLIPPERY!
SPLAT!
SPLAT!

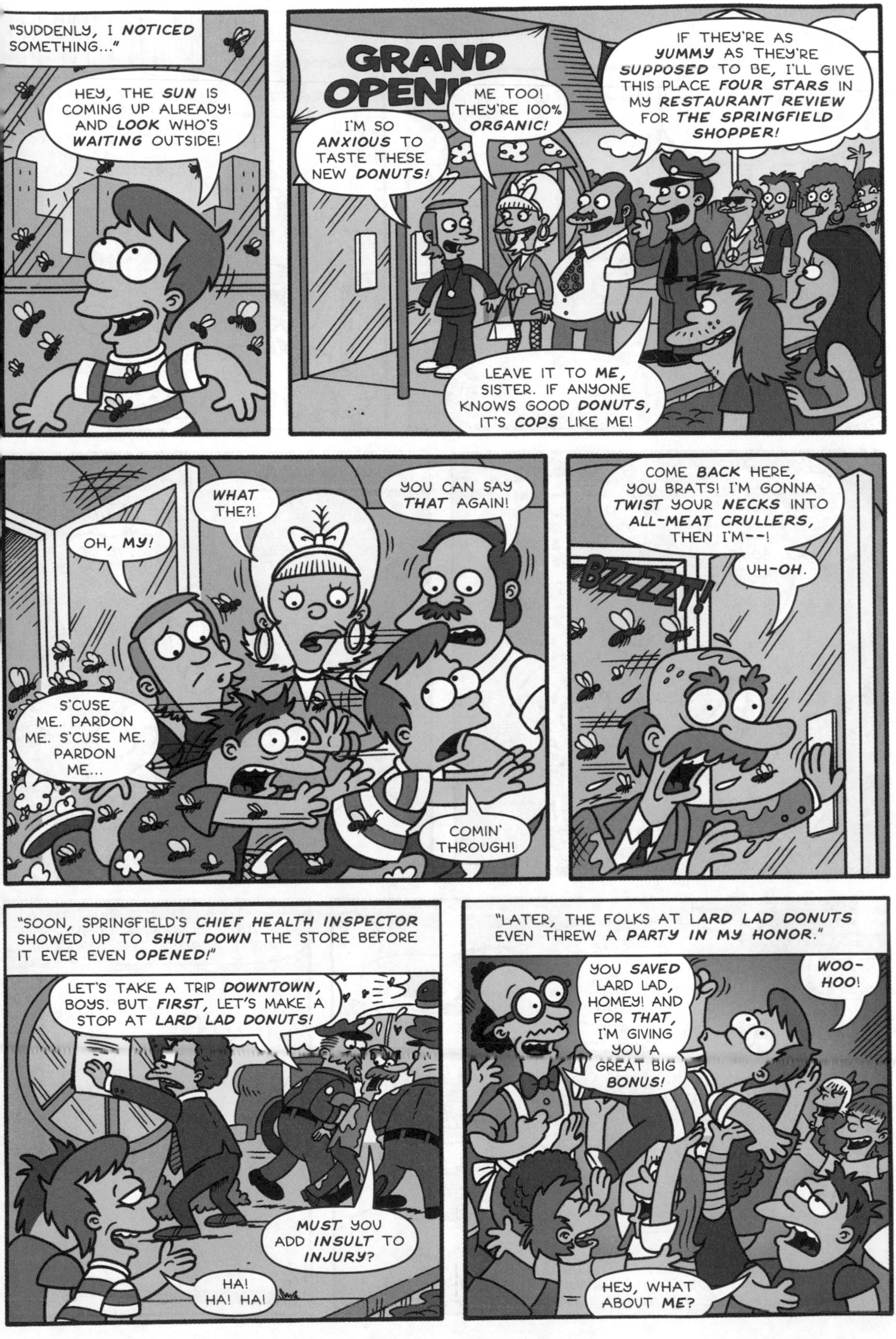
"SUDDENLY, I NOTICED SOMETHING..."
HEY, THE SUN IS COMING UP ALREADY! AND LOOK WHO'S WAITING OUTSIDE!
GRAND
OPEN
I'M SO ANXIOUS TO TASTE THESE NEW DONUTS!
ME TOO! THEY'RE 100% ORGANIC!
IF THEY'RE AS YUMMY AS THEY'RE SUPPOSED TO BE, I'LL GIVE THIS PLACE FOUR STARS IN MY RESTAURANT REVIEW FOR THE SPRINGFIELD SHOPPER!
LEAVE IT TO ME, SISTER. IF ANYONE KNOWS GOOD DONUTS, IT'S COPS LIKE ME!
OH, MY!
WHAT THE?!
YOU CAN SAY THAT AGAIN!
S'CUSE ME. PARDON ME. S'CUSE ME. PARDON ME...
COMIN' THROUGH!
COME BACK HERE, YOU BRATS! I'M GONNA TWIST YOUR NECKS INTO ALL-MEAT CRULLERS, THEN I'M--!
BZZZZZT!
UH-OH.
"SOON, SPRINGFIELD'S CHIEF HEALTH INSPECTOR SHOWED UP TO SHUT DOWN THE STORE BEFORE IT EVER EVEN OPENED!"
LET'S TAKE A TRIP DOWNTOWN, BOYS. BUT FIRST, LET'S MAKE A STOP AT LARD LAD DONUTS!
MUST YOU ADD INSULT TO INJURY?
HA! HA! HA!
"LATER, THE FOLKS AT LARD LAD DONUTS EVEN THREW A PARTY IN MY HONOR."
YOU SAVED LARD LAD, HOMEY! AND FOR THAT, I'M GIVING YOU A GREAT BIG BONUS!
WOO-HOO!
HEY, WHAT ABOUT ME?

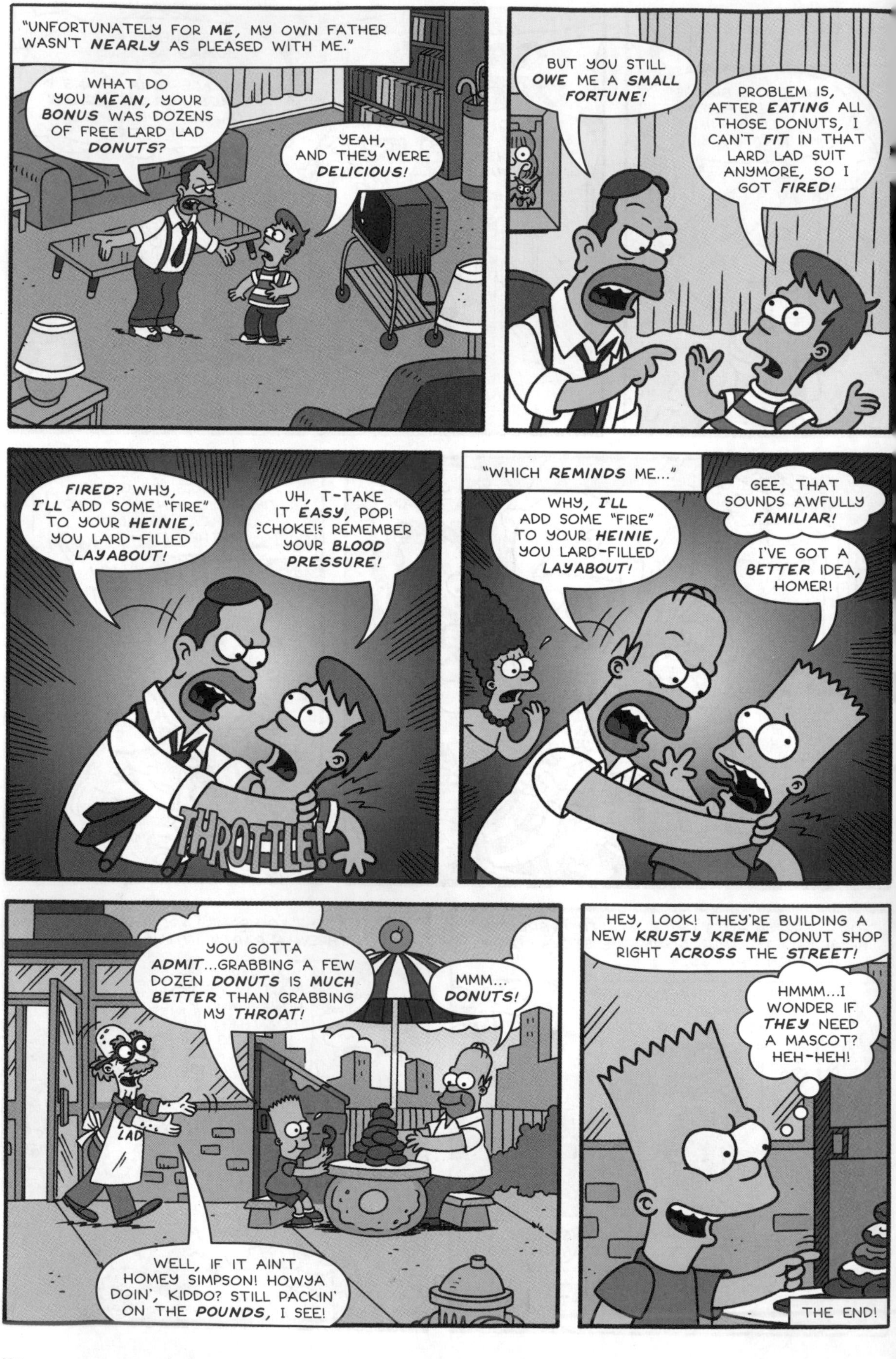

"UNFORTUNATELY FOR ME, MY OWN FATHER WASN'T NEARLY AS PLEASED WITH ME."
WHAT DO YOU MEAN, YOUR BONUS WAS DOZENS OF FREE LARD LAD DONUTS?
YEAH, AND THEY WERE DELICIOUS!
BUT YOU STILL OWE ME A SMALL FORTUNE!
PROBLEM IS, AFTER EATING ALL THOSE DONUTS, I CAN'T FIT IN THAT LARD LAD SUIT ANYMORE, SO I GOT FIRED!
FIRED? WHY, I'LL ADD SOME "FIRE" TO YOUR HEINIE, YOU LARD-FILLED LAYABOUT!
UH, T-TAKE IT EASY, POP! CHOKE! REMEMBER YOUR BLOOD PRESSURE!
THROTTLE!
"WHICH REMINDS ME..."
WHY, I'LL ADD SOME "FIRE" TO YOUR HEINIE, YOU LARD-FILLED LAYABOUT!
GEE, THAT SOUNDS AWFULLY FAMILIAR!
I'VE GOT A BETTER IDEA, HOMER!
YOU GOTTA ADMIT...GRABBING A FEW DOZEN DONUTS IS MUCH BETTER THAN GRABBING MY THROAT!
MMM... DONUTS!
LAD
WELL, IF IT AIN'T HOMEY SIMPSON! HOWYA DOIN', KIDDO? STILL PACKIN' ON THE POUNDS, I SEE!
HEY, LOOK! THEY'RE BUILDING A NEW KRUSTY KREME DONUT SHOP RIGHT ACROSS THE STREET!
HMMM...I WONDER IF THEY NEED A MASCOT? HEH-HEH!
THE END!

HEY DUDES AND DUDETTES! I'M INTERRUPTING THIS REALLY GREAT COMIC WITH EVEN GREATER NEWS. STARTING WITH THIS ISSUE, YOUR FRIENDS AT BONGO COMICS ARE PRESENTING A NEW PULLOUT SECTION CALLED...

BART'S FUN PAGES!

IT'S GOT GAMES AND PUZZLES AND OTHER FUN STUFF. DON'T WORRY, THESE PUZZLES WON'T MAKE YOU ANY SMARTER. IN FACT, SOME OF THEM ARE JUST DUMB, POINTLESS JOKES.

WHAT WILL MAKE YOU SMARTER (OR AT LEAST MAKE YOU LOOK SMARTER) IS THE TWO-PAGE WRAPAROUND THAT YOU CAN WRAP AROUND THIS COMIC BOOK SO IT *LOOKS* LIKE YOU'RE READING SOMETHING *INTELLIGENT*...

...LIKE THIS!

101 Ways to Improve

TAKE *THAT*, EGGHEAD.

OOF! SEE, IT *WORKS!* WELL, ENJOY. I GOTTA GO THROW UP.

POW

EL BARTO'S REBUS

SOLVE THE REBUSES BY FIGURING OUT WHAT THE PICTURES REPRESENT IN WORDS. THE ANSWER IS PRINTED UPSIDE DOWN ON THE BOTTOM, BUT DON'T PEEK UNLESS YOU'RE AS DUMB AS *PRINCIPAL SKINNER* AND THOSE OTHER *LOSERS*.

L + BAR + [thumb] + [bowling pins] + [man] — BILLIONS AND BILLIONS

[flash figure] + [alien] + [comb] + [eggs in pan]

RE: YOUR NL DEAR SIR, + [buses] + [dog] ARF! + [oar] + [people]

ANSWERS: 1) L BAR TOE STRIKE SAGAN (EL BARTO STRIKES AGAIN), 2) REED BONGO COMB EGGS (READ BONGO COMICS), 3) RE: BUSES ARF OAR LOSERS (DO I REALLY HAVE TO SPELL IT OUT FOR YOU?)

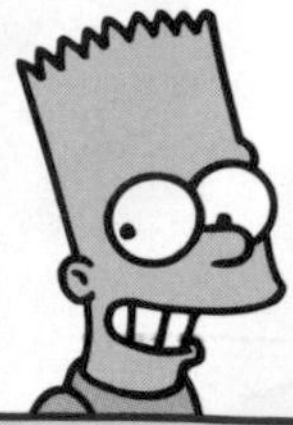

BART'S FUN PAGES PART II

KRUSTY'S COMPUTER-GENERATED CRYPTOGRAM

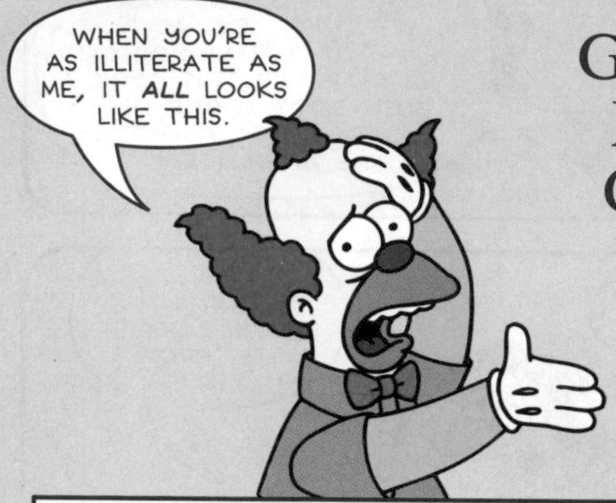
WHEN YOU'RE AS ILLITERATE AS ME, IT *ALL* LOOKS LIKE THIS.

CRYPTOGRAM INSTRUCTIONS: DECODE THIS TIMELY INSTRUCTION BY CHANGING EACH LETTER TO ITS CORRESPONDING LETTER. THEN DECODE THE AUTHOR'S NAME.

"WVXLWV GSRH GRNVOB RMHGIFXGRLM YB XSZMTRMT VZXS OVGGVI GL RGH XLIIVHKLMWRMT OVGGVI. GSVM WVXLWV GSV ZFGSLIH MZNV."

–XIBKGLTIZN RMHGIFXGRLMH

ANSWER KEY:
A=Z, B=Y, C=X, D=W, E=V, F=U, G=T, H=S, I=R, J=Q, K=P, L=O, M=N

COMIC BOOK GUY'S CATCHPHRASE JUMBLE

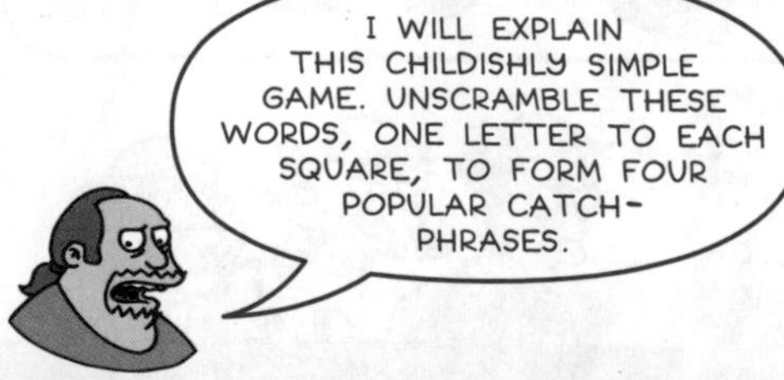
I WILL EXPLAIN THIS CHILDISHLY SIMPLE GAME. UNSCRAMBLE THESE WORDS, ONE LETTER TO EACH SQUARE, TO FORM FOUR POPULAR CATCH-PHRASES.

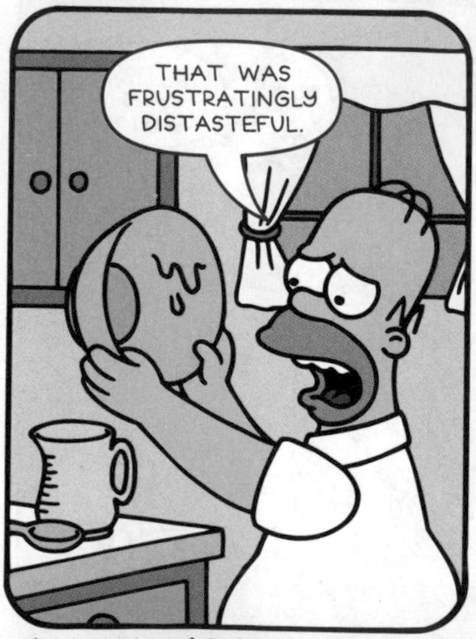
THAT WAS FRUSTRATINGLY DISTASTEFUL.

WHAT DID HOMER SAY WHEN HE ATE THE UNCOOKED CAKE?

KOYIN
yoink

DYHKEIS
hey Kids

BURACAM
Carumba

GIMNEBEG
Embiggen

DOUGH

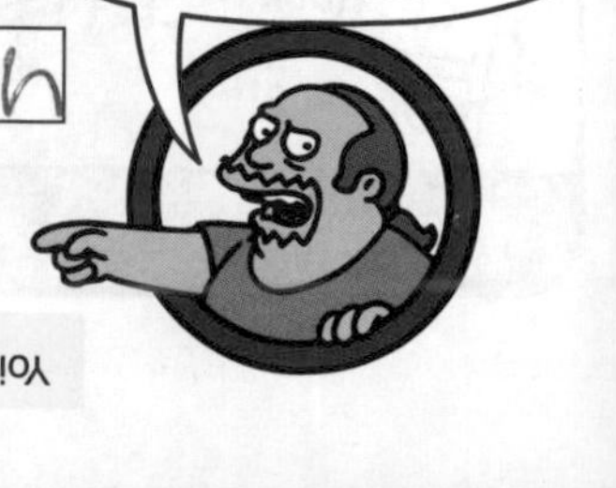
NOW ARRANGE THE CIRCLED LETTERS TO FORM THE ANSWER THAT *I* ALREADY FIGURED OUT WITHOUT THE CLUES ANY-WAY BECAUSE PUNS ARE MORE OBVIOUS THAN ANAGRAMS.

Yoink, Hey kids, Carumba, Embiggen "DOUGH!"

BART SIMPSON

IN

MOVIE MAYHEM

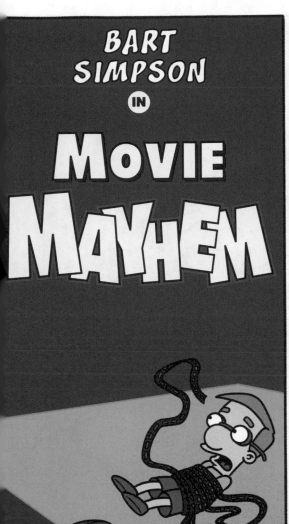

JAMES BATES
WRITER

MIKE ROTE
INKS

CHRIS UNGAR
LETTERS

LUIS ESCOBAR
PENCILS

NATHAN HAMILL
COLORS

BILL MORRISON
EDITS

THAT TAPE'S GOTTA BE UP HERE!

GIVE IT UP, BART. WE'VE LOOKED EVERYWHERE. IT'S JUST A MOVIE.

"ZOMBIE OR NOT ZOMBIE" IS NOT JUST A MOVIE, IT'S A CULT CLASSIC.

YOU CAN'T RENT IT. I TAPED IT OFF OF "COUNT BROCKULA'S MIDNIGHT MONSTER MADNESS STARRING KENT BROCKMAN!"

YOU'LL NEVER FIND IT.

I FOUND IT!

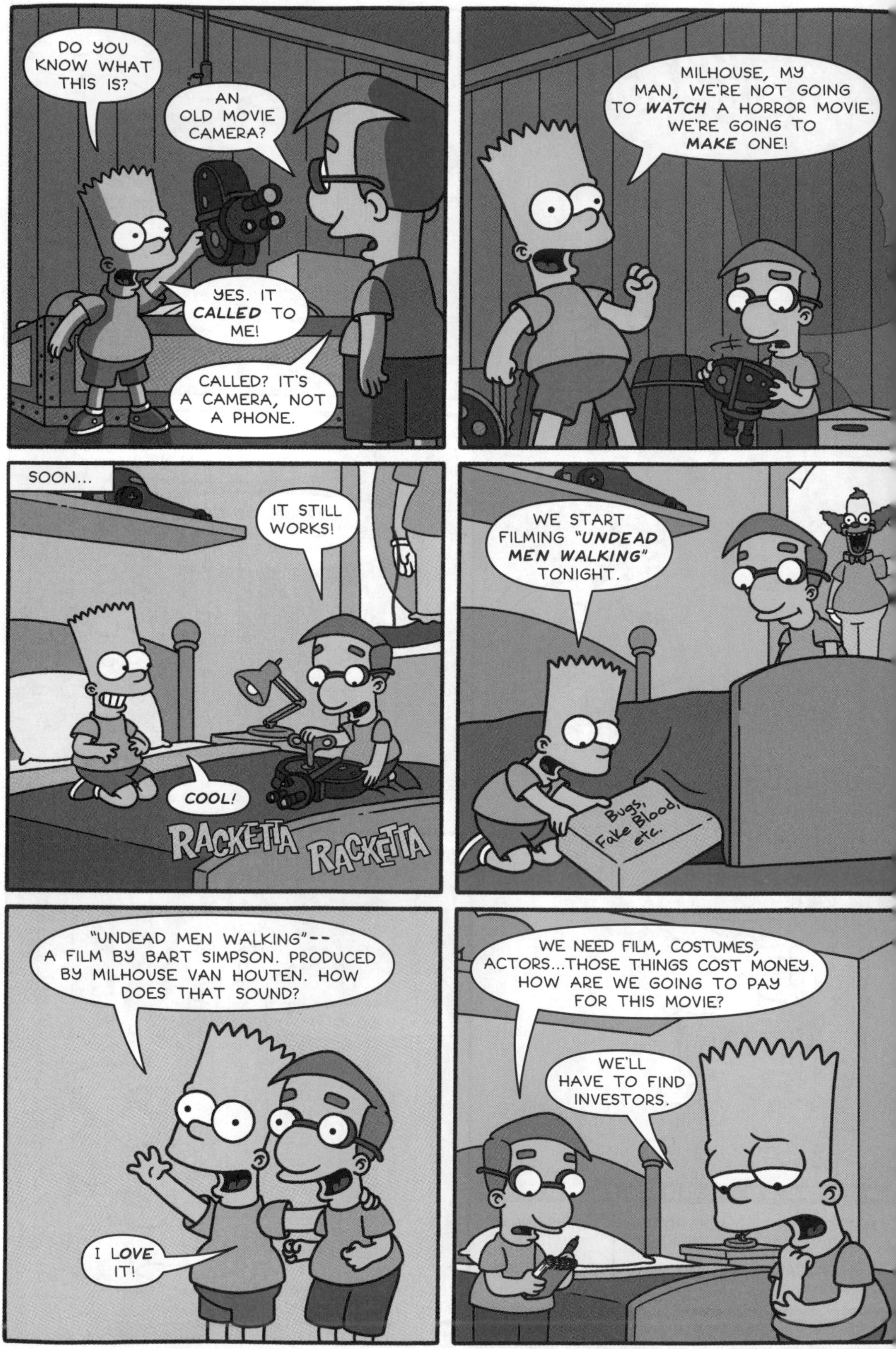
DO YOU KNOW WHAT THIS IS?
AN OLD MOVIE CAMERA?
YES. IT CALLED TO ME!
CALLED? IT'S A CAMERA, NOT A PHONE.
MILHOUSE, MY MAN, WE'RE NOT GOING TO WATCH A HORROR MOVIE. WE'RE GOING TO MAKE ONE!
SOON...
IT STILL WORKS!
COOL!
RACKETTA RACKETTA
WE START FILMING "UNDEAD MEN WALKING" TONIGHT.
Bugs, Fake Blood, etc.
"UNDEAD MEN WALKING"-- A FILM BY BART SIMPSON. PRODUCED BY MILHOUSE VAN HOUTEN. HOW DOES THAT SOUND?
I LOVE IT!
WE NEED FILM, COSTUMES, ACTORS...THOSE THINGS COST MONEY. HOW ARE WE GOING TO PAY FOR THIS MOVIE?
WE'LL HAVE TO FIND INVESTORS.

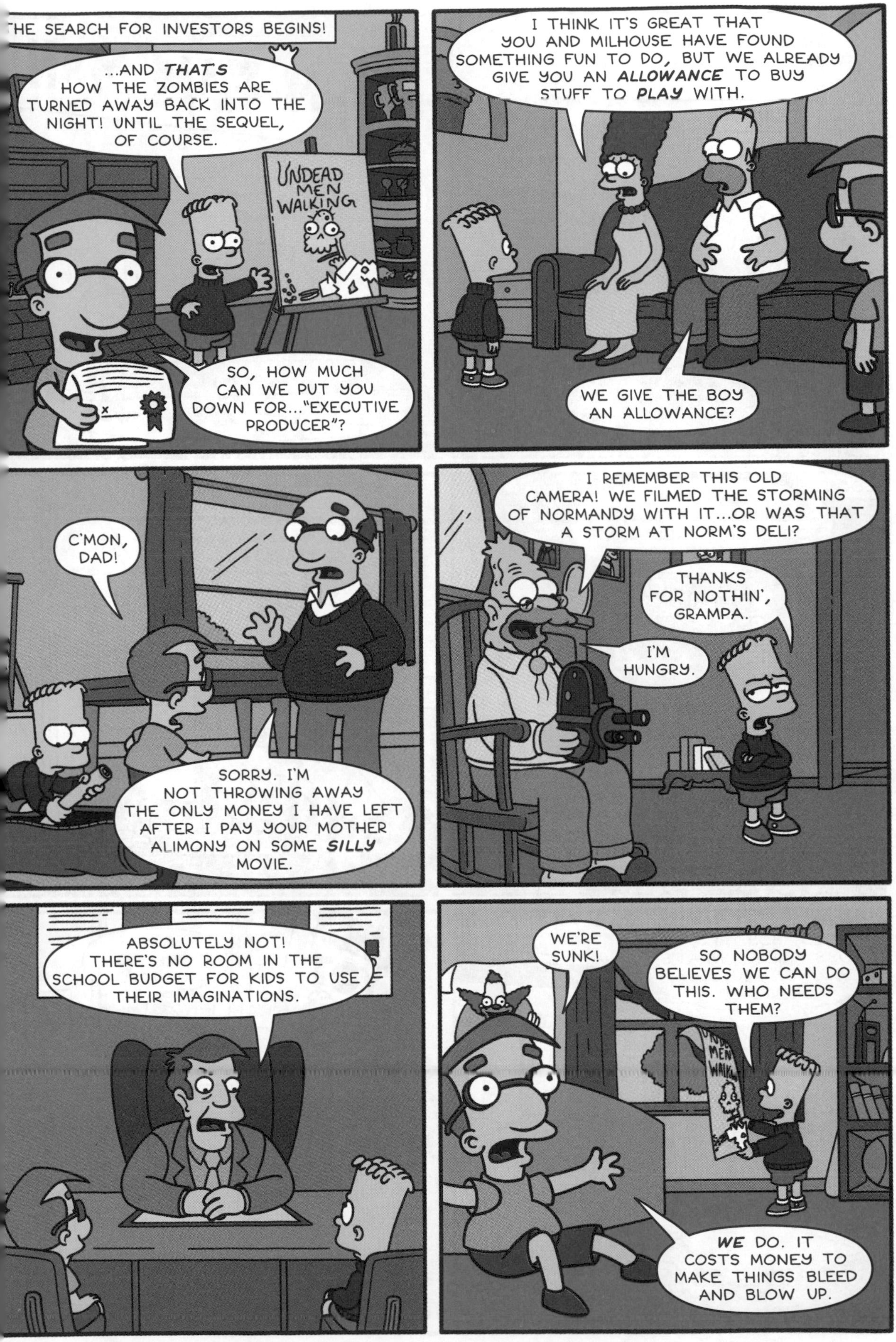
THE SEARCH FOR INVESTORS BEGINS!
...AND THAT'S HOW THE ZOMBIES ARE TURNED AWAY BACK INTO THE NIGHT! UNTIL THE SEQUEL, OF COURSE.
UNDEAD MEN WALKING
SO, HOW MUCH CAN WE PUT YOU DOWN FOR..."EXECUTIVE PRODUCER"?
I THINK IT'S GREAT THAT YOU AND MILHOUSE HAVE FOUND SOMETHING FUN TO DO, BUT WE ALREADY GIVE YOU AN ALLOWANCE TO BUY STUFF TO PLAY WITH.
WE GIVE THE BOY AN ALLOWANCE?
C'MON, DAD!
SORRY. I'M NOT THROWING AWAY THE ONLY MONEY I HAVE LEFT AFTER I PAY YOUR MOTHER ALIMONY ON SOME SILLY MOVIE.
I REMEMBER THIS OLD CAMERA! WE FILMED THE STORMING OF NORMANDY WITH IT...OR WAS THAT A STORM AT NORM'S DELI?
I'M HUNGRY.
THANKS FOR NOTHIN', GRAMPA.
ABSOLUTELY NOT! THERE'S NO ROOM IN THE SCHOOL BUDGET FOR KIDS TO USE THEIR IMAGINATIONS.
WE'RE SUNK!
SO NOBODY BELIEVES WE CAN DO THIS. WHO NEEDS THEM?
WE DO. IT COSTS MONEY TO MAKE THINGS BLEED AND BLOW UP.

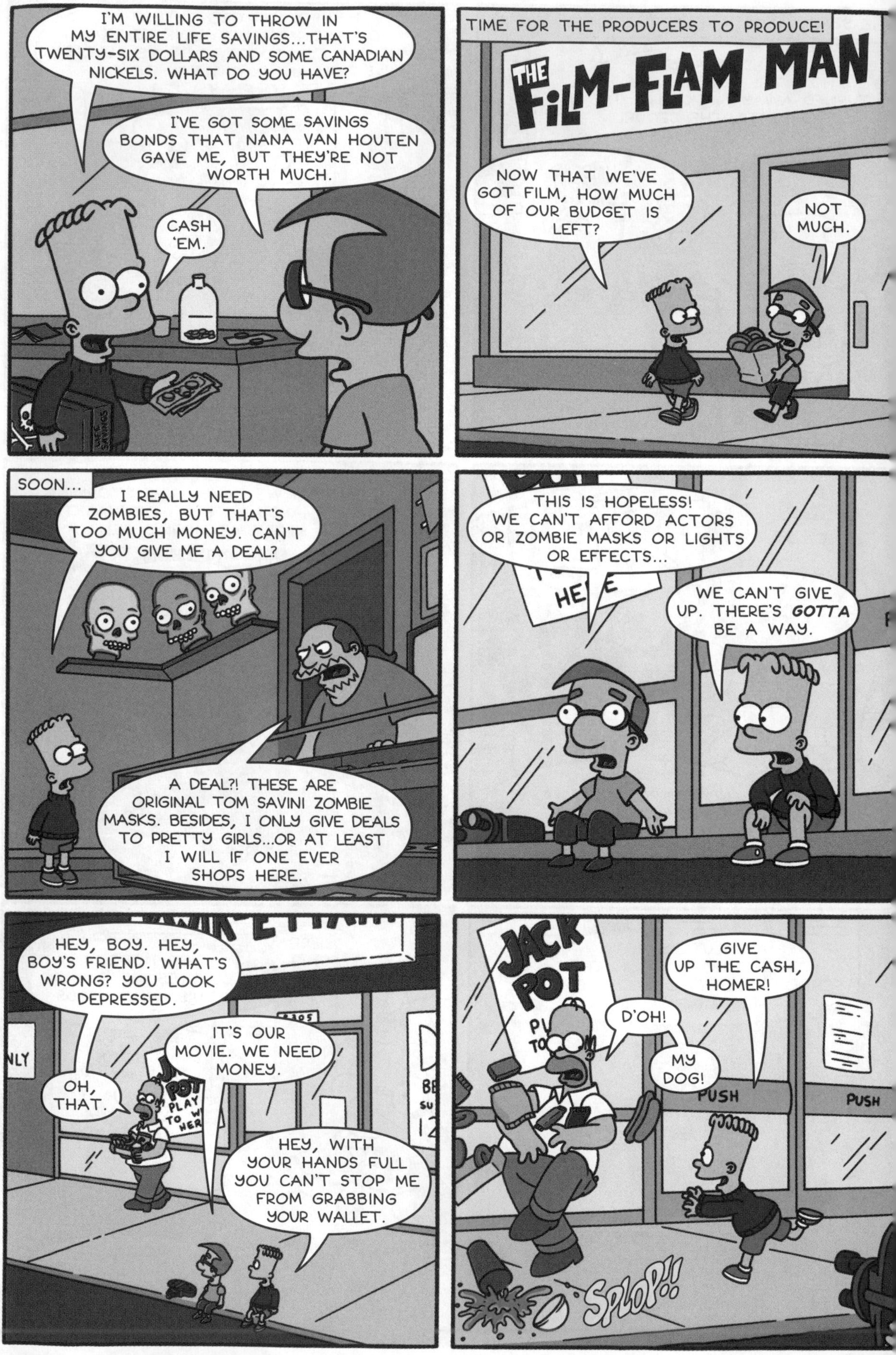
I'M WILLING TO THROW IN MY ENTIRE LIFE SAVINGS...THAT'S TWENTY-SIX DOLLARS AND SOME CANADIAN NICKELS. WHAT DO YOU HAVE?
I'VE GOT SOME SAVINGS BONDS THAT NANA VAN HOUTEN GAVE ME, BUT THEY'RE NOT WORTH MUCH.
CASH 'EM.
LIFE SAVINGS
TIME FOR THE PRODUCERS TO PRODUCE!
THE FILM-FLAM MAN
NOW THAT WE'VE GOT FILM, HOW MUCH OF OUR BUDGET IS LEFT?
NOT MUCH.
SOON...
I REALLY NEED ZOMBIES, BUT THAT'S TOO MUCH MONEY. CAN'T YOU GIVE ME A DEAL?
A DEAL?! THESE ARE ORIGINAL TOM SAVINI ZOMBIE MASKS. BESIDES, I ONLY GIVE DEALS TO PRETTY GIRLS...OR AT LEAST I WILL IF ONE EVER SHOPS HERE.
THIS IS HOPELESS! WE CAN'T AFFORD ACTORS OR ZOMBIE MASKS OR LIGHTS OR EFFECTS...
WE CAN'T GIVE UP. THERE'S ***GOTTA*** BE A WAY.
HEY, BOY. HEY, BOY'S FRIEND. WHAT'S WRONG? YOU LOOK DEPRESSED.
IT'S OUR MOVIE. WE NEED MONEY.
OH, THAT.
HEY, WITH YOUR HANDS FULL YOU CAN'T STOP ME FROM GRABBING YOUR WALLET.
JACK POT
GIVE UP THE CASH, HOMER!
D'OH!
MY DOG!
PUSH
PUSH
SPLOP!!

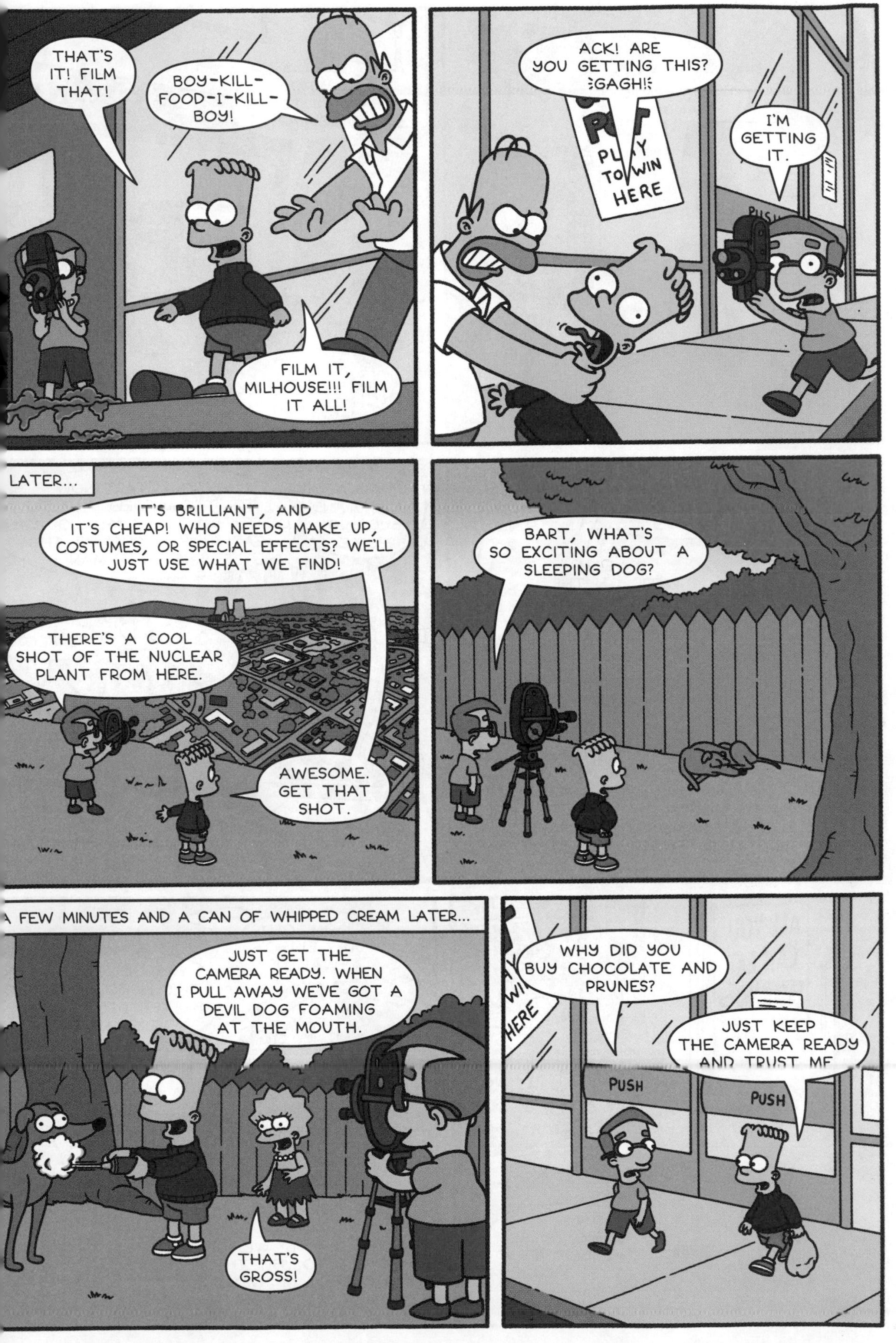

THAT'S IT! FILM THAT!
BOY-KILL-FOOD-I-KILL-BOY!
FILM IT, MILHOUSE!!! FILM IT ALL!
ACK! ARE YOU GETTING THIS? GAGH!
PLAY TO WIN HERE
I'M GETTING IT.
PUSH
LATER...
IT'S BRILLIANT, AND IT'S CHEAP! WHO NEEDS MAKE UP, COSTUMES, OR SPECIAL EFFECTS? WE'LL JUST USE WHAT WE FIND!
THERE'S A COOL SHOT OF THE NUCLEAR PLANT FROM HERE.
AWESOME. GET THAT SHOT.
BART, WHAT'S SO EXCITING ABOUT A SLEEPING DOG?
A FEW MINUTES AND A CAN OF WHIPPED CREAM LATER...
JUST GET THE CAMERA READY. WHEN I PULL AWAY WE'VE GOT A DEVIL DOG FOAMING AT THE MOUTH.
THAT'S GROSS!
WHY DID YOU BUY CHOCOLATE AND PRUNES?
JUST KEEP THE CAMERA READY AND TRUST ME
HERE
PUSH
PUSH

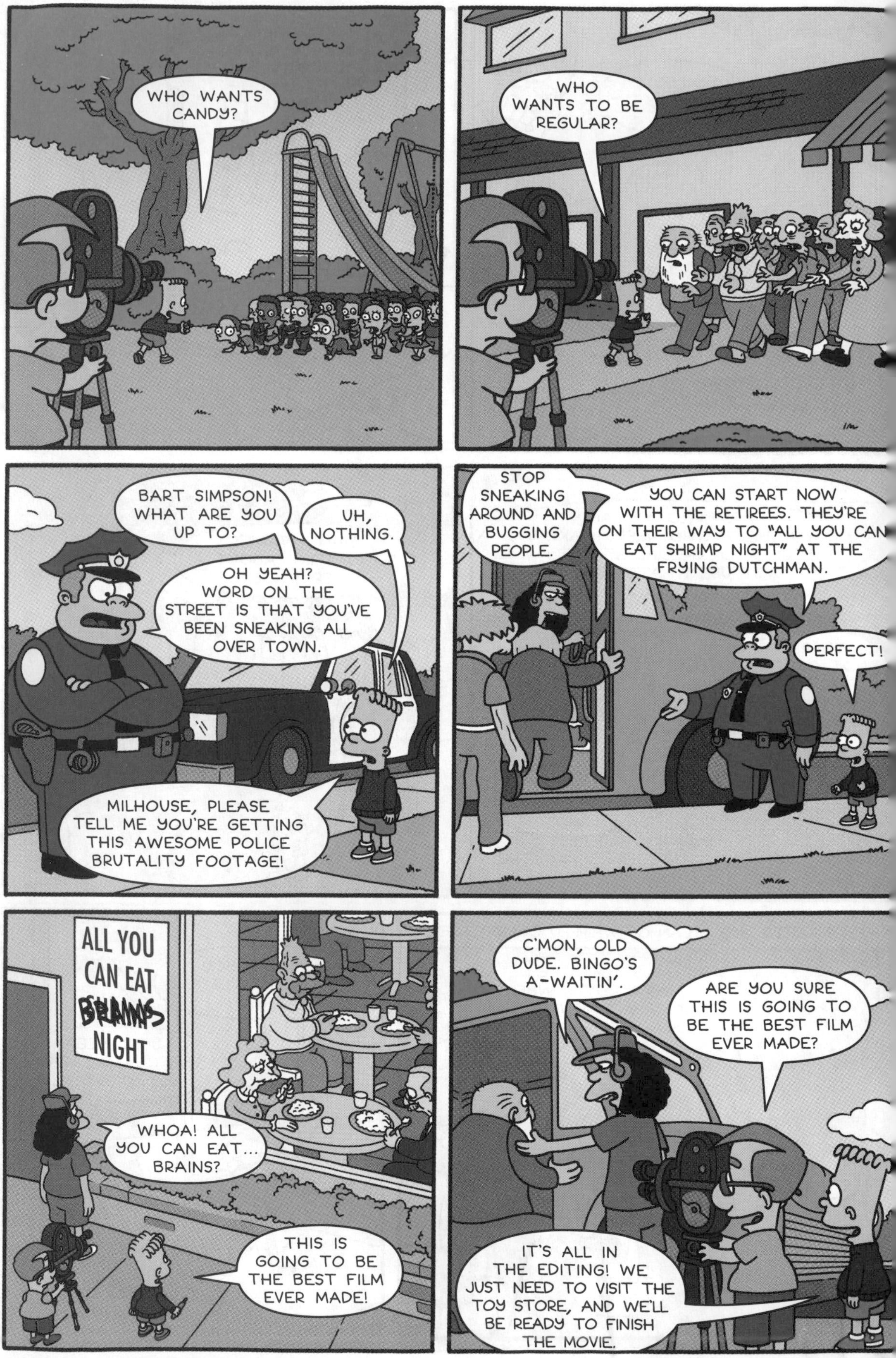
WHO WANTS CANDY?
WHO WANTS TO BE REGULAR?
BART SIMPSON! WHAT ARE YOU UP TO?
UH, NOTHING.
OH YEAH? WORD ON THE STREET IS THAT YOU'VE BEEN SNEAKING ALL OVER TOWN.
MILHOUSE, PLEASE TELL ME YOU'RE GETTING THIS AWESOME POLICE BRUTALITY FOOTAGE!
STOP SNEAKING AROUND AND BUGGING PEOPLE.
YOU CAN START NOW WITH THE RETIREES. THEY'RE ON THEIR WAY TO "ALL YOU CAN EAT SHRIMP NIGHT" AT THE FRYING DUTCHMAN.
PERFECT!
ALL YOU CAN EAT BRAINS NIGHT
WHOA! ALL YOU CAN EAT... BRAINS?
THIS IS GOING TO BE THE BEST FILM EVER MADE!
C'MON, OLD DUDE. BINGO'S A-WAITIN'.
ARE YOU SURE THIS IS GOING TO BE THE BEST FILM EVER MADE?
IT'S ALL IN THE EDITING! WE JUST NEED TO VISIT THE TOY STORE, AND WE'LL BE READY TO FINISH THE MOVIE.

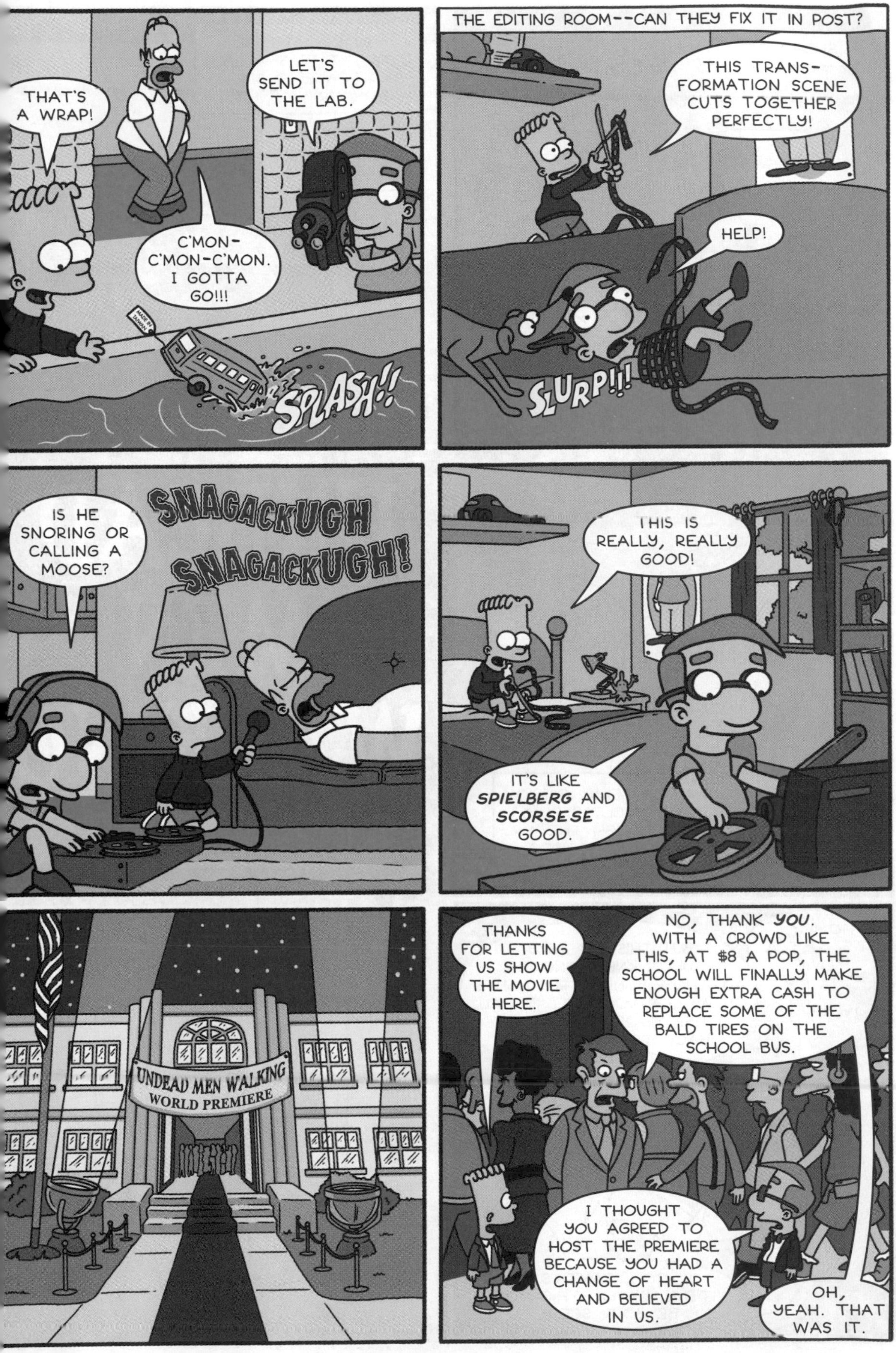
THAT'S A WRAP!
LET'S SEND IT TO THE LAB.
C'MON-C'MON-C'MON. I GOTTA GO!!!
SPLASH!!
THE EDITING ROOM--CAN THEY FIX IT IN POST?
THIS TRANS-FORMATION SCENE CUTS TOGETHER PERFECTLY!
HELP!
SLURP!!!
IS HE SNORING OR CALLING A MOOSE?
SNAGACKUGH
SNAGACKUGH!
THIS IS REALLY, REALLY GOOD!
IT'S LIKE SPIELBERG AND SCORSESE GOOD.
UNDEAD MEN WALKING
WORLD PREMIERE
THANKS FOR LETTING US SHOW THE MOVIE HERE.
NO, THANK YOU. WITH A CROWD LIKE THIS, AT $8 A POP, THE SCHOOL WILL FINALLY MAKE ENOUGH EXTRA CASH TO REPLACE SOME OF THE BALD TIRES ON THE SCHOOL BUS.
I THOUGHT YOU AGREED TO HOST THE PREMIERE BECAUSE YOU HAD A CHANGE OF HEART AND BELIEVED IN US.
OH, YEAH. THAT WAS IT.

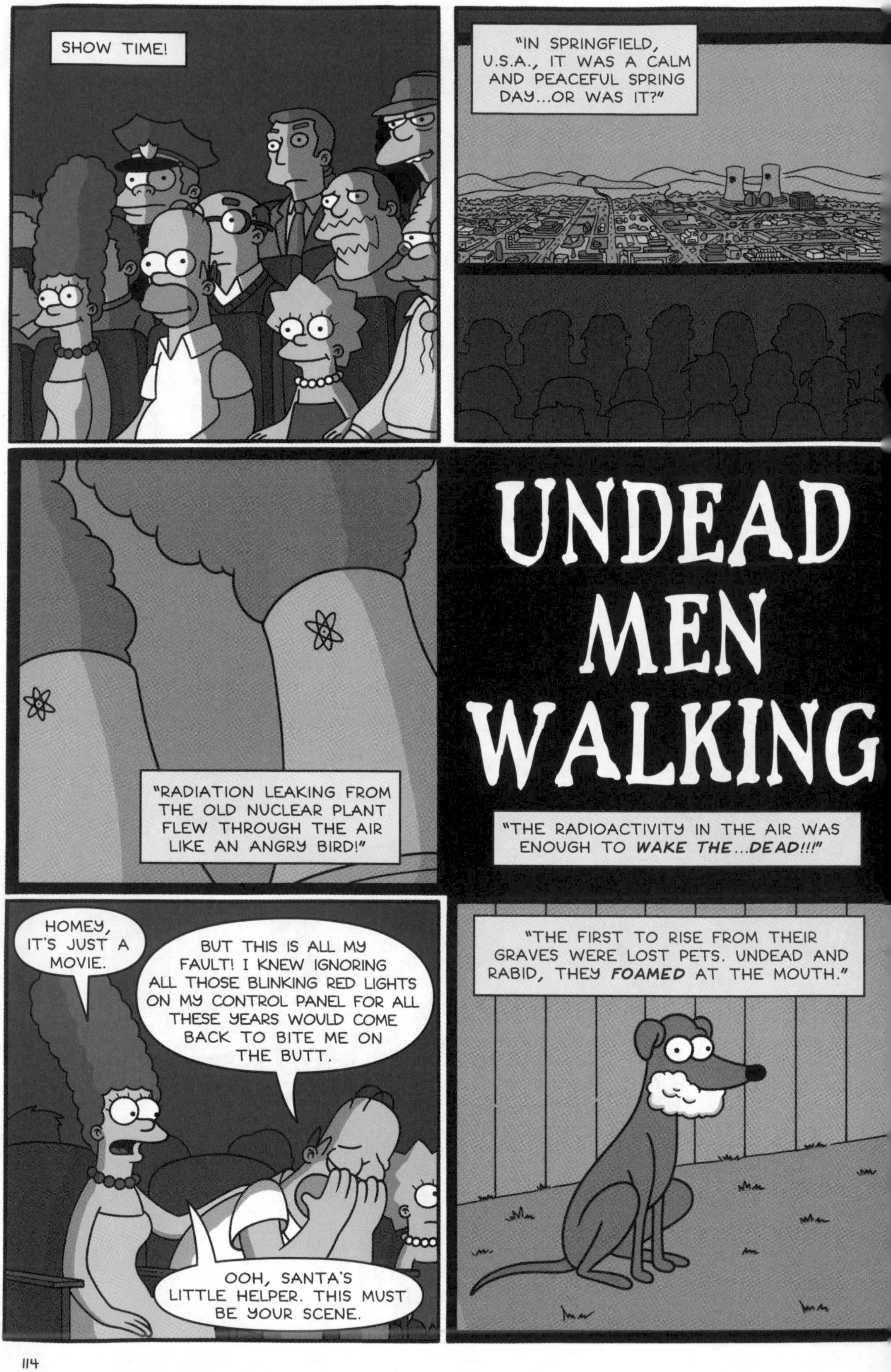
SHOW TIME!
"IN SPRINGFIELD, U.S.A., IT WAS A CALM AND PEACEFUL SPRING DAY...OR WAS IT?"
"RADIATION LEAKING FROM THE OLD NUCLEAR PLANT FLEW THROUGH THE AIR LIKE AN ANGRY BIRD!"
UNDEAD MEN WALKING
"THE RADIOACTIVITY IN THE AIR WAS ENOUGH TO WAKE THE...DEAD!!!"
HOMEY, IT'S JUST A MOVIE.
BUT THIS IS ALL MY FAULT! I KNEW IGNORING ALL THOSE BLINKING RED LIGHTS ON MY CONTROL PANEL FOR ALL THESE YEARS WOULD COME BACK TO BITE ME ON THE BUTT.
OOH, SANTA'S LITTLE HELPER. THIS MUST BE YOUR SCENE.
"THE FIRST TO RISE FROM THEIR GRAVES WERE LOST PETS. UNDEAD AND RABID, THEY FOAMED AT THE MOUTH."

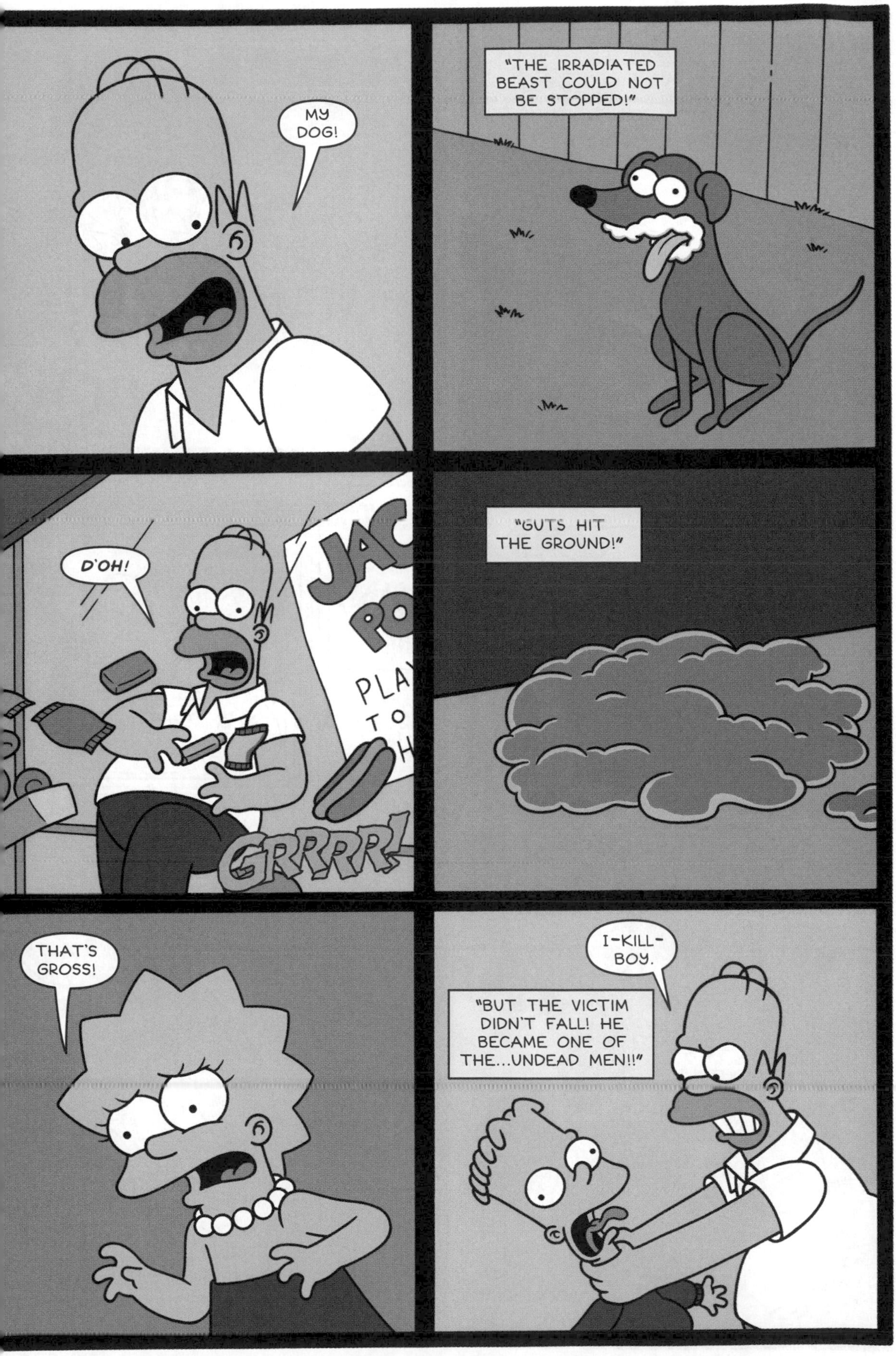
MY DOG!
"THE IRRADIATED BEAST COULD NOT BE STOPPED!"
D'OH!
JAC PO PLAY TO H
GRRRR!
"GUTS HIT THE GROUND!"
THAT'S GROSS!
I-KILL-BOY.
"BUT THE VICTIM DIDN'T FALL! HE BECAME ONE OF THE...UNDEAD MEN!!"

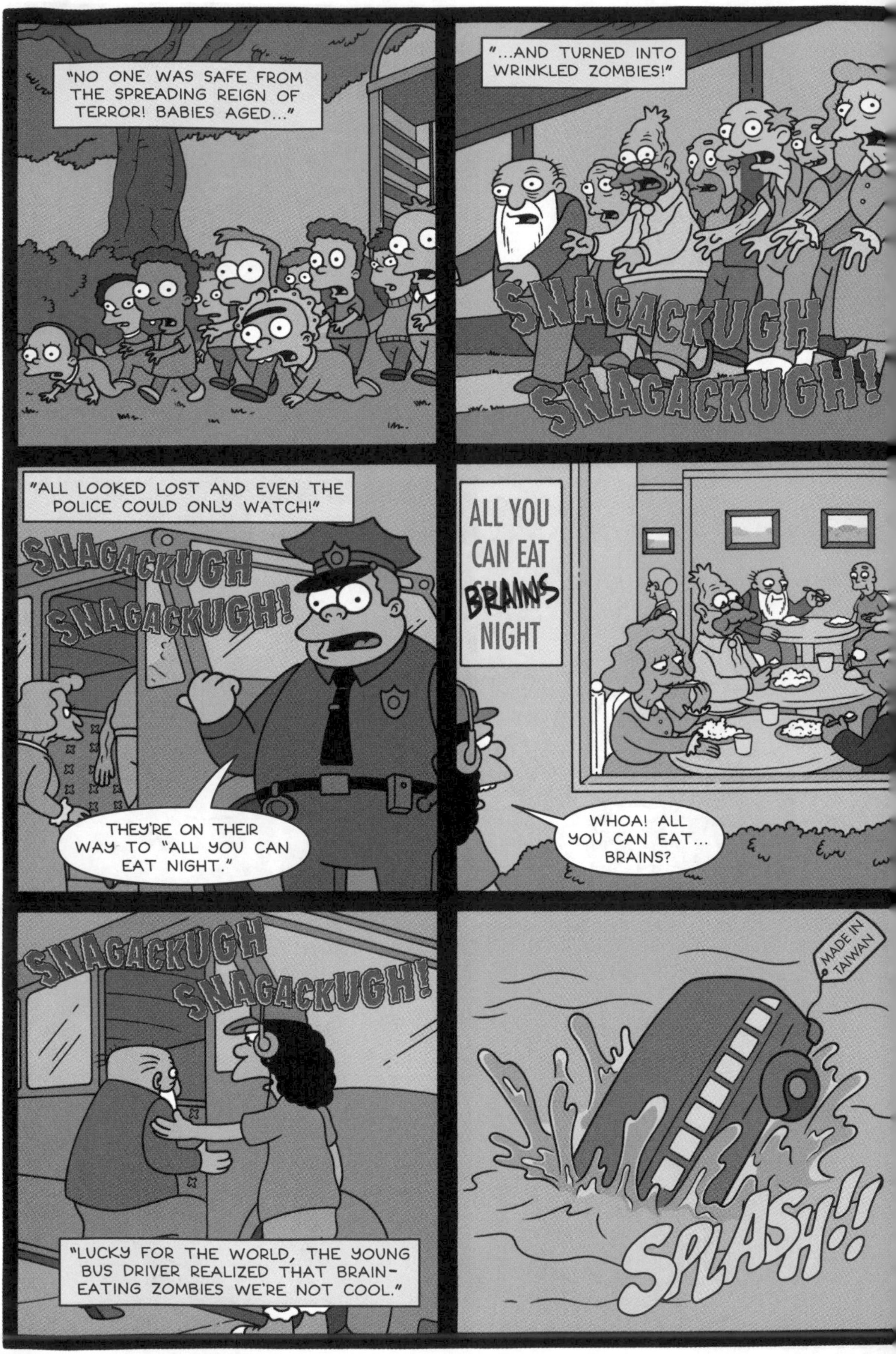
"NO ONE WAS SAFE FROM THE SPREADING REIGN OF TERROR! BABIES AGED..."
"...AND TURNED INTO WRINKLED ZOMBIES!"
SNAGACKUGH
SNAGACKUGH!
"ALL LOOKED LOST AND EVEN THE POLICE COULD ONLY WATCH!"
SNAGACKUGH
SNAGACKUGH!
THEY'RE ON THEIR WAY TO "ALL YOU CAN EAT NIGHT."
ALL YOU CAN EAT BRAINS NIGHT
WHOA! ALL YOU CAN EAT... BRAINS?
SNAGACKUGH
SNAGACKUGH!
"LUCKY FOR THE WORLD, THE YOUNG BUS DRIVER REALIZED THAT BRAIN-EATING ZOMBIES WE'RE NOT COOL."
MADE IN TAIWAN
SPLASH!!

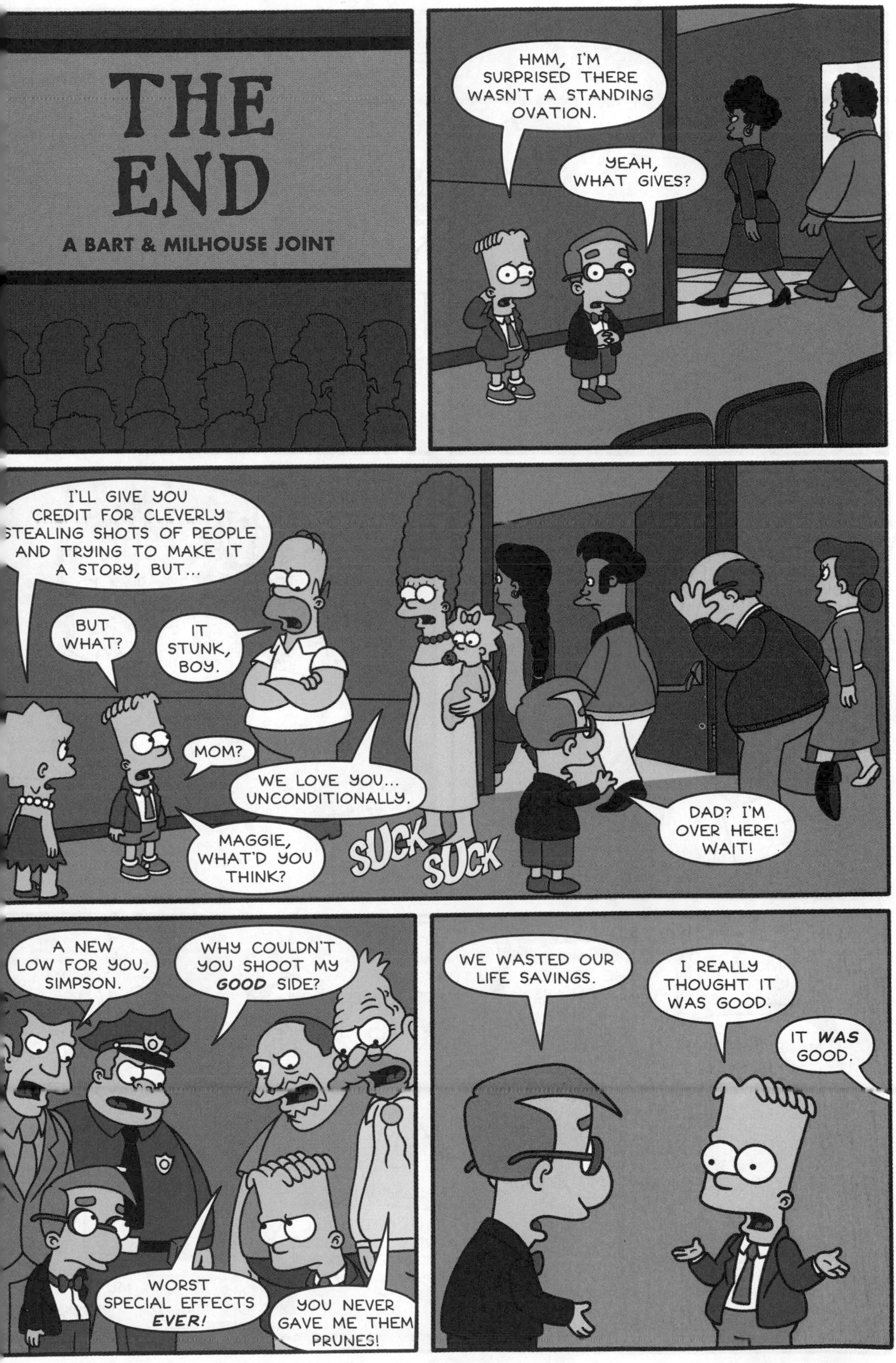
THE END
A BART & MILHOUSE JOINT
HMM, I'M SURPRISED THERE WASN'T A STANDING OVATION.
YEAH, WHAT GIVES?
I'LL GIVE YOU CREDIT FOR CLEVERLY STEALING SHOTS OF PEOPLE AND TRYING TO MAKE IT A STORY, BUT...
BUT WHAT?
IT STUNK, BOY.
MOM?
WE LOVE YOU... UNCONDITIONALLY.
MAGGIE, WHAT'D YOU THINK?
SUCK SUCK
DAD? I'M OVER HERE! WAIT!
A NEW LOW FOR YOU, SIMPSON.
WHY COULDN'T YOU SHOOT MY **GOOD** SIDE?
WORST SPECIAL EFFECTS **EVER!**
YOU NEVER GAVE ME THEM PRUNES!
WE WASTED OUR LIFE SAVINGS.
I REALLY THOUGHT IT WAS GOOD.
IT **WAS** GOOD.

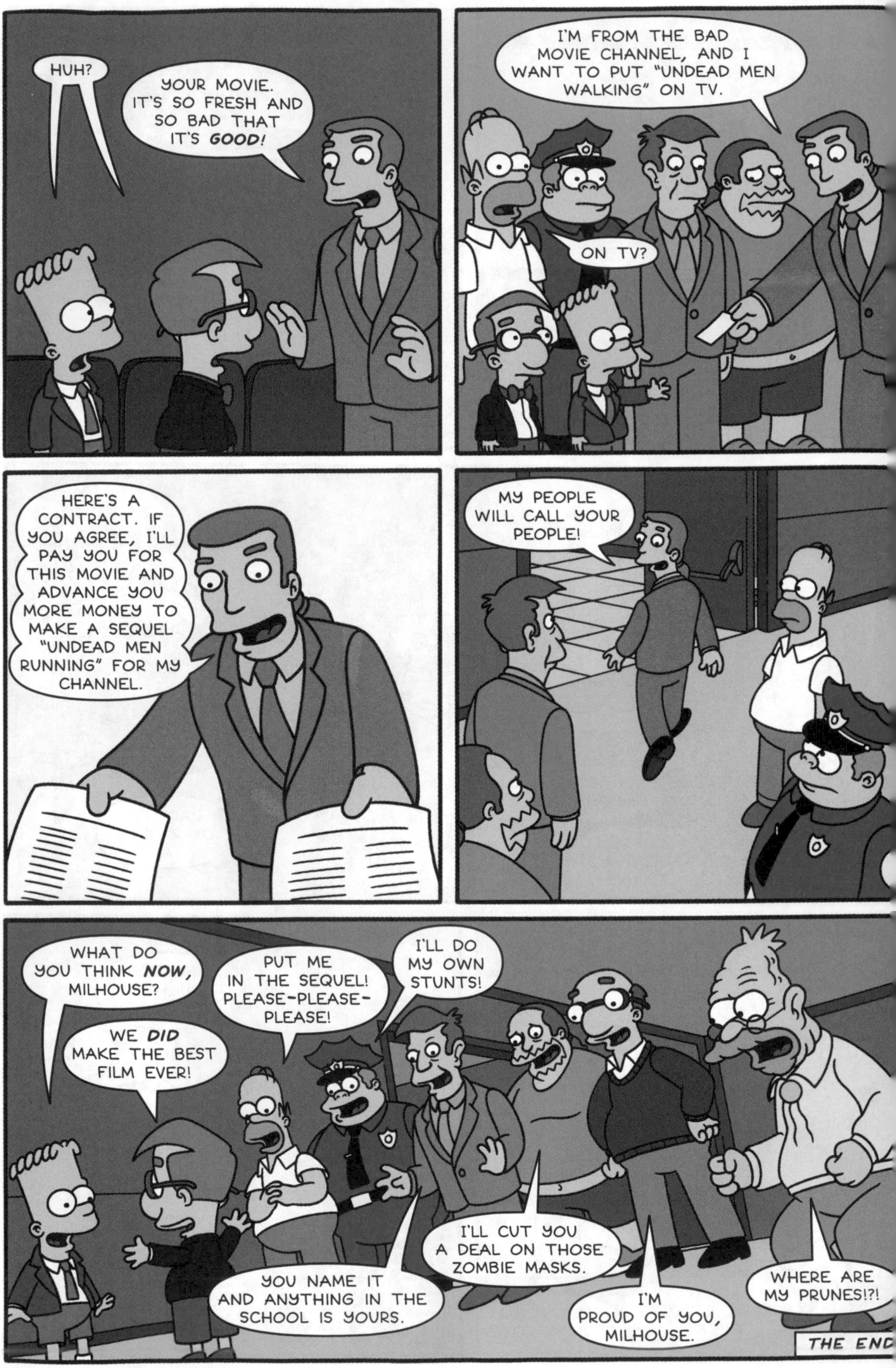
HUH?
YOUR MOVIE. IT'S SO FRESH AND SO BAD THAT IT'S *GOOD!*
I'M FROM THE BAD MOVIE CHANNEL, AND I WANT TO PUT "UNDEAD MEN WALKING" ON TV.
ON TV?
HERE'S A CONTRACT. IF YOU AGREE, I'LL PAY YOU FOR THIS MOVIE AND ADVANCE YOU MORE MONEY TO MAKE A SEQUEL "UNDEAD MEN RUNNING" FOR MY CHANNEL.
MY PEOPLE WILL CALL YOUR PEOPLE!
WHAT DO YOU THINK *NOW,* MILHOUSE?
WE *DID* MAKE THE BEST FILM EVER!
PUT ME IN THE SEQUEL! PLEASE-PLEASE-PLEASE!
I'LL DO MY OWN STUNTS!
YOU NAME IT AND ANYTHING IN THE SCHOOL IS YOURS.
I'LL CUT YOU A DEAL ON THOSE ZOMBIE MASKS.
I'M PROUD OF YOU, MILHOUSE.
WHERE ARE MY PRUNES!?!
THE END

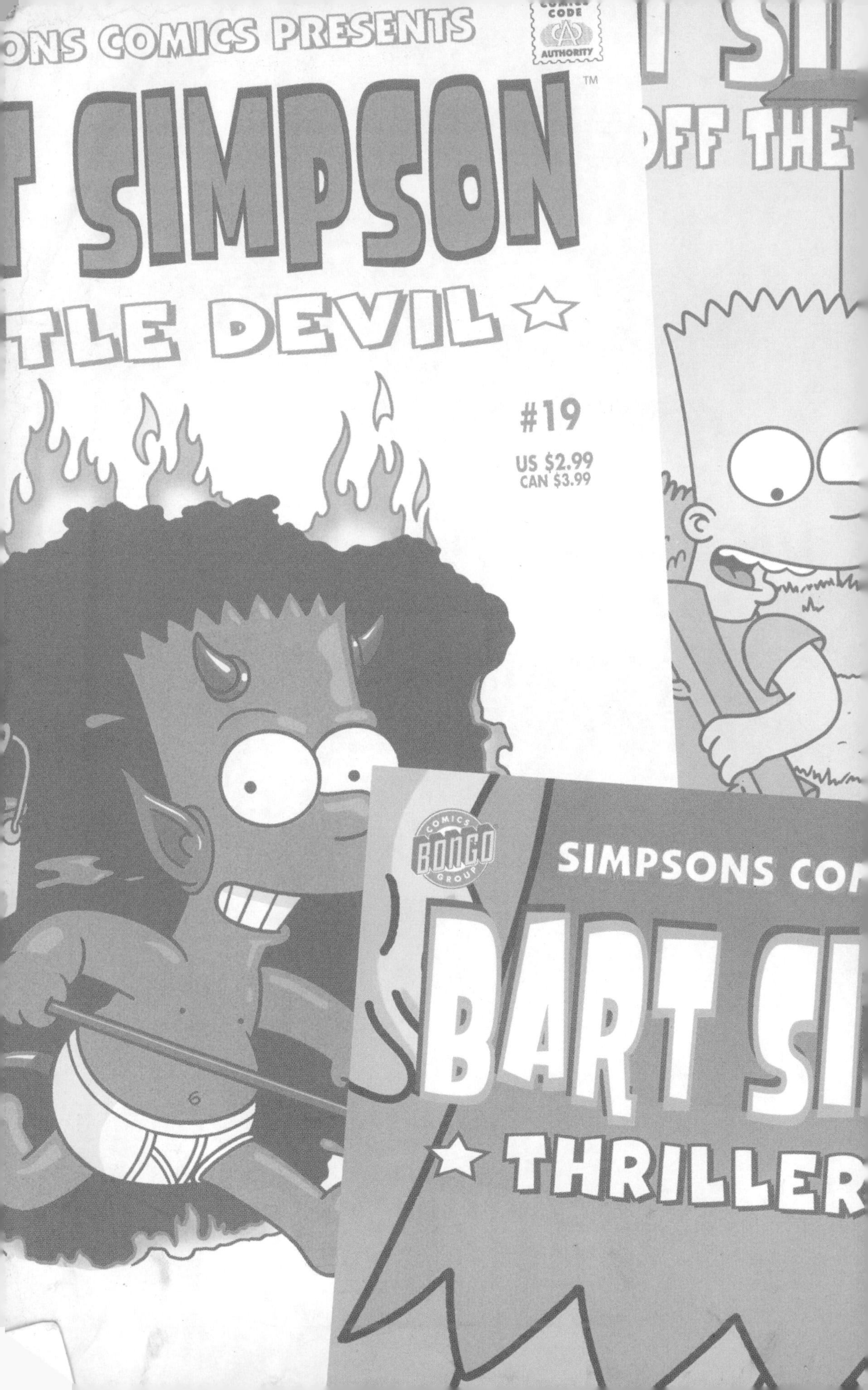

ONS COMICS PRESENTS
COMICS CODE AUTHORITY
T SIMPSON
TM
TLE DEVIL
#19
US $2.99
CAN $3.99
OFF THE
COMICS BONGO GROUP
SIMPSONS CO
BART SI
THRILLER